McGraw-Hill
Mathematics

Answer Key

- ▶ Practice
- ▶ Reteach
- ▶ Enrich
- ▶ Daily Homework

2

D1511737

Mc Graw Hill **Macmillan McGraw-Hill**
New York   Farmington

The **Answer Key** provides answers for the Practice, Reteach, Enrich, and Daily Homework blackline masters that accompany lessons in the Student Book. Each page in the **Answer Key** contains the blackline masters that support one lesson.

Macmillan/McGraw-Hill

A Division of The McGraw·Hill Companies

Macmillan/McGraw-Hill
Two Penn Plaza
New York, New York 10121-2298

ISBN 0-02-100419-6
3 4 5 6 7 8 9 024 04 03 02 01

Chapter 1 ~ Lesson 1

Practice

Addition Strategies
P 1-1 PRACTICE

Add. You can use the number line to count on.

0 1 2 3 4 5 6 7 8 9 10 11 12

1. $6 + 1 = \underline{7}$ $3 + 2 = \underline{5}$ $4 + 3 = \underline{7}$

2. $7 + 1 = \underline{8}$ $5 + 2 = \underline{7}$ $6 + 3 = \underline{9}$

3. $5 + 3 = \underline{8}$ $9 + 3 = \underline{12}$ $8 + 2 = \underline{10}$

4.
9	4	7	6	5	8	5
$+3$	$+3$	$+2$	$+1$	$+0$	$+2$	$+4$
12	7	9	7	5	10	9

5.
8	2	6	5	6	7	4
$+3$	$+3$	$+2$	$+1$	$+3$	$+1$	$+0$
11	5	8	6	9	8	4

6.
8	7	9	8	5	9	7
$+1$	$+3$	$+1$	$+0$	$+2$	$+2$	$+5$
9	10	10	8	7	11	12

Problem Solving

7. A frog jumps over 6 rocks.

Then he jumps over 2 more.

How many rocks does he jump over in all?

$\underline{8}$ rocks

A turtle lays 4 eggs

Then she lays 3 more.

How many eggs does she lay in all?

$\underline{7}$ eggs

Reteach

Addition Strategies
R 1-1 RETEACH

You can use squares to count on.

Find 5 + 3. Start at 5. Count on 3.

1 2 3 4 5 6 7 8 $5 + 3 = \underline{8}$ $\begin{array}{r} 5 \\ +3 \\ \hline 8 \end{array}$

Add. Draw squares to count on.

1. $8 + 1 = \underline{9}$

2. $6 + 2 = \underline{8}$

3. $7 + 3 = \underline{10}$

4. $5 + 1 = \underline{6}$

5. $9 + 3 = \underline{12}$

6. $7 + 2 = \underline{9}$

Enrich

Addition Strategies
E 1-1 ENRICH

Count On to Add

Write an addition sentence for each riddle.

1. Alex started at 4.
He counted on 3.
Where did he land?

$\underline{4 + 3 = 7}$

Karen started at 5.
She counted on 4.
Where did she land?

$\underline{5 + 4 = 9}$

2. Maria started at 6.
She counted on 2.
Where did she land?

$\underline{6 + 2 = 8}$

Ricky started at 6.
He counted on 4.
Where did he land?

$\underline{6 + 4 = 10}$

3. Ann started at 9.
She counted on 3.
Where did she land?

$\underline{9 + 3 = 12}$

John started at 8.
He counted on 3.
Where did he land?

$\underline{8 + 3 = 11}$

4. Brian started at 7.
He counted on 5.
Where did he land?

$\underline{7 + 5 = 12}$

Cara started at 6.
She counted on 5.
Where did she land?

$\underline{6 + 5 = 11}$

Daily Homework

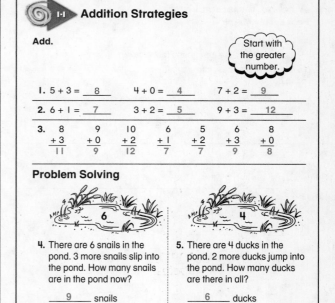

Addition Strategies
1-1

Add.

Start with the greater number.

1. $5 + 3 = \underline{8}$ $4 + 0 = \underline{4}$ $7 + 2 = \underline{9}$

2. $6 + 1 = \underline{7}$ $3 + 2 = \underline{5}$ $9 + 3 = \underline{12}$

3.
8	9	10	6	5	6	8
$+3$	$+0$	$+2$	$+1$	$+2$	$+3$	$+0$
11	9	12	7	7	9	8

Problem Solving

4. There are 6 snails in the pond. 3 more snails slip into the pond. How many snails are in the pond now?

$\underline{9}$ snails

5. There are 4 ducks in the pond. 2 more ducks jump into the pond. How many ducks are there in all?

$\underline{6}$ ducks

Spiral Review

Add.

6.
2	3	5	4	3	2	4
$+2$	$+2$	$+1$	$+3$	$+1$	$+0$	$+2$
4	5	6	7	4	2	6

Chapter 1 ~ Lesson 2

Practice

Algebra: Turnaround Facts

Find each sum.

1.
$$3 + 2 = 5 \quad 2 + 3 = 5 \quad 5 + 7 = 12 \quad 7 + 5 = 12 \quad 2 + 0 = 2 \quad 0 + 2 = 2$$

2.
$$4 + 5 = 9 \quad 5 + 4 = 9 \quad 7 + 1 = 8 \quad 1 + 7 = 8 \quad 4 + 2 = 6 \quad 2 + 4 = 6$$

3.
$$5 + 6 = 11 \quad 6 + 5 = 11 \quad 3 + 4 = 7 \quad 4 + 3 = 7 \quad 7 + 4 = 11 \quad 4 + 7 = 11$$

4.
$$7 + 2 = 9 \quad 2 + 7 = 9 \quad 5 + 3 = 8 \quad 3 + 5 = 8 \quad 2 + 8 = 10 \quad 8 + 2 = 10$$

Are these turnaround facts?
Write yes or no.

5.

$7 + 2$	$6 + 6$	$1 + 9$
$2 + 7$	$5 + 5$	$9 + 1$
yes	no	yes

Problem Solving

6. There are 2 brown frogs.
There are 8 green frogs.
How many frogs are there?
___10___ frogs

There are 4 spotted turtles.
There are 2 striped turtles.
How many turtles are there?
___6___ turtles

Use with Grade 2, Chapter 1, Lesson 2, pages 5–6. (4)

Reteach

Algebra: Turnaround Facts

 $2 + 3 = \underline{5}$

The order of the addends is changed.
The sum is the same.

 $3 + 2 = \underline{5}$

Draw dots to show the numbers. Add.

1. $8 + 4 = \underline{12}$ $5 + 2 = \underline{7}$
$4 + 8 = \underline{12}$ $2 + 5 = \underline{7}$

2. $3 + 4 = \underline{7}$ $1 + 8 = \underline{9}$
$4 + 3 = \underline{7}$ $8 + 1 = \underline{9}$

3. $5 + 3 = \underline{8}$ $6 + 5 = \underline{11}$
$3 + 5 = \underline{8}$ $5 + 6 = \underline{11}$

Use with Grade 2, Chapter 1, Lesson 2, pages 5–6. (5)

Enrich

Algebra: Turnaround Facts
Fact Letter Match

Find each sum.

Match the letter to the turnaround fact below.

To find the secret message, write the correct letters in the boxes.

1.

$4 + 2 = 6$	**A**	$3 + 2 = 5$	**T**	$1 + 5 = 6$	**F**
$2 + 6 = 8$	**U**	$1 + 3 = 4$	**D**	$7 + 2 = 9$	**N**
$3 + 7 = 10$	**O**	$4 + 3 = 7$	**R**	$5 + 6 = 11$	**C**

| **T** $2 + 3 = 5$ | **U** $6 + 2 = 8$ | **R** $3 + 4 = 7$ | **N** $2 + 7 = 9$ |

| **A** $2 + 4 = 6$ | **R** $3 + 4 = 7$ | **O** $7 + 3 = 10$ | **U** $6 + 2 = 8$ | **N** $2 + 7 = 9$ | **D** $3 + 1 = 4$ |

| **F** $5 + 1 = 6$ | **A** $2 + 4 = 6$ | **C** $6 + 5 = 11$ | **T** $2 + 3 = 5$ |

Use with Grade 2, Chapter 1, Lesson 2, pages 5–6. (6)

Daily Homework

1-2 Turnaround Facts

Find each sum.

1.
$$4 + 3 = 7 \quad 3 + 4 = 7 \quad 4 + 6 = 10 \quad 6 + 4 = 10 \quad 2 + 5 = 7 \quad 5 + 2 = 7$$

2.
$$3 + 8 = 11 \quad 8 + 3 = 11 \quad 4 + 5 = 9 \quad 5 + 4 = 9 \quad 3 + 9 = 12 \quad 9 + 3 = 12$$

3.
$$3 + 7 = 10 \quad 7 + 3 = 10 \quad 8 + 4 = 12 \quad 4 + 8 = 12 \quad 6 + 5 = 11 \quad 5 + 6 = 11$$

Are these turnaround facts?
Write *yes* or *no*.

4.

$4 + 5$	$4 + 6$	$7 + 4$
$5 + 4$	$6 + 6$	$4 + 7$
Yes.	No.	Yes.

Spiral Review

Find each sum.

5.
$$7 + 3 = 10 \quad 8 + 2 = 10 \quad 4 + 1 = 5 \quad 10 + 2 = 12 \quad 2 + 8 = 10 \quad 6 + 3 = 9 \quad 5 + 1 = 6$$

Chapter 1 ~ Lesson 3

Practice

Problem Solving: Reading for Math
Read to Set a Purpose

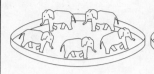

Kathy and Nick are at the circus.
They see 4 clowns on the tightrope.
They see 3 clowns on the trapeze.
How many clowns do they see in all?

Solve.

1. How many clowns are on the tightrope? __4__ clowns

2. How many clowns are on the trapeze? __3__ clowns

3. How many clowns do Kathy and Nick see in all? __7__ clowns

   Write an addition sentence to show your thinking.
   __4 + 3 = 7__

4. What information helped you find the answer?
   There were 4 clowns on the tightrope and
   3 clowns on the trapeze.

Use with Grade 2, Chapter 1, Lesson 3, pages 9–10. (7)

Practice

Problem Solving: Reading for Math
Read to Set a Purpose

There are many animals in the circus.
There are 5 elephants in one ring.
There are 4 horses in another ring.
How many animals are in the rings?

Choose the best answer. Fill in the ○.

1. How many elephants are in a ring?
   Ⓐ 4 Ⓑ 7 Ⓒ 5 Ⓓ 9

2. How many horses are in a ring?
   Ⓕ 5 Ⓖ 7 Ⓗ 4 Ⓙ 9

3. How many animals are in the rings?
   Ⓐ 6 Ⓑ 7 Ⓒ 8 Ⓓ 9

4. What information helped you find how many animals are in the rings?
   Ⓕ There are many animals in the circus.
   Ⓖ There are 5 elephants in one ring and 4 horses in another ring.
   Ⓗ There are more elephants than horses.

Use with Grade 2, Chapter 1, Lesson 3, pages 9–10. (8)

Practice

Problem Solving: Reading for Math
Read to Set a Purpose

A tiny car is in the middle of the circus ring.
There are 5 clowns in the car.
6 more clowns will try to get into the car.
How many clowns are there in all?

Choose the best answer. Fill in the ○.

1. How many clowns are in the car?
   Ⓐ 5 Ⓑ 2 Ⓒ 11 Ⓓ 6

2. How many clowns will try to get into the car?
   Ⓕ 5 Ⓖ 12 Ⓗ 3 Ⓙ 6

Solve.

3. How many clowns are there in all? __11__ clowns

   Write an addition sentence to show your thinking.
   __5 + 6 = 11__

4. What information helped you find the answer?
   There are 5 clowns in the car and 6 clowns that will try to get into the car.

Use with Grade 2, Chapter 1, Lesson 3, pages 9–10. (9)

Daily Homework

Problem Solving: Reading for Math
Read to Set a Purpose

Kelly saw 5 frogs in the pond.
Matt saw 3 frogs in the grass.

Solve.

1. How many frogs did Kelly see in the pond? __5__ frogs

2. How many frogs did Matt see in the grass? __3__ frogs

3. How many frogs did they see in all? __8__ frogs

   Write a number sentence to show your thinking.
   __5 + 3 = 8__

4. What information helped you find the answer?
   There were 5 frogs in the pond and 3 frogs in the grass.

Spiral Review
Add.

5.
$$\frac{8}{+2} \quad \frac{5}{+3} \quad \frac{10}{+2} \quad \frac{7}{+3} \quad \frac{6}{+1} \quad \frac{9}{+3} \quad \frac{4}{+2}$$
   10   8   12   10   7   12   6

Grade 2, Chapter 1, Lesson 3, Cluster A **3**

Chapter 1 ~ Lesson 4

Practice

Problem Solving: Strategy
Draw a Picture

Draw a picture. Solve.

1. There are 4 kittens in the basket. 5 more kittens climb into the basket. How many kittens are in the basket?

   __9__ kittens

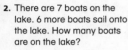

2. There are 7 boats on the lake. 6 more boats sail onto the lake. How many boats are on the lake?

   __13__ boats

3. Joe counted 3 nests in the tree. Then he counted 4 more. How many nests are in the tree?

   __7__ nests

Mixed Strategy Review
Solve.

4. Meg ate 5 grapes. Ray ate the same number. How many grapes did they eat in all?

   __10__ grapes

5. **Create a problem** for which you would draw a picture to solve. Share it with others.

   _____

   _____

Use with Grade 2, Chapter 1, Lesson 4, pages 13–14. (10)

Reteach

Problem Solving: Strategy
Draw a Picture

Page 14, Problem 4
Mandy catches 4 fish. Her brother catches the same number of fish. How many fish do they catch altogether?

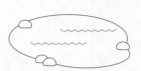

Step 1 **Read**	**Be sure you understand the problem.**
	What do you know?
	• Mandy catches __4__ fish.
	• Her brother catches __4__ fish.
	What do you need to find?
	• You need to find __how many fish they catch altogether__

Step 2 **Plan**	**Make a plan.** Choose a strategy.
▪ Draw a Picture	Draw a picture.
▪ Write a Number Sentence	
▪ Use Logical Reasoning	Describe what is happening in the picture.
▪ Act it Out	
▪ Choose the Operation	
▪ Make a Table	
▪ Guess and Check	
▪ Find a Pattern	
▪ Make a Graph	

Use with Grade 2, Chapter 1, Lesson 4, pages 13–14. (11)

Reteach

Problem Solving: Strategy
Draw a Picture

Step 3 **Solve**	**Carry out your plan.**
	• Draw a picture.
	• Tell about the picture.

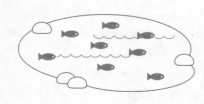

How many fish do they catch altogether?

__8__ fish

Step 4 **Look Back**	**Is the solution reasonable?**
	Does your answer make sense? (Yes) No
	Did you answer the question? (Yes) No

Use with Grade 2, Chapter 1, Lesson 4, pages 13–14. (12)

Daily Homework

1·4   Problem Solving: Strategy
Draw a Picture

Draw a picture. Solve.

1. There are 2 ducks on the pond. 4 more ducks land on the pond. How many ducks are there now?

   __6__ ducks

2. There are 9 ants in the grass. 3 more ants walk into the grass. How many ants are there now?

   __12__ ants

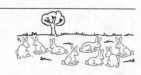

3. There are 5 bugs on a log. 4 more bugs fly onto the log. How many bugs are there now?

   __9__ bugs

4. There are 5 rabbits in a field. 3 more rabbits hop into the field. How many rabbits are there now?

   __8__ rabbits

Spiral Review
Add.

5.
8	8	7	6	3	3	5
+3	+0	+3	+1	+9	+7	+3
11	8	10	7	12	10	8

Chapter 1 ~ Lesson 5

Practice

Count Back to Subtract

P 1-5 PRACTICE

Subtract. You can use the number line to count back.

```
←—+—+—+—+—+—+—+—+—+—+—+—+—→
  0  1  2  3  4  5  6  7  8  9  10 11 12
```

1. $10 - 1 = 9$ $5 - 2 = 3$ $11 - 2 = 9$

2. $9 - 3 = 6$ $7 - 2 = 5$ $8 - 3 = 5$

3. $6 - 2 = 4$ $9 - 1 = 8$ $12 - 3 = 9$

4.
2	5	7	10	12	7	9
−2	−1	−1	−3	−3	−2	−8
0	4	6	7	9	5	1

5.
7	3	8	11	5	8	12
−3	−3	−2	−4	−3	−1	−5
4	0	6	7	2	7	7

6.
6	10	11	0	8	9	11
−1	−3	−3	−0	−3	−2	−6
5	7	8	0	5	7	5

Problem Solving

7. There are 9 ducks in the pond.
   3 ducks swim away.
   How many ducks are left?
   __6__ ducks

   There are 12 beavers on a dam.
   3 beavers swim away.
   How many beavers are left?
   __9__ beavers

Use with Grade 2, Chapter 1, Lesson 5, pages 15–16. (13)

Reteach

Count Back to Subtract

R 1-5 RETEACH

You can use a number line to count back to subtract.

Find $10 - 3$. Start at 10. Count back 3.

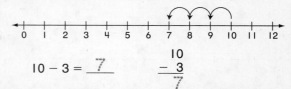

```
←—+—+—+—+—+—+—+—+—+—+—+—+—→
  0  1  2  3  4  5  6  7  8  9  10 11 12
```

$10 - 3 = 7$ $\begin{array}{r} 10 \\ -3 \\ \hline 7 \end{array}$

Count back to subtract.
Tell where you start.
Tell how many you count back.

1. $6 - 2 = 4$ Start at _6_.   Count back _2_.

2. $8 - 1 = 7$ Start at _8_.   Count back _1_.

3. $11 - 2 = 9$ Start at _11_.   Count back _2_.

4. $7 - 2 = 5$ Start at _7_.   Count back _2_.

5. $9 - 3 = 6$ Start at _9_.   Count back _3_.

6. $12 - 3 = 9$ Start at _12_.   Count back _3_.

7. $10 - 1 = 9$ Start at _10_.   Count back _1_.

Use with Grade 2, Chapter 1, Lesson 5, pages 15–16. (14)

Enrich

Count Back to Subtract
Rock Hop

E 1-5 ENRICH

Murray Frog, Freddy Frog, and Franny Frog jump on rocks across the pond.

Write a subtraction sentence that tells about the jumps.

1. Murray Frog jumps back 1.
   He starts on 9.
   Where does he land?
   __9 − 1 = 8__
   Murray Frog lands on _8_.

   Franny Frog jumps back 3.
   She starts on 9.
   Where does she land?
   __9 − 3 = 6__
   Franny Frog lands on _6_.

2. Freddy Frog jumps back 2.
   He starts on 10.
   Where does he land?
   __10 − 2 = 8__
   Freddy Frog lands on _8_.

   Franny Frog jumps back 3.
   She starts on 12.
   Where does she land?
   __12 − 3 = 9__
   Franny Frog lands on _9_.

3. Murray Frog jumps back 2.
   He lands on 5.
   Where did he start?
   __7 − 2 = 5__
   Murray Frog starts on _7_.

   Freddy Frog jumps back 3.
   He lands on 8.
   Where did he start?
   __11 − 3 = 8__
   Freddy Frog starts on _11_.

Use with Grade 2, Chapter 1, Lesson 5, pages 15–16. (15)

Daily Homework

1-5 Count Back to Subtract

Subtract. You can use a number line to count back.

```
←—+—+—+—+—+—+—+—+—+—+—+—+—→
  0  1  2  3  4  5  6  7  8  9  10 11 12
```

1. $9 - 3 = 6$ $12 - 1 = 11$ $7 - 2 = 5$

2. $5 - 3 = 2$ $8 - 2 = 6$ $12 - 3 = 9$

3. $9 - 2 = 7$ $11 - 3 = 8$ $10 - 3 = 7$

4.
9	7	6	0	11	6
−1	−3	−1	−0	−2	−2
8	4	5	0	9	4

5.
5	12	5	9	10	5
−0	−2	−2	−0	−2	−2
5	10	3	9	8	3

Problem Solving

6. 8 frogs sit on a log. 3 frogs hop away. How many frogs are left?
   __5__ frogs

8

Spiral Review

Add.

7.
5	9	6	8	3	7	10
+2	+3	+1	+0	+8	+2	+1
7	12	7	8	11	9	11

Chapter 1 ~ Lesson 6

Practice

Relate Addition and Subtraction

P 1-6 PRACTICE

Add. Then write a related subtraction sentence.

1. $6 + 2 =$ __8__
   $8 - 2 = 6$ or $8 - 6 = 2$

$4 + 5 =$ __9__
   $9 - 5 = 4$ or $9 - 4 = 5$

2. $3 + 6 =$ __9__
   $9 - 6 = 3$ or $9 - 3 = 6$

$2 + 4 =$ __6__
   $6 - 4 = 2$ or $6 - 2 = 4$

3. $5 + 6 =$ __11__
   $11 - 6 = 5$ or $11 - 5 = 6$

$3 + 7 =$ __10__
   $10 - 7 = 3$ or $10 - 3 = 7$

4. $1 + 5 =$ __6__
   $6 - 5 = 1$ or $6 - 1 = 5$

$9 + 3 =$ __12__
   $12 - 3 = 9$ or $12 - 9 = 3$

Is the addition related to the subtraction? Write yes or no.

5. $5 + 5 = 10$
   $10 - 5 = 5$
   __yes__

$8 + 2 = 10$
   $8 - 2 = 6$
   __no__

$1 + 9 = 10$
   $10 - 1 = 9$
   __yes__

6. $2 + 9 = 11$
   $11 - 2 = 9$
   __yes__

$6 + 6 = 12$
   $6 - 6 = 0$
   __no__

$4 + 3 = 7$
   $4 - 3 = 1$
   __no__

Problem Solving

7. Keesha counts 9 bugs. Ronnie counts 2 bugs. How many bugs are there in all?

__11__ bugs

There are 11 grasshoppers. 2 grasshoppers jump away. How many grasshoppers are left?

__9__ grasshoppers

Use with Grade 2, Chapter 1, Lesson 6, pages 17–18. (16)

Reteach

Relate Addition and Subtraction

R 1-6 RETEACH

$8 + 4 =$ __12__
$12 - 4 =$ __8__

These addition and subtraction facts have the same three numbers.

Add or subtract.

1. $4 + 7 =$ __11__
   $11 - 7 =$ __4__

$3 + 6 =$ __9__
   $9 - 3 =$ __6__

2. $9 + 3 =$ __12__
   $12 - 3 =$ __9__

$2 + 5 =$ __7__
   $7 - 5 =$ __2__

3. $2 + 8 =$ __10__
   $10 - 2 =$ __8__

$1 + 6 =$ __7__
   $7 - 6 =$ __1__

Use with Grade 2, Chapter 1, Lesson 6, pages 17–18. (17)

Enrich

Relate Addition and Subtraction
Matching Facts

E 1-6 ENRICH

Add or subtract.
Cross out the fact that is not related.

1.
$3 + 2 = 5$ $4 + 1 = 5$ $5 - 2 = 3$ $4 + 5 = 9$ $5 - 4 = 1$ $9 - 5 = 4$

2.
$6 - 2 = 4$ $10 - 6 = 4$ $4 + 6 = 10$ $4 + 3 = 7$ $7 - 3 = 4$ $7 - 0 = 7$

3.
$8 - 2 = 6$ $2 + 8 = 10$ $6 + 2 = 8$ $4 + 4 = 8$ $8 - 4 = 4$ $8 - 0 = 8$

4.
$5 + 0 = 5$ $5 - 0 = 5$ $10 - 5 = 5$ $11 - 5 = 6$ $6 + 3 = 9$ $6 + 5 = 11$

What if the shapes are numbers?
Cross out the facts that are not related.

5.

Use with Grade 2, Chapter 1, Lesson 6, pages 17–18. (18)

Daily Homework

1-6 Relate Addition and Subtraction

Add. Write a related subtraction sentence.

> Remember you can use addition facts to find subtraction facts.

1. $7 + 5 =$ __12__
   $12 - 7 =$ __5__
   or $12 - 5 = 7$

$3 + 6 =$ __9__
   $9 - 3 =$ __6__
   or $9 - 6 = 3$

$6 + 4 =$ __10__
   $10 - 6 =$ __4__
   or $10 - 4 = 6$

2. $5 + 3 =$ __8__
   $8 - 5 =$ __3__
   or $8 - 3 = 5$

$5 + 6 =$ __11__
   $11 - 5 =$ __6__
   or $11 - 6 = 5$

$3 + 4 =$ __7__
   $7 - 3 =$ __4__
   or $7 - 4 = 3$

3. $9 + 3 =$ __12__
   $12 - 9 =$ __3__
   or $12 - 3 = 9$

$5 + 4 =$ __9__
   $9 - 5 =$ __4__
   or $9 - 4 = 5$

$4 + 7 =$ __11__
   $11 - 4 =$ __7__
   or $11 - 7 = 4$

Is the addition related to the subtraction? Write *yes* or *no*.

4. $3 + 6 = 9$
   $9 - 6 = 3$
   Yes.

$3 + 5 = 8$
   $5 - 2 = 3$
   No.

$5 + 7 = 12$
   $12 - 5 = 7$
   Yes.

Spiral Review
Add or subtract.

5.
$8 + 2 = 10$ $12 - 8 = 4$ $6 + 3 = 9$ $10 - 3 = 7$ $8 - 0 = 8$ $5 + 1 = 6$ $7 + 3 = 10$

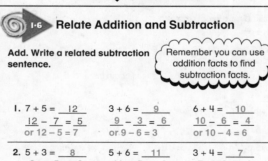

Chapter 1 ~ Lesson 7

Practice

Fact Families

Add or subtract. Complete each fact family.

1. $6 + 1 = \underline{7}$
    $1 + 6 = \underline{7}$
    $7 - 1 = \underline{6}$
    $7 - 6 = \underline{1}$

    $4 + 5 = \underline{9}$
    $5 + \underline{4} = 9$
    $9 - \underline{4} = 4$
    $9 - \underline{4} = 5$

2. $3 + \underline{9} = 12$
    $9 + 3 = \underline{12}$
    $12 - 9 = \underline{3}$
    $12 - \underline{3} = 9$

    $\underline{8} + 2 = 10$
    $2 + \underline{8} = 10$
    $10 - \underline{8} = 2$
    $10 - 2 = \underline{8}$

3. $3 + 3 = \underline{6}$
    $6 - 3 = \underline{3}$

    $5 + \underline{5} = 10$
    $10 - \underline{5} = 5$

4. $\underline{4} + 4 = 8$
    $8 - 4 = \underline{4}$

    $\underline{6} + 6 = 12$
    $12 - \underline{6} = 6$

Problem Solving

5. There are 8 birds on a branch.
    4 birds fly away.
    How many birds are left?
    $\underline{4}$ birds

    There are 7 birds on a branch.
    5 birds come to join them.
    How many birds are there in all?
    $\underline{12}$ birds

Use with Grade 2, Chapter 1, Lesson 7, pages 19–20. (19)

Reteach

Fact Families

Fact families use the same three numbers.

$2 + 4 = \underline{6}$ $6 - 4 = \underline{2}$
$4 + 2 = \underline{6}$ $6 - 2 = \underline{4}$

Add or subtract. Complete the fact family.

1.
    $3 + 5 = \underline{8}$ $8 - 5 = \underline{3}$
    $5 + 3 = \underline{8}$ $8 - 3 = \underline{5}$

2. $6 + 1 = \underline{7}$ $7 - 6 = \underline{1}$
    $1 + 6 = \underline{7}$ $7 - 1 = \underline{6}$

3. $9 + 3 = \underline{12}$ $12 - 3 = \underline{9}$
    $3 + 9 = \underline{12}$ $12 - 9 = \underline{3}$

4. $5 + 5 = \underline{10}$ $10 - 5 = \underline{5}$

Use with Grade 2, Chapter 1, Lesson 7, pages 19–20. (20)

Enrich

Fact Families

It's in the Beads

Color some beads red. Color some beads blue.
Write a fact family. For ex. 1–3, check students' work.

1.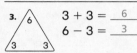
    $\underline{\quad} + \underline{\quad} = \underline{\quad}$ $\underline{\quad} + \underline{\quad} = \underline{\quad}$
    $\underline{\quad} - \underline{\quad} = \underline{\quad}$ $\underline{\quad} - \underline{\quad} = \underline{\quad}$

2.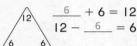
    $\underline{\quad} + \underline{\quad} = \underline{\quad}$ $\underline{\quad} + \underline{\quad} = \underline{\quad}$
    $\underline{\quad} - \underline{\quad} = \underline{\quad}$ $\underline{\quad} - \underline{\quad} = \underline{\quad}$

3.
    $\underline{\quad} + \underline{\quad} = \underline{\quad}$ $\underline{\quad} + \underline{\quad} = \underline{\quad}$
    $\underline{\quad} - \underline{\quad} = \underline{\quad}$ $\underline{\quad} - \underline{\quad} = \underline{\quad}$

Use with Grade 2, Chapter 1, Lesson 7, pages 19–20. (21)

Daily Homework

1-7 Fact Families

Add or subtract.
Complete each fact family.

1. (11) (8) (3)
    $8 + 3 = \underline{11}$ $11 - 8 = \underline{3}$
    $3 + \underline{8} = 11$ $\underline{11} - 3 = 8$

2. (11) (6) (5)
    $6 + 5 = \underline{11}$ $11 - \underline{5} = 6$
    $5 + \underline{6} = 11$ $11 - 6 = \underline{5}$

Complete each fact family triangle.

3.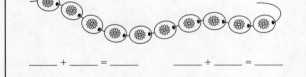
    (11) (7) (4)   (12) (3) (9)   (10) (8) (2)

4.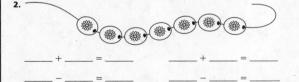
    (12) (5) (7)   (12) (4) (8)   (11) (2) (9)

Spiral Review

Complete each number sentence.

5. $9 + 2 = \underline{11}$ $12 - \underline{5} = 7$ $10 - 7 = \underline{3}$

6. $6 + \underline{4} = 10$ $10 - 0 = \underline{10}$ $\underline{6} - 1 = 7$

Chapter 1 ~ Lesson 8

Part A Worksheet

Problem Solving: Application
Draw a Pond

Make a pond diagram.

Draw a large pond.

Cut out the animals and plants.

Paste them on your pond.

frogs

dragonflies

ducks

fish

beaver

cattails

lily pads

raccoons

turtles

Use with Grade 2, Chapter 1, Lesson 8, pages 23–26. (22)

Part A Worksheet

Problem Solving: Application
Draw a Pond

1. Show the number of each animal and plant you used to make your diagram. Answers may vary.

Animals and Plants	Number
frogs	
ducks	
bugs	
fish	
turtles	
raccoons	
beaver	
cattails	
lilypads	

2. Write a problem that you could solve by looking at your pond diagram. Share it with others.

_____

_____

Use with Grade 2, Chapter 1, Lesson 8, pages 23–26. (23)

Part B Worksheet

Problem Solving: Application
Why Do Ducks Stay Warm?

1. Record what happened to each side of the feather.

Side of Feather	Got Wet	Water Rolled Off
Colored		X
Not Colored	X	

2. What side of the feather did the water roll off?

_____ colored side

Tell why you think that happened.

Answers may vary. Possible answer: Something in the crayon makes water roll off.

3. How do you think a duck's feathers keep a duck dry?

Answers may vary. Possible answer: There is something on a duck's feathers that makes the water roll off.

_____

_____

_____

Use with Grade 2, Chapter 1, Lesson 8, pages 23–26. (24)

Chapter 2 ~ Lesson 1

Practice

Doubles to Add

Add.

1. $6 + 6 = \underline{12}$ $6 + 7 = \underline{13}$ $8 + 7 = \underline{15}$

2. $8 + 8 = \underline{16}$ $8 + 9 = \underline{17}$ $10¢ + 10¢ = \underline{20¢}$

3.
$\begin{array}{r}3\\+3\\\hline 6\end{array}$
$\begin{array}{r}3¢\\+4¢\\\hline 7¢\end{array}$
$\begin{array}{r}3\\+2\\\hline 5\end{array}$
$\begin{array}{r}4\\+4\\\hline 8\end{array}$
$\begin{array}{r}4\\+5\\\hline 9\end{array}$
$\begin{array}{r}4\\+3\\\hline 7\end{array}$

4.
$\begin{array}{r}8\\+8\\\hline 16\end{array}$
$\begin{array}{r}8\\+9\\\hline 17\end{array}$
$\begin{array}{r}8¢\\+7¢\\\hline 15¢\end{array}$
$\begin{array}{r}5\\+5\\\hline 10\end{array}$
$\begin{array}{r}5\\+6\\\hline 11\end{array}$
$\begin{array}{r}5¢\\+4¢\\\hline 9¢\end{array}$

5.
$\begin{array}{r}9¢\\+9¢\\\hline 18¢\end{array}$
$\begin{array}{r}9\\+10\\\hline 19\end{array}$
$\begin{array}{r}9\\+8\\\hline 17\end{array}$
$\begin{array}{r}0\\+0\\\hline 0\end{array}$
$\begin{array}{r}0\\+1\\\hline 1\end{array}$
$\begin{array}{r}6\\+7\\\hline 13\end{array}$

6.
$\begin{array}{r}6¢\\+9¢\\\hline 15¢\end{array}$
$\begin{array}{r}7\\+6\\\hline 13\end{array}$
$\begin{array}{r}10\\+10\\\hline 20\end{array}$
$\begin{array}{r}10¢\\+9¢\\\hline 19¢\end{array}$
$\begin{array}{r}6\\+6\\\hline 12\end{array}$
$\begin{array}{r}8\\+9\\\hline 17\end{array}$

Problem Solving

7. There is one more bird stamp than cat stamp. There are 9 bird stamps.

   How many stamps are there in all?

   $\underline{17}$ stamps

8. Jack has 7 baseball stamps. Jill has 8 baseball stamps.

   How many stamps do they have in all?

   $\underline{15}$ stamps

Reteach

Doubles to Add

○○○○○○
○○○○○○◌

$7 + 7 = \underline{14}$ $7 + 8 = \underline{15}$

$\begin{array}{r}7\\+7\\\hline 14\end{array}$
$\begin{array}{r}7\\+8\\\hline 15\end{array}$

Draw one more to add.

1. ○○○○○○○○
   ○○○○○○○○○

   $\begin{array}{r}8\\+8\\\hline 16\end{array}$
   $\begin{array}{r}8\\+9\\\hline 17\end{array}$

   $8 + 8 = \underline{16}$ $8 + 9 = \underline{17}$

2. ○○○○○○○○○
   ○○○○○○○○○○

   $\begin{array}{r}9\\+9\\\hline 18\end{array}$
   $\begin{array}{r}9\\+10\\\hline 19\end{array}$

Add.

3. $7 + 8 = \underline{15}$ $9¢ + 9¢ = \underline{18¢}$ $10 + 10 = \underline{20}$

4.
$\begin{array}{r}5¢\\+5¢\\\hline 10¢\end{array}$
$\begin{array}{r}5¢\\+6¢\\\hline 11¢\end{array}$
$\begin{array}{r}7\\+7\\\hline 14\end{array}$
$\begin{array}{r}7\\+8\\\hline 15\end{array}$
$\begin{array}{r}9\\+9\\\hline 18\end{array}$
$\begin{array}{r}9\\+10\\\hline 19\end{array}$

5.
$\begin{array}{r}6\\+6\\\hline 12\end{array}$
$\begin{array}{r}6\\+7\\\hline 13\end{array}$
$\begin{array}{r}8\\+8\\\hline 16\end{array}$
$\begin{array}{r}8\\+9\\\hline 17\end{array}$
$\begin{array}{r}4¢\\+4¢\\\hline 8¢\end{array}$
$\begin{array}{r}4¢\\+5¢\\\hline 9¢\end{array}$

Enrich

Doubles to Add
Doubles Patterns

1. Billy saves 1¢.
   Each day he doubles the cents he saves.
   Write the amount Billy saves each day.

Monday	Tuesday	Wednesday	Thursday	Friday
1¢	2¢	4¢	8¢	16¢

   How much does Billy save on Friday? $\underline{16¢}$

2. Sara saves 3¢.
   Each day she doubles the cents she saves.
   Write the amount Sara saves each day.

Friday	Saturday	Sunday
3¢	6¢	12¢

   How much does Sara save on Sunday? $\underline{12¢}$

3. Nico saves 5¢.
   Each day he doubles the cents he saves.
   Write the amount Nico saves each day.

Friday	Saturday	Sunday
5¢	10¢	20¢

   How much does Nico save on Sunday? $\underline{20¢}$

4. Who saves the most money? $\underline{Nico}$

5. Who saves the least money? $\underline{Sara}$

Daily Homework

2-1 Doubles to Add

Add.

1. $5 + 5 = \underline{10}$ $5 + 6 = \underline{11}$ $5 + 4 = \underline{9}$

2. $3 + 3 = \underline{6}$ $3 + 2 = \underline{5}$ $3 + 4 = \underline{7}$

3. $4 + 4 = \underline{8}$ $4 + 3 = \underline{7}$ $4 + 5 = \underline{9}$

4.
$\begin{array}{r}6\\+6\\\hline 12\end{array}$
$\begin{array}{r}6\\+7\\\hline 13\end{array}$
$\begin{array}{r}6\\+5\\\hline 11\end{array}$
$\begin{array}{r}7\\+7\\\hline 14\end{array}$
$\begin{array}{r}7\\+8\\\hline 15\end{array}$
$\begin{array}{r}7\\+6\\\hline 13\end{array}$

5.
$\begin{array}{r}8\\+8\\\hline 16\end{array}$
$\begin{array}{r}8\\+9\\\hline 17\end{array}$
$\begin{array}{r}8\\+7\\\hline 15\end{array}$
$\begin{array}{r}9\\+9\\\hline 18\end{array}$
$\begin{array}{r}9\\+10\\\hline 19\end{array}$
$\begin{array}{r}9\\+8\\\hline 17\end{array}$

Problem Solving

6. Pete has 6 Grand Canyon postcards. Lisa has the same number of postcards from Yellowstone. How many postcards do they have in all?

   $\underline{12}$ postcards

Spiral Review

Complete each number sentence.

7. $6 + 5 = \underline{11}$ $\underline{11} - 6 = 5$ $6 + \underline{5} = 11$

Chapter 2 ~ Lesson 2

Practice

Make a Ten to Add 7, 8, 9

Add. You can use counters and a 10-frame.

1. $9 + 4 = 13$

$\begin{array}{r} 9 \\ +\ 4 \\ \hline 13 \end{array}$

$8 + 6 = 14$
$\begin{array}{r} 8 \\ +\ 6 \\ \hline 14 \end{array}$

2. $8 + 5 = 13$ $7 + 4 = 11$ $9 + 6 = 15$

3. $5 + 7 = 12$ $6 + 8 = 14$ $7 + 7 = 14$

4.
$\begin{array}{r} 9 \\ +3 \\ \hline 12 \end{array}$
$\begin{array}{r} 9 \\ +5 \\ \hline 14 \end{array}$
$\begin{array}{r} 5 \\ +8 \\ \hline 13 \end{array}$
$\begin{array}{r} 8 \\ +4 \\ \hline 12 \end{array}$
$\begin{array}{r} 6 \\ +9 \\ \hline 15 \end{array}$
$\begin{array}{r} 7 \\ +9 \\ \hline 16 \end{array}$
$\begin{array}{r} 2 \\ +9 \\ \hline 11 \end{array}$

5.
$\begin{array}{r} 6 \\ +8 \\ \hline 14 \end{array}$
$\begin{array}{r} 9 \\ +9 \\ \hline 18 \end{array}$
$\begin{array}{r} 7 \\ +8 \\ \hline 15 \end{array}$
$\begin{array}{r} 5 \\ +6 \\ \hline 11 \end{array}$
$\begin{array}{r} 9 \\ +7 \\ \hline 16 \end{array}$
$\begin{array}{r} 8 \\ +9 \\ \hline 17 \end{array}$
$\begin{array}{r} 8 \\ +6 \\ \hline 14 \end{array}$

6.
$\begin{array}{r} 5 \\ +9 \\ \hline 14 \end{array}$
$\begin{array}{r} 7 \\ +6 \\ \hline 13 \end{array}$
$\begin{array}{r} 4 \\ +9 \\ \hline 13 \end{array}$
$\begin{array}{r} 8 \\ +3 \\ \hline 11 \end{array}$
$\begin{array}{r} 7 \\ +5 \\ \hline 12 \end{array}$
$\begin{array}{r} 8 \\ +8 \\ \hline 16 \end{array}$
$\begin{array}{r} 3 \\ +9 \\ \hline 12 \end{array}$

Problem Solving

7. Sam has 7 postcards. Terry has 6 postcards. How many postcards do they have in all?

____13____ postcards

There are 9 postcards from Ohio. There are 4 postcards from Maine. How many postcards are there in all?

____13____ postcards

Reteach

Make a Ten to Add 7, 8, 9

Add $8 + 5$.

Show 8.	Make a 10.	$8 + 5$ is the same as
Show 5 more.	Move 2.	$10 + 3$, so

      $8 + 5 = 13$.

$\begin{array}{r} 8 \\ +5 \\ \hline 13 \end{array}$

Add. You can use counters and a 10-frame.

1. $8 + 6$ $9 + 7$

$8 + 6$ is the same as $9 + 7$ is the same as

$10 + \underline{\ 4\ }$, so $10 + \underline{\ 6\ }$, so

$8 + 6 = \underline{\ 14\ }$. $9 + 7 = \underline{\ 16\ }$.

2.
$\begin{array}{r} 7 \\ +4 \\ \hline 11 \end{array}$
$\begin{array}{r} 9 \\ +5 \\ \hline 14 \end{array}$
$\begin{array}{r} 8 \\ +9 \\ \hline 17 \end{array}$
$\begin{array}{r} 9 \\ +6 \\ \hline 15 \end{array}$
$\begin{array}{r} 5 \\ +8 \\ \hline 13 \end{array}$
$\begin{array}{r} 2 \\ +9 \\ \hline 11 \end{array}$
$\begin{array}{r} 6 \\ +7 \\ \hline 13 \end{array}$

Enrich

Make a Ten to Add 7, 8, 9
Match Sums

Cut out the cards.
Play with a partner.
Take turns.

- Turn the cards over.
- Choose two cards.
- Keep the cards if the sums match. Put the cards back if they do not match.

The player with more cards wins.

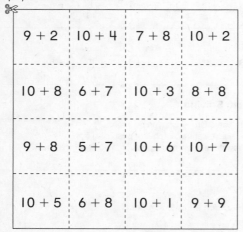

$9 + 2$	$10 + 4$	$7 + 8$	$10 + 2$
$10 + 8$	$6 + 7$	$10 + 3$	$8 + 8$
$9 + 8$	$5 + 7$	$10 + 6$	$10 + 7$
$10 + 5$	$6 + 8$	$10 + 1$	$9 + 9$

Daily Homework

2-2 Make a Ten to Add 7, 8, 9

Add. You can use ⬤ and the 10-frame.

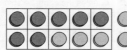

1. $7 + 6 = 13$

2. $9 + 4 = 13$ $6 + 8 = 14$ $3 + 7 = 10$

3. $8 + 5 = 13$ $2 + 9 = 11$ $7 + 7 = 14$

4.
$\begin{array}{r} 8 \\ +3 \\ \hline 11 \end{array}$
$\begin{array}{r} 6 \\ +9 \\ \hline 15 \end{array}$
$\begin{array}{r} 5¢ \\ +7¢ \\ \hline 12¢ \end{array}$
$\begin{array}{r} 2 \\ +8 \\ \hline 10 \end{array}$
$\begin{array}{r} 9 \\ +5 \\ \hline 14 \end{array}$
$\begin{array}{r} 7 \\ +6 \\ \hline 13 \end{array}$
$\begin{array}{r} 4¢ \\ +8¢ \\ \hline 12¢ \end{array}$

5.
$\begin{array}{r} 4 \\ +7 \\ \hline 11 \end{array}$
$\begin{array}{r} 9¢ \\ +3¢ \\ \hline 12¢ \end{array}$
$\begin{array}{r} 5 \\ +9 \\ \hline 14 \end{array}$
$\begin{array}{r} 6 \\ +7 \\ \hline 13 \end{array}$
$\begin{array}{r} 7 \\ +3 \\ \hline 10 \end{array}$
$\begin{array}{r} 5 \\ +8 \\ \hline 13 \end{array}$
$\begin{array}{r} 8 \\ +6 \\ \hline 14 \end{array}$

Solve.

6. Matt saw 5 kittens and 7 puppies. How many animals did he see?

____12____ animals

Spiral Review
Add.

7.
$\begin{array}{r} 8 \\ +8 \\ \hline 16 \end{array}$
$\begin{array}{r} 8 \\ +7 \\ \hline 15 \end{array}$
$\begin{array}{r} 6 \\ +6 \\ \hline 12 \end{array}$
$\begin{array}{r} 7 \\ +6 \\ \hline 13 \end{array}$
$\begin{array}{r} 7 \\ +7 \\ \hline 14 \end{array}$
$\begin{array}{r} 7 \\ +8 \\ \hline 15 \end{array}$
$\begin{array}{r} 9 \\ +9 \\ \hline 18 \end{array}$

Chapter 2 ~ Lesson 3

Practice

Three Addends

Add.

1.
$$3 + 2 + 3 = 8$$
$$4 + 5 + 4 = 13$$
$$8 + 0 + 2 = 10$$
$$4 + 3 + 4 = 11$$
$$5 + 4 + 6 = 15$$
$$9 + 1 + 5 = 15$$
$$2 + 3 + 4 = 9$$

2.
$$4 + 8 + 2 = 14$$
$$7 + 6 + 6 = 19$$
$$9 + 1 + 4 = 14$$
$$8 + 3 + 8 = 19$$
$$7 + 3 + 6 = 16$$
$$5 + 5 + 5 = 15$$
$$5 + 3 + 0 = 8$$

3.
$$4 + 6 + 8 = 18$$
$$3 + 5 + 2 = 10$$
$$0 + 7 + 9 = 16$$
$$2 + 4 + 3 = 9$$
$$8 + 2 + 3 = 13$$
$$5 + 6 + 7 = 18$$
$$1 + 9 + 2 = 12$$

4.
$$6 + 5 + 6 = 17$$
$$5 + 4 + 7 = 16$$
$$8 + 3 + 4 = 15$$
$$5 + 3 + 4 = 12$$
$$1 + 9 + 6 = 16$$
$$3 + 8 + 2 = 13$$
$$6 + 8 + 6 = 20$$

Problem Solving

5. Bess has 4 stamps. Tim has 9 stamps. Ben has 3 stamps. How many stamps do they have in all?

___16___ stamps

There are 4 bear stamps, 6 wolf stamps, and 7 fox stamps. How many stamps are there in all?

___17___ stamps

Reteach

Three Addends

Use addition strategies to help you find the sum of three addends.

Find a double.
$$4 + 3 + 4 = 11$$ 8

Make a ten.
$$6 + 5 + 5 = 15$$ 10

Circle names for doubles. Add.

1.
$$(3) + (3) + 7 = 13$$ 6
$$4 + (2) + (2) = 8$$
$$(4) + 5 + (4) = 13$$
$$(3) + 7 + (3) = 13$$
$$(5) + (5) + 2 = 12$$

Circle names for tens. Add.

2.
$$(8) + (2) + 4 = 14$$ 10
$$(4) + 3 + (6) = 13$$
$$(1) + (9) + 4 = 14$$
$$8 + (7) + (3) = 18$$
$$(5) + 6 + (5) = 16$$

Add. Use any strategy.

3.
$$8 + 3 + 8 = 19$$
$$7 + 4 + 4 = 15$$
$$8 + 9 + 1 = 18$$
$$9 + 9 + 2 = 20$$
$$2 + 7 + 8 = 17$$
$$2 + 9 + 2 = 13$$
$$8 + 0 + 8 = 16$$

Enrich

Three Addends

Pete's Playground

This is a map of the playground at Pete's school.
The map shows the number of units between each playground toy.

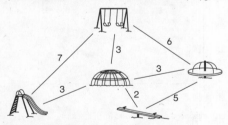

Find the total number of units for each path.
Write a number sentence to show how you found the total.

1. slide to swings to UFO to dome

___7___ units + ___6___ units + ___3___ units = ___16___ units

2. seesaw to dome to swings to UFO

___2___ units + ___3___ units + ___6___ units = ___11___ units

3. dome to seesaw to UFO to swings

___2___ units + ___5___ units + ___6___ units = ___13___ units

Daily Homework

2-3 Three Addends

Add. Use different strategies.

1.
$$6 + 6 + 2 = 14$$
$$5 + 8 + 5 = 18$$
$$6 + 2 + 4 = 12$$
$$3 + 7 + 5 = 15$$
$$3 + 4 + 4 = 11$$
$$2 + 7 + 8 = 17$$
$$6 + 3 + 3 = 12$$

2.
$$7 + 2 + 7 = 16$$
$$3 + 9 + 1 = 13$$
$$8 + 8 + 3 = 19$$
$$4 + 6 + 5 = 15$$
$$5 + 5 + 6 = 16$$
$$9 + 8 + 1 = 18$$
$$8 + 2 + 3 = 13$$

3.
$$1 + 7 + 3 = 11$$
$$4 + 9 + 4 = 17$$
$$5 + 7 + 7 = 19$$
$$6 + 5 + 6 = 17$$
$$3 + 1 + 8 = 17$$
$$6 + 6 + 4 = 16$$
$$3 + 5 + 7 = 15$$

4. $$5 + 5 + 2 = 12$$ $$9 + 6 + 4 = 19$$ $$3 + 8 + 7 = 18$$

Solve.

5. Karen bought 3 postcards on the first day of her trip. She bought 6 postcards on the second day, and 5 postcards on the third day. How many postcards did she buy in all?

___14___ postcards

Spiral Review

Add or subtract.

6.
$$4 + 7 = 11$$
$$11 - 4 = 7$$
$$8 + 4 = 12$$
$$12 - 8 = 4$$
$$12 - 4 = 8$$
$$9 + 5 = 14$$
$$14 - 5 = 9$$

Chapter 2 ~ Lesson 4

Practice

Problem Solving: Reading for Math
Use a Summary

Dear Diary,
Today I went swimming in Lena's pool. There were 4 of us in the pool. Then 5 more of our friends jumped in. It was fun!

Solve.

1. Write two important number facts from the story.
There were 4 children in the pool. Then 5 more children jumped in.

2. Use the facts to write a sentence.
4 children were in the pool, and then 5 more children jumped in.

3. How many children were in the pool in all? ___ 9 children

Write a number sentence to show your thinking.
4 + 5 = 9

Use with Grade 2, Chapter 2, Lesson 4, pages 47–48. (34)

Practice

Problem Solving: Reading for Math
Use a Summary

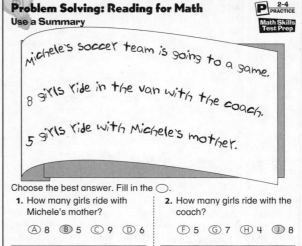

Michele's soccer team is going to a game. 8 girls ride in the van with the coach. 5 girls ride with Michele's mother.

Choose the best answer. Fill in the ◯.

1. How many girls ride with Michele's mother?
Ⓐ 8 Ⓑ 5 Ⓒ 9 Ⓓ 6

2. How many girls ride with the coach?
Ⓕ 5 Ⓖ 7 Ⓗ 4 Ⓙ 8

3. Which sentence tells the facts in the story?
Ⓐ 8 girls ride with the coach, and 5 girls ride with Michele's mother.
Ⓑ The score of the game is 8 to 5.
Ⓒ 8 girls ride with the coach, and 5 girls stay home.

4. Which number sentence shows how many girls went to the soccer game?
Ⓕ 5 + 5 = 10
Ⓖ 8 − 5 = 3
Ⓗ 8 + 5 = 13
Ⓙ 8 + 8 = 16

Use with Grade 2, Chapter 2, Lesson 4, pages 47–48. (35)

Practice

Problem Solving: Reading for Math
Use a Summary

Kevin likes to read. He read 5 pages of his book on Tuesday. He read 9 more pages of his book on Wednesday.

Choose the best answer. Fill in the ◯.

1. How many pages did Kevin read on Tuesday?
Ⓐ 4 Ⓑ 2 Ⓒ 5 Ⓓ 6

2. How many pages did Kevin read on Wednesday?
Ⓕ 9 Ⓖ 5 Ⓗ 3 Ⓙ 6

Solve.

3. Use the number facts from the story to write a sentence.
Kevin read 5 pages and 9 more pages.

4. How many pages did Kevin read in all? __14__ pages
Write a number sentence to show your thinking.
5 + 9 = 14

Use with Grade 2, Chapter 2, Lesson 4, pages 47–48. (36)

Daily Homework

2-4 Problem Solving: Reading for Math
Use a Summary

Dear Grandpa,
The Grand Canyon is neat! I took a walk to learn about the plants and animals here. There were 5 grown-ups on the walk. There were 8 kids. Wish you were here.
Love, Pete

Mr. Joseph Reyes
100 Smith Ave.
Mapleville, MA
12345

Solve.

1. Write 2 important number facts from the story.
5 grown-ups; 8 kids

2. Use both facts to write one sentence that tells a number story.
There were 5 grown-ups and 8 kids on the walk.

3. How many people went on the walk in all? ___ 13 people

Write a number sentence to show your thinking.
5 + 8 = 13

Spiral Review
Add.

4.	8	8	1	2	6	8	6
	2	2	3	7	6	9	9
	+ 8	+ 7	+ 7	+ 7	+ 3	+ 1	+ 4
	18	17	11	16	15	18	19

Grade 2, Chapter 2, Lesson 4, Cluster A **11**

Chapter 2 ~ Lesson 5

Practice

Problem Solving: Strategy
Write a Number Sentence

Write a number sentence. Solve.

1. Kelly buys 7 apples and 8 oranges. How many pieces of fruit does she buy altogether?

   $\underline{7}$ $(+)$ $\underline{8}$ = $\underline{15}$
   pieces of fruit

2. Joe has 13 baseball cards. Mike has 7 baseball cards. How many more cards does Joe have than Mike?

   $\underline{13}$ $(-)$ $\underline{7}$ = $\underline{6}$
   cards

3. Max caught 11 fish. He threw 3 fish back. How many fish did Max keep?

   $\underline{11}$ $(-)$ $\underline{3}$ = $\underline{8}$
   fish

4. Eric buys 2 stickers. Each sticker costs 9¢. How much does Eric spend?

   $\underline{9¢}$ $(+)$ $\underline{9¢}$ = $\underline{18¢}$

5. Rachel has 8 stickers. Jenny has 6 more stickers than Rachel does. How many stickers does Jenny have?

   $\underline{8}$ $(+)$ $\underline{6}$ = $\underline{14}$
   stickers

6. Sue caught 8 fish before lunch. She caught 4 more fish after lunch. How many fish did Sue catch altogether?

   $\underline{8}$ $(+)$ $\underline{4}$ = $\underline{12}$
   fish

Mixed Strategy Review

Solve.

7. Grace has 7 red beads and 5 blue beads. How many beads does she have in all?

   $\underline{12}$ beads

8. **Create a problem** for which you would write a number sentence to solve. Share it with others.

Use with Grade 2, Chapter 2, Lesson 5, pages 51–52. (37)

Reteach

Problem Solving: Strategy
Write a Number Sentence

Page 52, Problem 3

David has 7 air mail stamps and 6 letter stamps. How many stamps does he have altogether?

_____ $(+)$ _____ = _____ stamps

Step 1
Read

Be sure you understand the problem.

What do you know?

• David has $\underline{7}$ air mail stamps.

• He has $\underline{6}$ letter stamps.

What do you need to find?

• You need to find $\underline{how\ many\ stamps}$ $\underline{David\ has\ altogether}$

Step 2
Plan

- Draw a Picture
- Write a Number Sentence
- Use Logical Reasoning
- Act it Out
- Choose the Operation
- Make a Table
- Guess and Check
- Find a Pattern
- Make a Graph

Make a plan.
Choose a strategy.

Write an addition sentence to find the number of stamps altogether.

Use with Grade 2, Chapter 2, Lesson 5, pages 51–52. (38)

Reteach

Problem Solving: Strategy
Write a Number Sentence

Step 3
Solve

Carry out your plan.

• You know that David has $\underline{7}$ air mail stamps.

• You know that David has $\underline{6}$ letter stamps.

• Add to find out how many altogether. Write an addition sentence.

   $\underline{7}$ $(+)$ $\underline{6}$ = $\underline{13}$ stamps

• David has $\underline{13}$ stamps altogether.

Step 4
Look Back

Is the solution reasonable?

Does your answer make sense? (Yes) No

Did you answer the question? (Yes) No

Use with Grade 2, Chapter 2, Lesson 5, pages 51–52. (39)

© McGraw-Hill School Division

Daily Homework

2-5 Problem Solving: Strategy
Write a Number Sentence

Write a number sentence. Solve.

1. Kate has 9 postcards. Toby has 5 postcards. How many more postcards does Kate have than Toby?

   $\underline{9}$ $(-)$ $\underline{5}$ = $\underline{4}$ postcards

2. Jenny buys 5 fish postcards and 8 bear postcards. How many postcards does she have altogether?

   $\underline{5}$ $(+)$ $\underline{8}$ = $\underline{13}$ postcards

3. Mike has 12 postcards. He mails 8 postcards. How many does he have left?

   $\underline{12}$ $(-)$ $\underline{8}$ = $\underline{4}$ postcards

4. Carla buys 2 stamps. Each stamp costs 6¢. How much does Carla spend?

   $\underline{6¢}$ $(+)$ $\underline{6¢}$ = $\underline{12¢}$

Spiral Review

Add or subtract.

5.
$\begin{array}{r} 5 \\ +4 \\ \hline 9 \end{array}$
$\begin{array}{r} 9 \\ -6 \\ \hline 3 \end{array}$
$\begin{array}{r} 2 \\ +6 \\ \hline 8 \end{array}$
$\begin{array}{r} 10 \\ -5 \\ \hline 5 \end{array}$
$\begin{array}{r} 7 \\ +3 \\ \hline 10 \end{array}$
$\begin{array}{r} 10 \\ -2 \\ \hline 8 \end{array}$
$\begin{array}{r} 3 \\ +4 \\ \hline 7 \end{array}$

Chapter 2 ~ Lesson 6

Practice

Doubles to Subtract

Add or subtract.

1. $8 + 8 = \underline{16}$ $16 - 8 = \underline{8}$

2. $7 + 7 = \underline{14}$ $14 - 7 = \underline{7}$

3.
3	6	8	16	6	12
+3	−3	+8	−8	+6	−6
6	3	16	8	12	6

4.
0	20	7	7	9	10	8
+0	−10	+8	+7	+9	+10	−4
0	10	15	14	18	20	4

5.
5	18	4	14	2	10	4
+5	−9	+4	−7	+2	−5	−2
10	9	8	7	4	5	2

6.
0	1	4	13	8	17	5
−0	+1	+7	−6	+7	−8	+5
0	2	11	7	15	9	10

Problem Solving

7. A flower has 18 petals. 9 of the petals fall off. How many petals are left?

   $\underline{9}$ petals

Delly picks 7 flowers. Dean picks 6 flowers. How many flowers do they pick in all?

   $\underline{13}$ flowers

Use with Grade 2, Chapter 2, Lesson 6, pages 53–54. (40)

Reteach

Doubles to Subtract

You can use a doubles fact to help you subtract. Cross out to subtract.

$7 + 7 = \underline{14}$ ○○○○○○○

$14 - 7 = \underline{7}$ ⊗⊗⊗⊗⊗⊗⊗

Add. Then cross out to subtract.

1. $8 + 8 = \underline{16}$ ○○○○○○○○

   $16 - 8 = \underline{8}$ ⊗⊗⊗⊗⊗⊗⊗⊗

2. $9 + 9 = \underline{18}$ ○○○○○○○○○

   $18 - 9 = \underline{9}$ ⊗⊗⊗⊗⊗⊗⊗⊗⊗

3. $10 + 10 = \underline{20}$ ○○○○○○○○○○

   $20 - 10 = \underline{10}$ ⊗⊗⊗⊗⊗⊗⊗⊗⊗⊗

4.
7	14	8	16	9	18
+7	−7	+8	−8	+9	−9
14	7	16	8	18	9

Use with Grade 2, Chapter 2, Lesson 6, pages 53–54. (41)

Enrich

Doubles to Subtract

Puzzle Doubles

Subtract.
Write the doubles fact that gives the same difference.

1.
14
−8
6

12
−6
6

12
−9
3

6
−3
3

2.
16
−7
9

18
−9
9

17
−9
8

16
−8
8

3.
13
−6
7

14
−7
7

13
−9
4

8
−4
4

Use with Grade 2, Chapter 2, Lesson 6, pages 53–54. (42)

Daily Homework

2·6 Doubles to Subtract

Add or subtract.

1. $8 + 8 = \underline{16}$ $16 - 8 = \underline{8}$

2. $10 + 10 = \underline{20}$ $20 - 10 = \underline{10}$

3. $5 + 5 = \underline{10}$ $10 - 5 = \underline{5}$

4. $6 + 6 = \underline{12}$ $12 - 6 = \underline{6}$

5.
7	14	9	18	10	20
+7	−7	+9	−9	+10	−10
14	7	18	9	20	10

6.
6	12	8	16	5	10
+6	−6	+8	−8	+5	−5
12	6	16	8	10	5

Solve.

7. It is 5 miles from Ashley's house to the mall. How many miles is the drive from Ashley's house to the mall and back home again?

   $\underline{10}$ miles

Spiral Review

Add.

8.
7	4	8	2	9	3
+4	+7	+2	+8	+3	+9
11	11	10	10	12	12

Grade 2, Chapter 2, Lesson 6, Cluster B   13

Chapter 2 ~ Lesson 7

Practice

Relate Addition and Subtraction

P 2-7 PRACTICE

Complete each number sentence.

1. $8 + 5 = \underline{13}$ | $6 + 8 = \underline{14}$ | $6 + 7 = \underline{13}$
$13 - 5 = \underline{8}$ | $14 - 8 = \underline{6}$ | $13 - 7 = \underline{6}$

2. $4 + 9 = \underline{13}$ | $8 + 8 = \underline{16}$ | $6 + 9 = \underline{15}$
$13 - 4 = \underline{9}$ | $16 - 8 = \underline{8}$ | $15 - 6 = \underline{9}$

3.
$\begin{array}{r} 3 \\ +8 \\ \hline 11 \end{array}$
$\begin{array}{r} 11 \\ -8 \\ \hline 3 \end{array}$
$\begin{array}{r} 4 \\ +8 \\ \hline 12 \end{array}$
$\begin{array}{r} 12 \\ -8 \\ \hline 4 \end{array}$
$\begin{array}{r} 7 \\ +7 \\ \hline 14 \end{array}$
$\begin{array}{r} 14 \\ -7 \\ \hline 7 \end{array}$

4.
$\begin{array}{r} 8 \\ +7 \\ \hline 15 \end{array}$
$\begin{array}{r} 15 \\ -8 \\ \hline 7 \end{array}$
$\begin{array}{r} 9 \\ +7 \\ \hline 16 \end{array}$
$\begin{array}{r} 16 \\ -9 \\ \hline 7 \end{array}$
$\begin{array}{r} 8 \\ +9 \\ \hline 17 \end{array}$
$\begin{array}{r} 17 \\ -8 \\ \hline 9 \end{array}$

5.
$\begin{array}{r} 5 \\ +9 \\ \hline 14 \end{array}$
$\begin{array}{r} 14 \\ -5 \\ \hline 9 \end{array}$
$\begin{array}{r} 6 \\ +9 \\ \hline 15 \end{array}$
$\begin{array}{r} 15 \\ -6 \\ \hline 9 \end{array}$
$\begin{array}{r} 9 \\ +9 \\ \hline 18 \end{array}$
$\begin{array}{r} 18 \\ -9 \\ \hline 9 \end{array}$

Problem Solving

6. There are 16 stamps in a book. Pete uses 8 of the stamps. How many stamps are left?

___8___ stamps

Megan wrote 4 letters on Monday. She wrote 9 letters on Tuesday. How many letters did Megan write?

___13___ letters

Use with Grade 2, Chapter 2, Lesson 7, pages 55–56. (43)

Reteach

Relate Addition and Subtraction

R 2-7 RETEACH

These addition and subtraction facts have the same three numbers.

$6 + 7 = \underline{13}$
$13 - 6 = \underline{7}$

$\begin{array}{r} 6 \\ +7 \\ \hline 13 \end{array}$
$\begin{array}{r} 13 \\ -6 \\ \hline 7 \end{array}$

Add or subtract.

1. $6 + 8 = \underline{14}$
$14 - 8 = \underline{6}$
$\begin{array}{r} 6 \\ +8 \\ \hline 14 \end{array}$
$\begin{array}{r} 14 \\ -8 \\ \hline 6 \end{array}$

2. $7 + 9 = \underline{16}$
$16 - 9 = \underline{7}$
$\begin{array}{r} 7 \\ +9 \\ \hline 16 \end{array}$
$\begin{array}{r} 16 \\ -9 \\ \hline 7 \end{array}$

3. $8 + 7 = \underline{15}$
$15 - 7 = \underline{8}$
$\begin{array}{r} 8 \\ +7 \\ \hline 15 \end{array}$
$\begin{array}{r} 15 \\ -7 \\ \hline 8 \end{array}$

4. $6 + 9 = \underline{15}$
$15 - 9 = \underline{6}$
$\begin{array}{r} 6 \\ +9 \\ \hline 15 \end{array}$
$\begin{array}{r} 15 \\ -9 \\ \hline 6 \end{array}$

Use with Grade 2, Chapter 2, Lesson 7, pages 55–56. (44)

Enrich

Relate Addition and Subtraction
Stamp Collections

E 2-7 ENRICH

Stamps in Our Collections

Pete	
Polly	
Paco	
Paula	

Each stands for 1 stamp.

Pete has ___8___ stamps.   Polly has ___7___ stamps.
Paco has ___6___ stamps.   Paula has ___9___ stamps.

Write an addition sentence.
Write a related subtraction sentence.

	Addition Sentence	Subtraction Sentence
1. Pete and Paco	8 + 6 = 14 or 6 + 8 = 14	14 − 6 = 8 or 14 − 8 = 6
2. Pete and Paula	8 + 9 = 17 or 9 + 8 = 17	17 − 9 = 8 or 17 − 8 = 9
3. Polly and Paco	7 + 6 = 13 or 6 + 7 = 13	13 − 6 = 7 or 13 − 7 = 6
4. Paco and Paula	6 + 9 = 15 or 9 + 6 = 15	15 − 9 = 6 or 15 − 6 = 9
5. Polly and Paula	7 + 9 = 16 or 9 + 7 = 16	16 − 9 = 7 or 16 − 7 = 9

Use with Grade 2, Chapter 2, Lesson 7, pages 55–56. (45)

Daily Homework

2-7 Relate Addition and Subtraction

Complete each number sentence.

1. $8 + 7 = \underline{15}$ | $9 + 9 = \underline{18}$ | $7 + 6 = \underline{13}$
$15 - 8 = \underline{7}$ | $18 - 9 = \underline{9}$ | $13 - 7 = \underline{6}$

2. $7 + 6 = \underline{13}$ | $9 + 8 = \underline{17}$ | $7 + 7 = \underline{14}$
$13 - 7 = \underline{6}$ | $17 - 9 = \underline{8}$ | $14 - 7 = \underline{7}$

3.
$\begin{array}{r} 8 \\ +5 \\ \hline 13 \end{array}$
$\begin{array}{r} 13 \\ -8 \\ \hline 5 \end{array}$
$\begin{array}{r} 9 \\ +5 \\ \hline 14 \end{array}$
$\begin{array}{r} 14 \\ -9 \\ \hline 5 \end{array}$
$\begin{array}{r} 9 \\ +6 \\ \hline 15 \end{array}$
$\begin{array}{r} 15 \\ -9 \\ \hline 6 \end{array}$

Problem Solving

Use the graph.

4. How many stamps are there in all?

___11___ stamps

5. How many more flower stamps are there than fish stamps?

___5___ stamps

Spiral Review

Add.

6.
$\begin{array}{r} 3 \\ 7 \\ +4 \\ \hline 14 \end{array}$
$\begin{array}{r} 2 \\ 7 \\ +7 \\ \hline 16 \end{array}$
$\begin{array}{r} 5 \\ 3 \\ +5 \\ \hline 13 \end{array}$
$\begin{array}{r} 2 \\ 7 \\ +8 \\ \hline 17 \end{array}$
$\begin{array}{r} 6 \\ 1 \\ +6 \\ \hline 13 \end{array}$
$\begin{array}{r} 6 \\ 4 \\ +2 \\ \hline 12 \end{array}$
$\begin{array}{r} 1 \\ 5 \\ +9 \\ \hline 15 \end{array}$

Chapter 2 ~ Lesson 8

Practice

Missing Addends   **P** 2-8 PRACTICE

Find each missing addend.

1. $3 + \boxed{9} = 12$ $14 - 7 = \boxed{7}$ $\boxed{6} + 8 = 14$

2. $15 - \boxed{7} = 8$ $6 + \boxed{5} = 11$ $13 - 9 = \boxed{4}$

3.
$\begin{array}{r} 4 \\ + 7 \\ \hline \boxed{11} \end{array}$
$\begin{array}{r} 12 \\ - \boxed{8} \\ \hline 4 \end{array}$
$\begin{array}{r} 6 \\ + 9 \\ \hline \boxed{15} \end{array}$
$\begin{array}{r} 14 \\ - 8 \\ \hline \boxed{6} \end{array}$
$\begin{array}{r} 7 \\ + 7 \\ \hline \boxed{14} \end{array}$
$\begin{array}{r} 15 \\ - 7 \\ \hline \boxed{8} \end{array}$

4.
$\begin{array}{r} \boxed{8} \\ + 5 \\ \hline 13 \end{array}$
$\begin{array}{r} 16 \\ - \boxed{8} \\ \hline 8 \end{array}$
$\begin{array}{r} 6 \\ + 7 \\ \hline \boxed{13} \end{array}$
$\begin{array}{r} 17 \\ - \boxed{9} \\ \hline 8 \end{array}$
$\begin{array}{r} \boxed{5} \\ + 9 \\ \hline 14 \end{array}$
$\begin{array}{r} 14 \\ - \boxed{5} \\ \hline 9 \end{array}$

5.
$\begin{array}{r} 7 \\ + \boxed{3} \\ \hline 10 \end{array}$
$\begin{array}{r} 11 \\ - \boxed{6} \\ \hline 5 \end{array}$
$\begin{array}{r} \boxed{5} \\ + 8 \\ \hline 13 \end{array}$
$\begin{array}{r} 18 \\ - 9 \\ \hline \boxed{9} \end{array}$
$\begin{array}{r} 7 \\ + 4 \\ \hline 11 \end{array}$
$\begin{array}{r} 15 \\ - \boxed{7} \\ \hline 8 \end{array}$

6.
$\begin{array}{r} \boxed{8} \\ + 4 \\ \hline 12 \end{array}$
$\begin{array}{r} 10 \\ - \boxed{6} \\ \hline 4 \end{array}$
$\begin{array}{r} 6 \\ + 6 \\ \hline \boxed{12} \end{array}$
$\begin{array}{r} 16 \\ - \boxed{9} \\ \hline 7 \end{array}$
$\begin{array}{r} 8 \\ + \boxed{9} \\ \hline 17 \end{array}$
$\begin{array}{r} 16 \\ - 9 \\ \hline \boxed{7} \end{array}$

Problem Solving

7. Jeff has 10 stamps. He gets 10 more. How many stamps does he have now?

____20____ stamps

Gina has 15 postcards. 7 are from the United States. How many are not from the United States?

____8____ postcards

Use with Grade 2, Chapter 2, Lesson 8, pages 57–58. (46)

Reteach

Missing Addends   **R** 2-8 RETEACH

$9 + \boxed{} = 14$

Related facts use the same three numbers.

Write a related fact.

$14 - 9 = \underline{5}$,

so, $9 + \boxed{5} = 14$.

Find the missing numbers.

1. $8 + \boxed{4} = 12$ $8 + \boxed{8} = 16$
   $12 - 8 = \boxed{4}$ $16 - 8 = \boxed{8}$

2. $7 + \boxed{5} = 12$ $6 + \boxed{7} = 13$
   $12 - 7 = \boxed{5}$ $13 - 6 = \boxed{7}$

3. $5 + \boxed{8} = 13$ $8 + \boxed{7} = 15$
   $13 - 5 = \boxed{8}$ $15 - 8 = \boxed{7}$

4. $9 + \boxed{8} = 17$ $10 + \boxed{10} = 20$
   $17 - 9 = \boxed{8}$ $20 - 10 = \boxed{10}$

5.
$\begin{array}{r} 9 \\ + \boxed{4} \\ \hline 13 \end{array}$
$\begin{array}{r} 13 \\ - \boxed{9} \\ \hline 4 \end{array}$
$\begin{array}{r} 7 \\ + \boxed{9} \\ \hline 16 \end{array}$
$\begin{array}{r} 16 \\ - \boxed{7} \\ \hline 9 \end{array}$
$\begin{array}{r} 6 \\ + \boxed{9} \\ \hline 15 \end{array}$
$\begin{array}{r} 15 \\ - \boxed{9} \\ \hline 6 \end{array}$

Use with Grade 2, Chapter 2, Lesson 8, pages 57–58. (47)

Enrich

Missing Addends   **E** 2-8 ENRICH
Mystery Number

Write a number sentence. Find the mystery number.

1. Add 8 to me to get 13.

   Who am I?

   $\boxed{5} + \boxed{8} = \boxed{13}$

   The mystery number is
   ____5____

   Add 7 to me to get 16.

   Who am I?

   $\boxed{9} + \boxed{7} = \boxed{16}$

   The mystery number is
   ____9____

2. Subtract me from 11 to get 5.

   Who am I?

   $\boxed{11} - \boxed{6} = \boxed{5}$

   The mystery number is
   ____6____

   Subtract me from 14 to get 6.

   Who am I?

   $\boxed{14} - \boxed{8} = \boxed{6}$

   The mystery number is
   ____8____

3. Add 9 to me to get 12.

   Who am I?

   $\boxed{3} + \boxed{9} = \boxed{12}$

   The mystery number is
   ____3____

   Subtract me from 15 to get 8.

   Who am I?

   $\boxed{15} - \boxed{7} = \boxed{8}$

   The mystery number is
   ____7____

Use with Grade 2, Chapter 2, Lesson 8, pages 57–58. (48)

Daily Homework

2·8 Missing Addends

Find each missing number.

1. $9 + \boxed{7} = 16$ $16 - 9 = \boxed{7}$

2. $8 + \boxed{6} = 14$ $14 - 8 = \boxed{6}$

3.
$\begin{array}{r} 8 \\ + \boxed{7} \\ \hline 15 \end{array}$
$\begin{array}{r} 15 \\ - 8 \\ \hline 7 \end{array}$
$\begin{array}{r} 7 \\ + \boxed{6} \\ \hline 13 \end{array}$
$\begin{array}{r} 13 \\ - 7 \\ \hline 6 \end{array}$
$\begin{array}{r} 9 \\ + \boxed{4} \\ \hline 13 \end{array}$
$\begin{array}{r} 13 \\ - 9 \\ \hline 4 \end{array}$

Complete each number sentence.

4. $9 + \boxed{6} = 15$ $8 + \boxed{5} = 13$ $9 + \boxed{5} = 14$

5. $7 \boxed{+} 8 = 15$ $13 \boxed{-} 5 = 8$ $7 \boxed{+} 9 = 16$

Find the doubles.

6. $\boxed{4} + \boxed{4} = 8$ $\boxed{2} + \boxed{2} = 4$

7. $\boxed{3} + \boxed{3} = 6$ $\boxed{1} + \boxed{1} = 2$

Spiral Review

Add.

8. $7 + 4 = \underline{11}$ $8 + 5 = \underline{13}$ $9 + 3 = \underline{12}$

9. $8 + 4 = \underline{12}$ $8 + 6 = \underline{14}$ $9 + 4 = \underline{13}$

Grade 2, Chapter 2, Lesson 8, Cluster B **15**

Chapter 2 ~ Lesson 9

Practice

Fact Families

Complete each fact family.

1.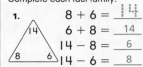

$8 + 6 = \underline{14}$ $9 + 4 = \underline{13}$
$6 + 8 = \underline{14}$ $4 + 9 = \underline{13}$
$14 - 8 = \underline{6}$ $13 - 9 = \underline{4}$
$14 - 6 = \underline{8}$ $13 - 4 = \underline{9}$

(triangle 14, 8, 6) (triangle 13, 9, 4)

2.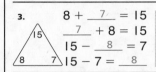

$8 + 9 = \underline{17}$ $5 + 8 = \underline{13}$
$9 + 8 = \underline{17}$ $8 + 5 = \underline{13}$
$17 - 8 = \underline{9}$ $13 - 5 = \underline{8}$
$17 - 9 = \underline{8}$ $13 - 8 = \underline{5}$

(triangle 17, 9, 8) (triangle 13, 8, 5)

3.

$8 + \underline{7} = 15$ $\underline{9} + 7 = 16$
$\underline{7} + 8 = 15$ $7 + \underline{9} = 16$
$15 - \underline{8} = 7$ $16 - 9 = \underline{7}$
$15 - 7 = \underline{8}$ $16 - \underline{7} = 9$

(triangle 15, 8, 7) (triangle 16, 9, 7)

4.

$\underline{7} + 7 = 14$ $\underline{9} + 9 = 18$
$14 - 7 = \underline{7}$ $18 - \underline{9} = 9$

(triangle 14, 7, 7) (triangle 18, 9, 9)

Problem Solving

5. Alex writes a fact family with these two numbers, 4 and 7. What number completes the fact family?

Possible answers: 3 or 11

David writes a fact family with these two numbers, 9 and 14. What number completes the fact family?

Possile answers: 5 or 23

Reteach

Fact Families

Some fact families have two addition facts and two subtraction facts.

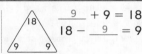 $9 + 7 = \underline{16}$ $16 - 7 = \underline{9}$
$7 + 9 = \underline{16}$ $16 - 9 = \underline{7}$

Some fact families have one addition fact and one subtraction fact.

$8 + 8 = \underline{16}$ $16 - 8 = \underline{8}$

Complete each fact family.

1. $4 + 9 = \underline{13}$ $13 - 9 = \underline{4}$
$9 + 4 = \underline{13}$ $13 - 4 = \underline{9}$

2. $6 + 5 = \underline{11}$ $11 - 5 = \underline{6}$
$5 + 6 = \underline{11}$ $11 - 6 = \underline{5}$

3. $8 + 9 = \underline{17}$ $17 - 9 = \underline{8}$
$9 + 8 = \underline{17}$ $17 - 8 = \underline{9}$

4. $7 + 7 = \underline{14}$ $14 - 7 = \underline{7}$

Enrich

Fact Families
Zoo Animal Families

Favorite Zoo Animal		Our Class	Mr. Ray's Class
	lion	7	4
	elephant	9	7
	zebra	5	8

Use the numbers to write a fact family.

1. How many children liked the elephant best?

Our class: $\underline{9}$
Mr. Ray's class: $\underline{7}$
Total: $\underline{16}$

$\underline{9} + \underline{7} = \underline{16}$
$\underline{7} + \underline{9} = \underline{16}$
$\underline{16} - \underline{7} = \underline{9}$
$\underline{16} - \underline{9} = \underline{7}$

2. How many children liked the lion best?

Our class: $\underline{7}$
Mr. Ray's class: $\underline{4}$
Total: $\underline{11}$

$\underline{7} + \underline{4} = \underline{11}$
$\underline{4} + \underline{7} = \underline{11}$
$\underline{11} - \underline{4} = \underline{7}$
$\underline{11} - \underline{7} = \underline{4}$

3. How many children liked the zebra best?

Our class: $\underline{5}$
Mr. Ray's class: $\underline{8}$
Total: $\underline{13}$

$\underline{5} + \underline{8} = \underline{13}$
$\underline{8} + \underline{5} = \underline{13}$
$\underline{13} - \underline{8} = \underline{5}$
$\underline{13} - \underline{5} = \underline{8}$

Daily Homework

2-9 Fact Families

Complete each fact family.

1. (triangle 13, 4, 9)

$9 + 4 = \underline{13}$ $4 + 9 = \underline{13}$
$13 - 9 = \underline{4}$ $13 - 4 = \underline{9}$

2. (triangle 16, 9, 7)

$9 + 7 = \underline{16}$ $7 + 9 = \underline{16}$
$16 - 9 = \underline{7}$ $16 - 7 = \underline{9}$

3. (triangle 14, 8, 6)

$8 + 6 = \underline{14}$ $6 + \underline{8} = 14$
$14 \underbigcirc{-} 8 = 6$ $14 - \underline{6} = 8$

4. (triangle 16, 8, 8)

$8 \underbigcirc{+} 8 = 16$ $16 \underbigcirc{-} 8 = 8$

Spiral Review

Draw a picture to solve this problem.

5. Brenda has 12 stamps.

She gives 4 stamps to Josh.

How many stamps does Brenda have left? $\underline{8}$ stamps

Chapter 2 ~ Lesson 10

Part A Worksheet

Problem Solving: Application
Design a Stamp

Part A 2-10 WORKSHEET
Decision Making

Design a state postcard stamp.

Draw a picture.

Show the cost.

Design a letter stamp for a place to visit.

Draw a picture.

Show the cost.

Check students' drawings.

Use with Grade 2, Chapter 2, Lesson 10, pages 63–64. (52)

Part A Worksheet

Problem Solving: Application
Design a Stamp

Part A 2-10 WORKSHEET
Decision Making

Answer these questions about the postcard stamp you designed. Answers will vary.

1. What state did you choose? _____

   Why did you choose that state?

   _____

2. What picture did you draw? _____

   Why did you draw that picture?

   _____

3. What cost did you choose? _____

   Why did you choose that cost?

   _____

Answer these questions about the letter stamp you designed.

4. What place did you choose? _____

   Why did you choose that place?

   _____

5. What cost did you choose? _____

   Why did you choose that cost?

   _____

Use with Grade 2, Chapter 2, Lesson 10, pages 63–64. (53)

Part B Worksheet

Problem Solving: Application
Stamp Glue

Part B 2-10 WORKSHEET
Math & Science

1. Record how much flour you put in each cup.

   Record how well each glue worked. Answers will vary.

Cup	Spoonfuls of Flour	How did the glue work?
A		
B		
C		

2. Which glue worked best?

   _____

   Tell why you think it worked best.

   _____

   _____

3. How do you think you could make a glue that works better?

   _____

   _____

   _____

   _____

Use with Grade 2, Chapter 2, Lesson 10, pages 65–66. (54)

Chapter 3 ~ Lesson 1

Practice

Tens

Write how many.

1. 4 groups of ten

_4_ tens = _40_ in all

7 groups of ten

_7_ tens = _70_ in all

2. 5 groups of ten

_5_ tens = _50_ in all

2 groups of ten

_2_ tens = _20_ in all

3. 8 groups of ten

_8_ tens = _80_ in all

3 groups of ten

_3_ tens = _30_ in all

4. 9 groups of ten

_9_ tens = _90_ in all

6 groups of ten

_6_ tens = _60_ in all

5. Circle all the ways to show 33.

(3 tens 3 ones)   30¢

(33)   (30 + 3)

6. Circle all the ways to show 67.

(60 + 7)   (6 tens 7 ones)

60 tens   76

Use with Grade 2, Chapter 3, Lesson 1, pages 79–80. (55)

Reteach

Tens

1 ten is the same as 10 ones.

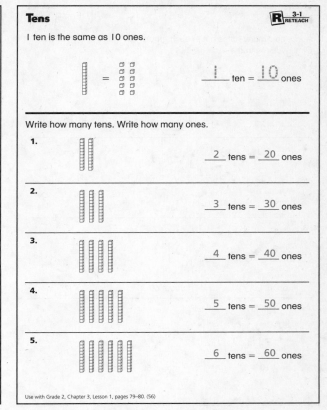

_1_ ten = _10_ ones

Write how many tens. Write how many ones.

1. _2_ tens = _20_ ones

2. _3_ tens = _30_ ones

3. _4_ tens = _40_ ones

4. _5_ tens = _50_ ones

5. _6_ tens = _60_ ones

Use with Grade 2, Chapter 3, Lesson 1, pages 79–80. (56)

Enrich

Tens
A Music Fair

Go with Ann and Mike through the music fair.
Look for tens and ones in order through 20.
Draw the path.

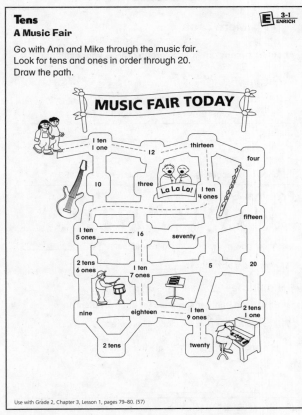

Use with Grade 2, Chapter 3, Lesson 1, pages 79–80. (57)

Daily Homework

3-1 Tens

Write how many.

1. 2 groups of ten

_2_ tens =
_20_ in all

4 groups of ten

_4_ tens =
_40_ in all

2. 6 groups of ten

_6_ tens =
_60_ in all

5 groups of ten

_5_ tens =
_50_ in all

3. 7 groups of ten

_7_ tens =
_70_ in all

9 groups of ten

_9_ tens =
_90_ in all

4. 10 groups of ten

_10_ tens =
_100_ in all

8 groups of ten

_8_ tens =
_80_ in all

5. 3 groups of ten

_3_ tens =
_30_ in all

1 group of ten

_1_ ten =
_10_ in all

Spiral Review
Subtract.

6. 11 − 8 = _3_   10 − 6 = _4_   12 − 7 = _5_

Grade 2, Chapter 3, Lesson 1, Cluster A **17**

Chapter 3 ~ Lesson 2

Practice

MORE Tens

About how many notes are in each group?
Circle your estimate.

1.
about 10   (about 30)

2.
(about 30)   about 80

3.
(about 20)   about 60

4.
about 10   (about 50)

Reteach

MORE Tens

An estimate tells about how many.

There are fewer than __10__ notes.

Estimate how many notes are in each group.
Circle your estimate.

1.
(more than 10)   less than 10

2.
more than 20   (less than 20)

3.
more than 30   (less than 30)

Enrich

MORE Tens

Make an Estimate   Answers may vary.

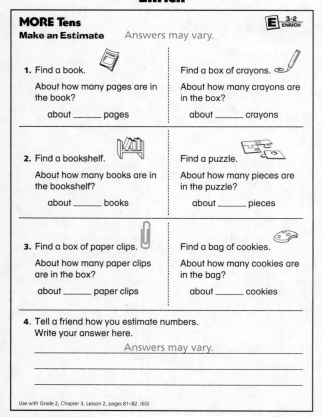

1. Find a book.

About how many pages are in
the book?

about _____ pages

Find a box of crayons.

About how many crayons are
in the box?

about _____ crayons

2. Find a bookshelf.

About how many books are in
the bookshelf?

about _____ books

Find a puzzle.

About how many pieces are
in the puzzle?

about _____ pieces

3. Find a box of paper clips.

About how many paper clips
are in the box?

about _____ paper clips

Find a bag of cookies.

About how many cookies are
in the bag?

about _____ cookies

4. Tell a friend how you estimate numbers.
Write your answer here.

_____ Answers may vary. _____

Daily Homework

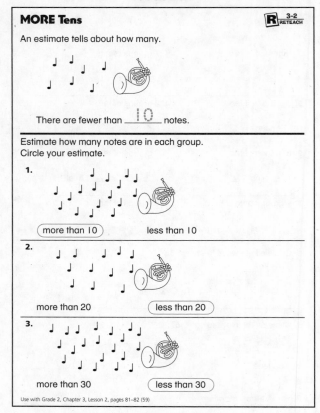

3-2 More Tens

About how many are in each group? Circle your estimate.

1. about 10 (about 20)

2. (about 30) about 60

3. about 10 (about 40)

4. (about 10) about 30

Problem Solving

5. About how many bells are in the picture? __Answers may vary__

6. Now count how many. __16__

Spiral Review

Solve. Write a number sentence for each problem.

7. There are 6 🥁 in the class. There are 3 △.

How many 🥁 and △ are there all together?

9

6 ⊕ 3 = 9

Chapter 3 ~ Lesson 3

Practice

Tens and Ones

P 3-3 PRACTICE

Write how many tens and ones.

1. 15 = __1__ ten __5__ ones

tens	ones
1	5

2. 43 = __4__ tens __3__ ones

tens	ones
4	3

3. 66 = __6__ tens __6__ ones

tens	ones
6	6

4. 18 = __1__ ten __8__ ones

tens	ones
1	8

5. 59 = __5__ tens __9__ ones

tens	ones
5	9

6. 21 = __2__ tens __1__ one

tens	ones
2	1

7. 74 = __7__ tens __4__ ones

tens	ones
7	4

8. 32 = __3__ tens __2__ ones

tens	ones
3	2

Use with Grade 2, Chapter 3, Lesson 3, pages 83–84. (61)

Reteach

Tens and Ones

R 3-3 RETEACH

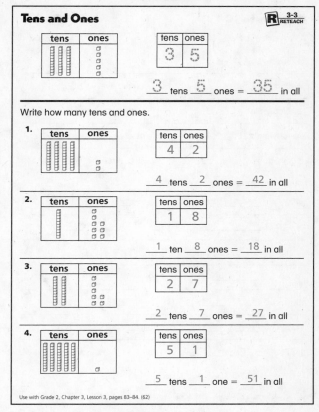

__3__ tens __5__ ones = __35__ in all

Write how many tens and ones.

1.

tens	ones
4	2

__4__ tens __2__ ones = __42__ in all

2.

tens	ones
1	8

__1__ ten __8__ ones = __18__ in all

3.

tens	ones
2	7

__2__ tens __7__ ones = __27__ in all

4.

tens	ones
5	1

__5__ tens __1__ one = __51__ in all

Use with Grade 2, Chapter 3, Lesson 3, pages 83–84. (62)

Enrich

Tens and Ones
Old Time Tens and Ones

E 3-3 ENRICH

Tens and ones have been written in many different ways.

A long time ago, the Egyptians wrote tens and ones with these marks.

A stick | means 1.   A ∩ means 10.

∩∩|||| is 24.

Write the number.

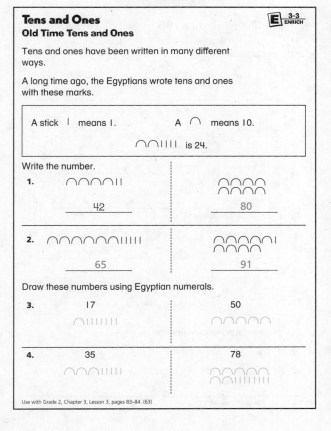

1. _____ 42   _____ 80

2. _____ 65   _____ 91

Draw these numbers using Egyptian numerals.

3.   17   50

4.   35   78

Use with Grade 2, Chapter 3, Lesson 3, pages 83–84. (63)

Daily Homework

3-3 Tens and Ones

Write how many tens and ones.

1. 36 = __3__ tens __6__ ones

tens	ones
3	6

2. 72 = __7__ tens __2__ ones

tens	ones
7	2

3. 45 = __4__ tens __5__ ones

tens	ones
4	5

Write each number.

4. 9 tens 4 ones   1 ten and 8 ones

Problem Solving

Draw a picture to solve.

5. Liz has 4 tens and 2 ones Mark has 2 tens and 2 ones. How many more tens does Liz have than Mark?
__2 tens__

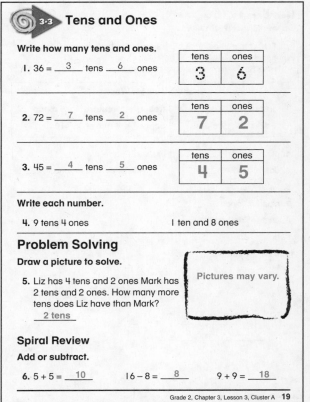

Pictures may vary.

Spiral Review

Add or subtract.

6. 5 + 5 = __10__   16 − 8 = __8__   9 + 9 = __18__

Grade 2, Chapter 3, Lesson 3, Cluster A **19**

© McGraw-Hill School Division

Chapter 3 ~ Lesson 4

Practice

Numbers to 100

Write each number.

1. seventy __70__   sixteen __16__

2. thirty-seven __37__   twenty-five __25__

3. eighty-nine __89__   twelve __12__

4. forty-eight __48__   ninety-two __92__

5. fifty-one __51__   sixty-three __63__

Write each word.

6. 23 __twenty-three__   45 __forty-five__

7. 78 __seventy-eight__   53 __fifty-three__

8. 13 __thirteen__   90 __ninety__

9. 84 __eighty-four__   29 __twenty-nine__

10. 35 __thirty-five__   18 __eighteen__

11. 59 __fifty-nine__   86 __eighty-six__

12. 31 __thirty-one__   66 __sixty-six__

Use with Grade 2, Chapter 3, Lesson 4, pages 85–86. (64)

Reteach

Numbers to 100

You can write word names for numbers.

1 one	11 eleven	30 thirty
2 two	12 twelve	40 forty
3 three	13 thirteen	50 fifty
4 four	14 fourteen	60 sixty
5 five	15 fifteen	70 seventy
6 six	16 sixteen	80 eighty
7 seven	17 seventeen	90 ninety
8 eight	18 eighteen	100 hundred
9 nine	19 nineteen	
10 ten	20 twenty	

Circle the number.

1. seventeen   7   (17)   70   twenty-one   1   20   (21)

2. forty-five   4   5   (45)   sixty   6   16   (60)

3. ninety-seven   9   (97)   7   thirty-two   (32)   3   2

Circle the word.

4. 56   five   sixty   (fifty-six)

5. 12   (twelve)   twenty   two

6. 74   seventy   seventeen   (seventy-four)

7. 89   (eighty-nine)   ninety   eighty

Use with Grade 2, Chapter 3, Lesson 4, pages 85–86. (65)

Enrich

Numbers to 100

Spanish Word Names

Spanish word names for numbers are in the box.
Write each sum.
Write the Spanish number word in the puzzle.

Spanish Number Words				
1 uno	2 dos	3 tres	4 cuatro	5 cinco
6 seis	7 siete	8 ocho	9 nueve	10 diez

1. diez − uno = __9__

2. uno + uno = __2__

3. dos − uno = __1__

4. dos + dos + uno = __5__

5. seis + uno = __7__

6. dos + uno = __3__

7. cinco + cinco = __10__

8. cuatro + cuatro = __8__

9. dos + dos = __4__

10. tres + tres = __6__

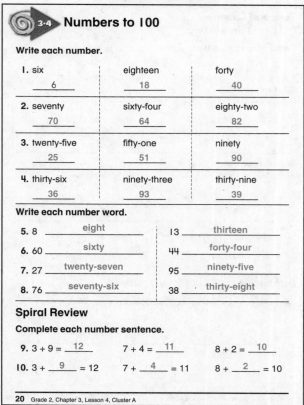

Use with Grade 2, Chapter 3, Lesson 4, pages 85–86. (66)

Daily Homework

3-4 **Numbers to 100**

Write each number.

1. six __6__   eighteen __18__   forty __40__

2. seventy __70__   sixty-four __64__   eighty-two __82__

3. twenty-five __25__   fifty-one __51__   ninety __90__

4. thirty-six __36__   ninety-three __93__   thirty-nine __39__

Write each number word.

5. 8 __eight__   13 __thirteen__

6. 60 __sixty__   44 __forty-four__

7. 27 __twenty-seven__   95 __ninety-five__

8. 76 __seventy-six__   38 __thirty-eight__

Spiral Review

Complete each number sentence.

9. 3 + 9 = __12__   7 + 4 = __11__   8 + 2 = __10__

10. 3 + __9__ = 12   7 + __4__ = 11   8 + __2__ = 10

© McGraw-Hill School Division

Chapter 3 ~ Lesson 5

Practice

Expanded Form P PRACTICE 3-5

Write each number in expanded form.

1.	56		39
	50 + 6		30 + 9
2.	23		67
	20 + 3		60 + 7
3.	34		70
	30 + 4		70 + 0
4.	96		46
	90 + 6		40 + 6
5.	33		18
	30 + 3		10 + 8
6.	14		81
	10 + 4		80 + 1
7.	99		77
	90 + 9		70 + 7
8.	65		92
	60 + 5		90 + 2

Reteach

Expanded Form R RETEACH 3-5

You can write numbers in expanded form.

27 in all	2 tens	7 ones
27 =	20	+ 7

Write each number in expanded form.

1.

35   30 + 5   61   60 + 1

2.

18   10 + 8   73   70 + 3

3.

49   40 + 9   54   50 + 4

Enrich

Expanded Form E ENRICH 3-5
Hidden Picture

Write the number shown by each expanded form.

Color numbers from 20 through 40 red.

Color numbers from 41 through 90 yellow.

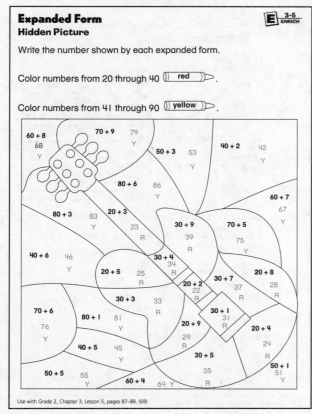

Daily Homework

3-5 Expanded Form

Write each number in expanded form.

1. **89**		**24**
80 + 9		20 + 4
2. **12**		**61**
10 + 2		60 + 1
3. **35**		**47**
30 + 5		40 + 7
4. **76**		**98**
70 + 6		90 + 8

Spiral Review

Add or subtract.

5.	8	7	18	16	4	9	17
	+ 7	+ 6	− 9	− 7	+ 8	+ 9	− 9
	15	13	9	9	12	18	8

Chapter 3 ~ Lesson 6

Practice

Problem Solving: Reading for Math
Draw Conclusions

P 3-6 PRACTICE Reading Skill

Rachel's class took a trip to the beach.
Some children are swimming.
Some children are building a sand castle.
Some children are playing volleyball.

Read the story. Look at the picture. Answer each question.

1. Are there more children building a sand castle or playing volleyball?
   playing volleyball

2. Are there more children swimming or building a sand castle?
   swimming

3. Do you think Rachel and her class are having fun? Why?
   Answers may vary. Possible answer: Yes, because
   everybody looks like they are having a good time.

Use with Grade 2, Chapter 3, Lesson 6, pages 89–90. (70)

Practice

Problem Solving: Reading for Math
Draw Conclusions

P 3-6 PRACTICE Math Skills Test Prep

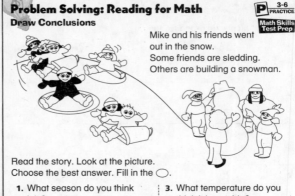

Mike and his friends went out in the snow.
Some friends are sledding.
Others are building a snowman.

Read the story. Look at the picture.
Choose the best answer. Fill in the ◯.

1. What season do you think it is?
   Ⓐ summer   Ⓑ winter
   Ⓒ spring   Ⓓ fall

2. Which sentence is true?
   Ⓕ More children are sledding than building a snowman.
   Ⓖ More children are building a snowman than sledding.
   Ⓗ As many children are sledding as are building a snowman.

3. What temperature do you think it is outside?
   Ⓐ hot
   Ⓑ cold
   Ⓒ warm

4. Which sentence do you think is true?
   Ⓕ Mike and his friends are not having fun.
   Ⓖ Mike and his friends are tired.
   Ⓗ Mike and his friends are having fun.

Use with Grade 2, Chapter 3, Lesson 6, pages 89–90. (71)

Practice

Problem Solving: Reading for Math
Draw Conclusions

P 3-6 PRACTICE Math Skills Test Prep

Mr. Hill's class is at the science museum.
Some children are looking at the dinosaur exhibit.
Some children are looking at the fish.
Other children are looking at the space exhibit.
Read the story. Look at the picture.
Choose the best answer. Fill in the ◯.

1. Which sentence is true?
   Ⓐ More children are looking at the dinosaur than at the fish.
   Ⓑ As many children are looking at the dinosaur as at the fish.
   Ⓒ More children are looking at the fish than at the dinosaur.

2. Which sentence is true?
   Ⓕ More children are looking at the fish than at the dinosaur.
   Ⓖ More children are looking at the rocket than at the fish.
   Ⓗ As many children are looking at the rocket as at the fish.

Answer the question.

3. Why do you think Mr. Hill's class went to the science museum?
   Answers may vary. Possible answer: To learn more
   about science

Use with Grade 2, Chapter 3, Lesson 6, pages 89–90. (72)

Daily Homework

3-6 **Problem Solving: Reading for Math**
Draw Conclusions

Sara and her friends are getting ready to eat. Some friends are making the meal. Some are making lemonade. Some are setting the table.

Read. Look at the pictures. Answer each question.

1. Are there more children making the meal or setting the table?
   There are more children making the meal.

2. Does everyone have a job to do? Why?
   Possible answers: Yes; because the work will get done
   more quickly, or everyone who wants to eat helps.

Spiral Review
Write each number in expanded form.

3. 83   46   25   91
   _80 + 3_   _40 + 6_   _20 + 5_   _90 + 1_

22 Grade 2, Chapter 3, Lesson 6, Cluster A

Chapter 3 ~ Lesson 7

Practice

Problem Solving: Strategy
Use Logical Reasoning

Solve.

1. How many birds are at the zoo?
   There are 7 tens in the number.
   The ones digit is less than 5.
   The number is greater than 73.
   __74__ birds

2. How long was the dolphin show?
   The number of minutes is between 40 and 60.
   The tens digit is one less than the ones digit.
   The number has 4 tens.
   __45__ minutes

3. How many snakes did Tim see?
   The number is greater than 20.
   The number is less than 30.
   The tens and ones digits are the same.
   __22__ snakes

4. How many fish did the seals eat?
   The number is between 30 and 50.
   The ones digit is 1 more than 8.
   The number has less than 4 tens.
   __39__ fish

Mixed Strategy Review

Solve.

5. Clare has 7 shells in her pail. Her brother gives her 11 more shells. How many shells does she have in all?
   __18__ shells

6. **Create a problem** for which you would use logical reasoning to solve. Share it with others.
   _____
   _____

Use with Grade 2, Chapter 3, Lesson 7, pages 93–94. (73)

Reteach

Problem Solving: Strategy
Use Logical Reasoning

Page 94, Problem 2
Lin, Billy and Ronny play in a band.
They play a violin, a guitar, and a drum.
Lin does not play violin.
Billy does not play an instrument with strings.
What does Billy play?

Step 1
Read
Be sure you understand the problem.
What do you know?
- Billy plays in a __band__ with Lin and Ronny.
- Billy's instrument does not have __strings__.

What do you need to find?
- You need to find __what instrument Billy plays.__

Step 2
Plan
Make a plan.
Choose a strategy.

- Draw a Picture
- Write a Number Sentence
- Use Logical Reasoning
- Act it Out
- Choose the Operation
- Make a Table
- Guess and Check
- Find a Pattern
- Make a Graph

Think about what you know.

Find clues.

Use logical reasoning to find the instrument Billy plays.

Use with Grade 2, Chapter 3, Lesson 7, pages 93–94. (74)

Reteach

Problem Solving: Strategy
Use Logical Reasoning

Step 3
Solve
Carry out your plan.
- List the instruments played in the band.
  __violin, guitar, drum__
- List the instruments that have strings.
  __violin and guitar__
- Use logical reasoning.
  What instrument does Billy play?
  __drum__

Step 4
Look Back
Is the solution reasonable?

Read the problem again.

Does your answer make sense? (Yes) No

Tell how you solved the problem by using the clues. __Answers may vary.__

Use with Grade 2, Chapter 3, Lesson 7, pages 93–94. (75)

Daily Homework

3·7
Problem Solving: Strategy
Use Logical Reasoning

Solve.

1. How many candy bars did Joe sell?
   The number of candy bars is between 20 and 30.
   The ones digit is just after 8.
   __29__ candy bars

2. How many meals were served at lunch?
   The number has a 7 in the tens place.
   The digit in the ones place is greater than 2.
   The number is less than 74.
   __73__ meals

3. How many flowers did the class plant?
   The number is greater than 40.
   The number is less than 50.
   The tens and ones digits are the same.
   _____ flowers

Spiral Review

Write each number.

4. four __4__   seventeen __17__   eighty-five __85__

Write each number word.

5. 7 __seven__   15 __fifteen__   32 __thirty-two__

Chapter 3 ~ Lesson 8

Practice

Compare Numbers

Compare. Write >, <, or =.

1. 47 $>$ 38	51 $>$ 45	19 $<$ 29
2. 36 $=$ 36	63 $<$ 72	23 $<$ 29
3. 95 $>$ 59	43 $<$ 49	78 $<$ 83
4. 31 $<$ 38	66 $>$ 6	45 $=$ 45
5. 27 $<$ 47	58 $<$ 81	49 $>$ 37
6. 83 $>$ 43	76 $>$ 57	58 $<$ 95
7. 28 $>$ 21	76 $>$ 69	40 $=$ 40
8. 80 $>$ 59	47 $<$ 59	68 $<$ 89
9. 33 $<$ 77	50 $<$ 60	32 $<$ 37
10. 16 $<$ 61	64 $<$ 82	95 $>$ 67
11. 28 $>$ 18	55 $>$ 34	47 $=$ 47
12. 92 $=$ 92	78 $<$ 87	36 $>$ 16

Use with Grade 2, Chapter 3, Lesson 8, pages 95–96. (76)

Reteach

Compare Numbers

You can use >, <, and = to compare numbers. Remember the arrow points to the lesser number.

16 is less than 24.	24 is greater than 16.	24 is equal to 24.
16 $<$ 24	24 $>$ 16	24 $=$ 24

Compare. Write >, <, or =.

1.

21 < 35	18 = 18	30 < 37

2. 25 $<$ 45	66 $>$ 6	72 $=$ 72
3. 52 $>$ 47	88 $>$ 81	31 $<$ 39
4. 41 $=$ 41	97 $>$ 79	63 $<$ 73

Use with Grade 2, Chapter 3, Lesson 8, pages 95–96. (77)

Enrich

Compare Numbers

Spin a Number

Use a [paperclip] and the spinners below.

Spin two 2-digit numbers.

Write the numbers in the boxes.

Write > or < in the circle.

Check students' work.

3 4 $<$ 7 5

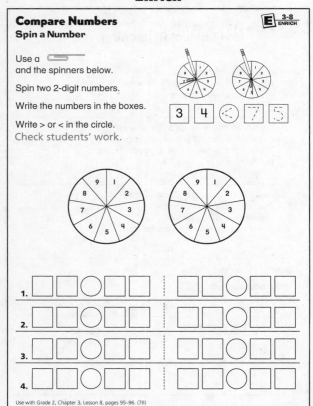

1.

2.

3.

4.

Use with Grade 2, Chapter 3, Lesson 8, pages 95–96. (78)

Daily Homework

3-8 Compare Numbers

Remember to compare the tens first.

Compare.

Use <, >, or =.

Use [box] if you like.

1. 58 $>$ 57	45 $=$ 45	42 $>$ 9	33 $<$ 44
2. 3 $<$ 34	98 $>$ 92	13 $>$ 2	65 $>$ 25
3. 22 $=$ 22	35 $<$ 64	19 $<$ 27	5 $<$ 63
4. 81 $>$ 26	17 $<$ 71	89 $=$ 89	99 $>$ 88
5. 49 $>$ 38	26 $=$ 26	78 $<$ 82	18 $<$ 19
6. 36 $>$ 29	12 $<$ 76	44 $<$ 46	77 $>$ 67

Spiral Review

Complete each number sentence.

7. $9 + 6 = \underline{15}$ $7 + 5 = \underline{12}$

$9 + \underline{6} = 15$ $7 \underline{+} 5 = 12$

$15 - 9 = \underline{6}$ $12 - 7 = \underline{5}$

$15 \underline{-} 6 = 9$ $12 - \underline{5} = 7$

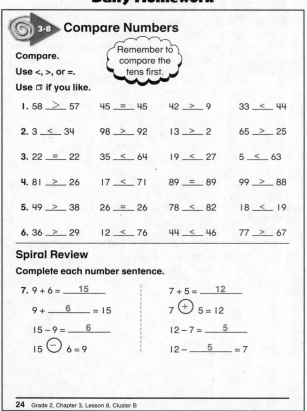

Chapter 3 ~ Lesson 9

Practice

Order Numbers

P 3-9 PRACTICE

Write the number that comes just before.

1. __44__, 45   __39__, 40   __77__, 78

2. __60__, 61   __18__, 19   __53__, 54

3. __23__, 24   __85__, 86   __19__, 20

4. __72__, 73   __39__, 40   __77__, 78

Write the number that comes just after.

5. 50, __51__   17, __18__   99, __100__

6. 42, __43__   87, __88__   13, __14__

7. 29, __30__   47, __48__   39, __40__

8. 27, __28__   59, __60__   66, __67__

Write the number that comes between.

9. 29, __30__, 31   91, __92__, 93   55, __56__, 57

10. 60, __61__, 62   77, __78__, 79   84, __85__, 86

11. 48, __49__, 50   39, __40__, 41   15, __16__, 17

Reteach

Order Numbers

R 3-9 RETEACH

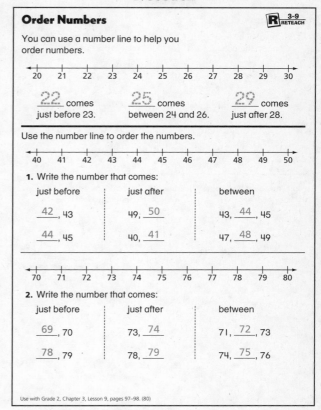

You can use a number line to help you order numbers.

20 21 22 23 24 25 26 27 28 29 30

__22__ comes just before 23.   __25__ comes between 24 and 26.   __29__ comes just after 28.

Use the number line to order the numbers.

40 41 42 43 44 45 46 47 48 49 50

1. Write the number that comes:

just before	just after	between
__42__, 43	49, __50__	43, __44__, 45
__44__, 45	40, __41__	47, __48__, 49

70 71 72 73 74 75 76 77 78 79 80

2. Write the number that comes:

just before	just after	between
__69__, 70	73, __74__	71, __72__, 73
__78__, 79	78, __79__	74, __75__, 76

Enrich

Order Numbers
Getting in Order

E 3-9 ENRICH

The numbers are mixed up.
Put them in order from least to greatest.

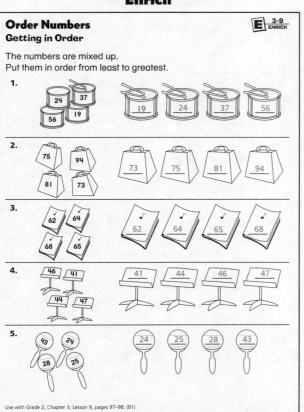

1. 24 37 56 19 → 19 24 37 56

2. 75 94 81 73 → 73 75 81 94

3. 62 64 68 65 → 62 64 65 68

4. 46 41 44 47 → 41 44 46 47

5. 43 24 28 25 → 24 25 28 43

Daily Homework

3·9 Order Numbers

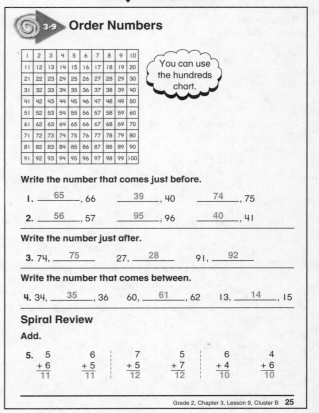

1	2	3	4	5	6	7	8	9	10
11	12	13	14	15	16	17	18	19	20
21	22	23	24	25	26	27	28	29	30
31	32	33	34	35	36	37	38	39	40
41	42	43	44	45	46	47	48	49	50
51	52	53	54	55	56	57	58	59	60
61	62	63	64	65	66	67	68	69	70
71	72	73	74	75	76	77	78	79	80
81	82	83	84	85	86	87	88	89	90
91	92	93	94	95	96	97	98	99	100

You can use the hundreds chart.

Write the number that comes just before.

1. __65__, 66   __39__, 40   __74__, 75

2. __56__, 57   __95__, 96   __40__, 41

Write the number just after.

3. 74, __75__   27, __28__   91, __92__

Write the number that comes between.

4. 34, __35__, 36   60, __61__, 62   13, __14__, 15

Spiral Review
Add.

5.
$$\begin{array}{r} 5 \\ +6 \\ \hline 11 \end{array} \quad \begin{array}{r} 6 \\ +5 \\ \hline 11 \end{array} \quad \begin{array}{r} 7 \\ +5 \\ \hline 12 \end{array} \quad \begin{array}{r} 5 \\ +7 \\ \hline 12 \end{array} \quad \begin{array}{r} 6 \\ +4 \\ \hline 10 \end{array} \quad \begin{array}{r} 4 \\ +6 \\ \hline 10 \end{array}$$

Chapter 3 ~ Lesson 10

Practice

Skip Count

1. Skip count by twos. Connect the dots.

36 38 40 End 24
Start 20 22
26
34 32 30 28

Skip count by fives. Connect the dots.

Start 30
End 80 35
75 40
70 45
65 50
55
60

2. Skip count by threes. Connect the dots.

6 9
15
Start 3 12
End 30 18
27 24 21

Skip count by fours. Connect the dots.

8 12
16
20
Start 4 24
28 32
40 36
End

Reteach

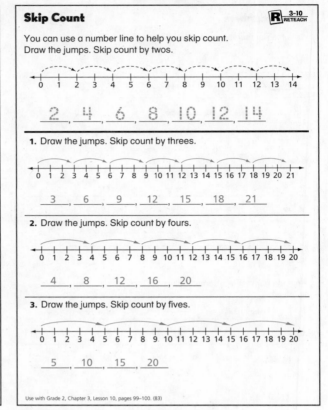

Skip Count

You can use a number line to help you skip count. Draw the jumps. Skip count by twos.

0 1 2 3 4 5 6 7 8 9 10 11 12 13 14

2, 4, 6, 8, 10, 12, 14

1. Draw the jumps. Skip count by threes.

0 1 2 3 4 5 6 7 8 9 10 11 12 13 14 15 16 17 18 19 20 21

3, 6, 9, 12, 15, 18, 21

2. Draw the jumps. Skip count by fours.

0 1 2 3 4 5 6 7 8 9 10 11 12 13 14 15 16 17 18 19 20

4, 8, 12, 16, 20

3. Draw the jumps. Skip count by fives.

0 1 2 3 4 5 6 7 8 9 10 11 12 13 14 15 16 17 18 19 20

5, 10, 15, 20

Enrich

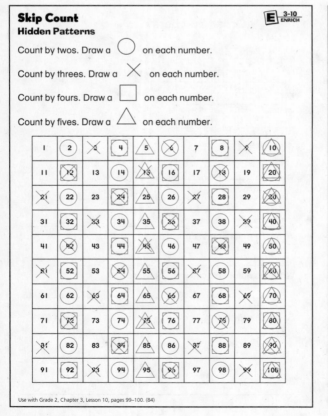

Skip Count
Hidden Patterns

Count by twos. Draw a ○ on each number.

Count by threes. Draw a ✕ on each number.

Count by fours. Draw a □ on each number.

Count by fives. Draw a △ on each number.

Daily Homework

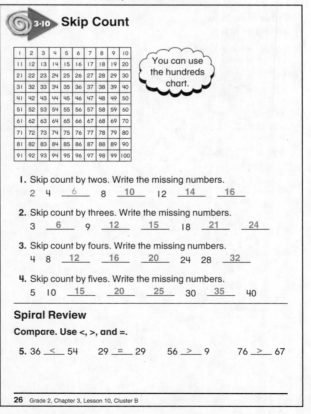

3-10 Skip Count

1	2	3	4	5	6	7	8	9	10
11	12	13	14	15	16	17	18	19	20
21	22	23	24	25	26	27	28	29	30
31	32	33	34	35	36	37	38	39	40
41	42	43	44	45	46	47	48	49	50
51	52	53	54	55	56	57	58	59	60
61	62	63	64	65	66	67	68	69	70
71	72	73	74	75	76	77	78	79	80
81	82	83	84	85	86	87	88	89	100
91	92	93	94	95	96	97	98	99	100

You can use the hundreds chart.

1. Skip count by twos. Write the missing numbers.

2 4 __6__ 8 __10__ 12 __14__ __16__

2. Skip count by threes. Write the missing numbers.

3 __6__ 9 __12__ __15__ 18 __21__ __24__

3. Skip count by fours. Write the missing numbers.

4 8 __12__ __16__ __20__ 24 28 __32__

4. Skip count by fives. Write the missing numbers.

5 10 __15__ __20__ __25__ 30 __35__ 40

Spiral Review

Compare. Use <, >, and =.

5. 36 __<__ 54   29 __=__ 29   56 __>__ 9   76 __>__ 67

Chapter 3 ~ Lesson 11

Practice

Odd and Even Numbers

P 3-11 PRACTICE

Write if the number is even or odd.

1. 13 <u>odd</u>   45 <u>odd</u>   68 <u>even</u>

2. 33 <u>odd</u>   70 <u>even</u>   28 <u>even</u>

3. 44 <u>even</u>   95 <u>odd</u>   67 <u>odd</u>

4. 72 <u>even</u>   9 <u>odd</u>   79 <u>odd</u>

Write the next three even numbers.

5. 24, <u>26</u>, <u>28</u>, <u>30</u>   36, <u>38</u>, <u>40</u>, <u>42</u>

6. 78, <u>80</u>, <u>82</u>, <u>84</u>   42, <u>44</u>, <u>46</u>, <u>48</u>

7. 50, <u>52</u>, <u>54</u>, <u>56</u>   94, <u>96</u>, <u>98</u>, <u>100</u>

Write the next three odd numbers

8. 31, <u>33</u>, <u>35</u>, <u>37</u>   47, <u>49</u>, <u>51</u>, <u>53</u>

9. 25, <u>27</u>, <u>29</u>, <u>31</u>   59, <u>61</u>, <u>63</u>, <u>65</u>

10. 73, <u>75</u>, <u>77</u>, <u>79</u>   87, <u>89</u>, <u>91</u>, <u>93</u>

Reteach

Odd and Even Numbers

R 3-11 RETEACH

An even number of objects can be matched in pairs.

4

○ --- ○
○ --- ○

<u>even</u>

An odd number of objects has one left over.

5

○ --- ○
○ --- ○
○

<u>odd</u>

Write if the number is even or odd.

1. 8

○ — ○
○ — ○
○ — ○
○ — ○

<u>even</u>

7

○ — ○
○ — ○
○ — ○
○

<u>odd</u>

Tell if the number is even or odd.

2. 16 <u>even</u>   23 <u>odd</u>   39 <u>odd</u>

3. 61 <u>odd</u>   34 <u>even</u>   88 <u>even</u>

Enrich

Odd and Even Numbers
Band Number Match

E 3-11 ENRICH

Five children march in a band.

Sam   Mary   Paco   Elena   Chin

Clues	Who Am I?	What Is My Number?
1. The tens digit is an odd number. The ones digit comes just after 7.	Chin	18
2. The ones digit is two more than the tens digit. Both digits are even numbers.	Paco	46
3. The tens digit is 2 less than the ones digit. Both digits are odd numbers.	Sam	35
4. The ones digit is 6 less than the tens digit. Both digits are odd numbers.	Mary	71
5. The tens digit is an even number. The ones digit comes just before 1.	Elena	80

Daily Homework

3-11 Odd and Even Numbers

Write if the number is even or odd.

1. 55 <u>odd</u>   62 <u>even</u>   16 <u>even</u>

2. 43 <u>odd</u>   21 <u>odd</u>   94 <u>even</u>

3. 60 <u>even</u>   87 <u>odd</u>   38 <u>even</u>

Write the next three even numbers.

4. 20 <u>22</u> <u>24</u> <u>26</u>   72 <u>74</u> <u>76</u> <u>78</u>

5. 46 <u>48</u> <u>50</u> <u>52</u>   88 <u>90</u> <u>92</u> <u>94</u>

Write the next three odd numbers.

6. 65 <u>67</u> <u>69</u> <u>71</u>   17 <u>19</u> <u>21</u> <u>23</u>

7. 33 <u>35</u> <u>37</u> <u>39</u>   81 <u>83</u> <u>85</u> <u>87</u>

Spiral Review

About how many notes are in each group? Circle your estimate.

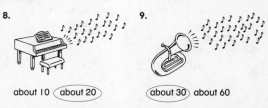

8. about 10   (about 20)

9. (about 30)   about 60

Chapter 3 ~ Lesson 12

Practice

Ordinal Numbers
P 3-12 PRACTICE

green   red purple blue yellow   orange

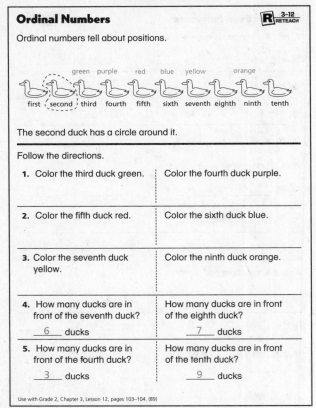

first

Follow the directions.

1. Color the sixth child blue. | Color the fourth child red.
2. Color the first child green. | Color the seventh child yellow.
3. Color the tenth child orange. | Color the fifth child purple.
4. How many children are in front of the third child? _2_ children | How many children are in front of the eighth child? _7_ children

Answer each question.

5. There are 10 children in line. How many children are in front of the tenth child? _9_ children | There are 10 children in the line. How many children are behind the sixth child? _4_ children

Reteach

Ordinal Numbers
R 3-12 RETEACH

Ordinal numbers tell about positions.

green purple   red   blue yellow   orange

first second third fourth fifth sixth seventh eighth ninth tenth

The second duck has a circle around it.

Follow the directions.

1. Color the third duck green. | Color the fourth duck purple.
2. Color the fifth duck red. | Color the sixth duck blue.
3. Color the seventh duck yellow. | Color the ninth duck orange.
4. How many ducks are in front of the seventh duck? _6_ ducks | How many ducks are in front of the eighth duck? _7_ ducks
5. How many ducks are in front of the fourth duck? _3_ ducks | How many ducks are in front of the tenth duck? _9_ ducks

Enrich

Ordinal Numbers
Who's in Line?
E 3-12 ENRICH

orange   green

red   blue   purple   yellow

1. Mary is second in line. Drew is right after Mary. Roger is two places behind Drew.

   In what place in line is Drew? Color Drew red.

   third

   In what place in line is Roger? Color Roger blue.

   fifth

   Jacob is ninth in line. Gail is right after Jacob. Sue is two places ahead of Gail.

   In what place in line is Gail? Color Gail yellow.

   tenth

   In what place in line is Sue? Color Sue green.

   eighth

2. Barry is fourth in line. There are two children between Barry and Lee. Lee is after Barry.

   In what place in line is Lee? Color Lee purple.

   seventh

   Deon is five places behind Bennett. Bennett is first in line of all the children.

   In what place in line is Deon? Color Deon orange.

   sixth

Daily Homework

3-12 Ordinal Numbers

Follow each direction.

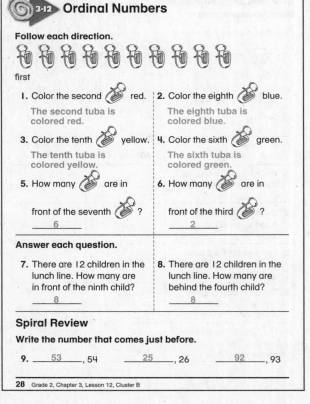

first

1. Color the second 🎺 red. | 2. Color the eighth 🎺 blue.
   The second tuba is colored red. | The eighth tuba is colored blue.
3. Color the tenth 🎺 yellow. | 4. Color the sixth 🎺 green.
   The tenth tuba is colored yellow. | The sixth tuba is colored green.
5. How many 🎺 are in front of the seventh 🎺? _6_ | 6. How many 🎺 are in front of the third 🎺? _2_

Answer each question.

7. There are 12 children in the lunch line. How many are in front of the ninth child? _8_ | 8. There are 12 children in the lunch line. How many are behind the fourth child? _8_

Spiral Review

Write the number that comes just before.

9. _53_, 54   _25_, 26   _92_, 93

Chapter 3 ~ Lesson 13

Part A Worksheet

Problem Solving: Application
Make a Drum

Part A 3-13 WORKSHEET Decision Making

Make a drum.

Cut out the parts you can buy.

You have 50¢.

Choose the parts you will buy.

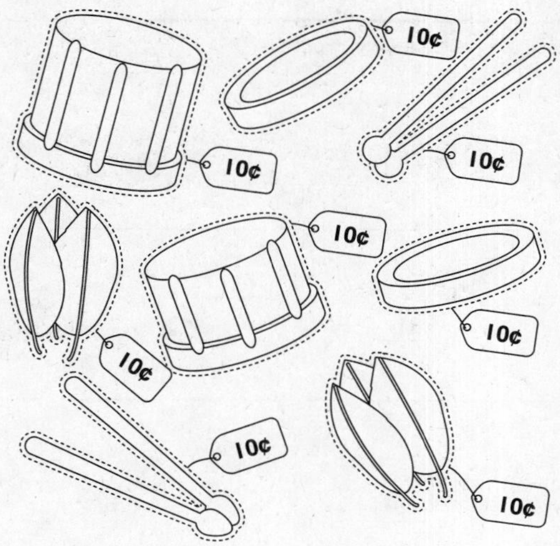

10¢
10¢
10¢
10¢
10¢
10¢
10¢
10¢

Use with Grade 2, Chapter 3, Lesson 13, pages 105–108. (91)

Part A Worksheet

Problem Solving: Application
Make a Drum

Part A 3-13 WORKSHEET Decision Making

1. How much did you spend for the parts you chose? _____ ¢

   Show your work. Check students' work.

2. How much money do you have left? _____ ¢

   Show your work.

3. What if you buy one more item? What would it be?

   _____

   How much more will your drum cost? _____ ¢

   How much will you spend in all? _____ ¢

   Show your work.

Use with Grade 2, Chapter 3, Lesson 13, pages 105–108. (92)

Part B Worksheet

Problem Solving: Application
What Sounds Can You Hear?

Part B 3-13 WORKSHEET Math & Science

1. Describe the sounds each tube made.

   Shortest tube

   _____

   Next longest tube

   _____

   Next longest tube

   _____

   Longest tube

   _____

2. Which tube made the loudest sound?

   _____

   Which tube made the softest sound?

   _____

3. What if you want to make a tube with a louder sound? How could you do this?

   _____

   _____

   _____

   Answers may vary.

Use with Grade 2, Chapter 3, Lesson 13, pages 105–108. (93)

Chapter 4 ~ Lesson 1

Practice

Coins

Use coins.
Show each price in two different ways.
Draw the coins. Answers may vary. Possible answers are given.

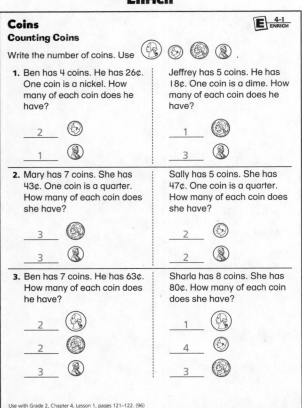

1. 19¢
2. 93¢
3. 58¢
4. 75¢

Use with Grade 2, Chapter 4, Lesson 1, pages 121–122. (94)

Reteach

Coins

Count the coin with the greatest value first.

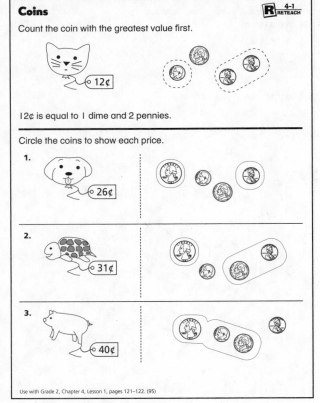

12¢

12¢ is equal to 1 dime and 2 pennies.

Circle the coins to show each price.

1. 26¢
2. 31¢
3. 40¢

Use with Grade 2, Chapter 4, Lesson 1, pages 121–122. (95)

Enrich

Coins
Counting Coins

Write the number of coins. Use 🪙 🪙 🪙 🪙 .

1. Ben has 4 coins. He has 26¢. One coin is a nickel. How many of each coin does he have?

   __2__ 🪙
   __1__ 🪙

   Jeffrey has 5 coins. He has 18¢. One coin is a dime. How many of each coin does he have?

   __1__ 🪙
   __3__ 🪙

2. Mary has 7 coins. She has 43¢. One coin is a quarter. How many of each coin does she have?

   __3__ 🪙
   __3__ 🪙

   Sally has 5 coins. She has 47¢. One coin is a quarter. How many of each coin does she have?

   __2__ 🪙
   __2__ 🪙

3. Ben has 7 coins. He has 63¢. How many of each coin does he have?

   __2__ 🪙
   __2__ 🪙
   __3__ 🪙

   Sharla has 8 coins. She has 80¢. How many of each coin does she have?

   __1__ 🪙
   __4__ 🪙
   __3__ 🪙

Use with Grade 2, Chapter 4, Lesson 1, pages 121–122. (96)

Daily Homework

Coins

Use coins.

Show each price two ways.

Draw the coins. Answers will vary.

penny   nickel   dime   quarter

1. 12¢

2. 23¢

3. 8¢

Problem Solving

4. Kate and Tim bought a 🫙. The 🫙 cost 17¢. Tim paid 8¢. Kate paid the rest. How much did Kate pay? __9¢__

Spiral Review

Subtract.

5.	20	17	15	13	16	18	14
	− 10	− 8	− 7	− 8	− 9	− 9	− 7
	10	9	8	7	7	9	7

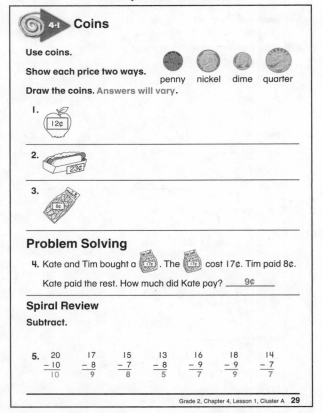

Chapter 4 ~ Lesson 2

Practice

Counting Money

P 4-2 PRACTICE

Do you have enough money to buy the charm?
Circle yes or no.

1. 27¢
10¢ 15¢ 20¢ 21¢ 22¢
yes (no)

2. 35¢
10¢ 20¢ 25¢ 30¢ 31¢ 32¢
yes (no)

3. 50¢
25¢ 35¢ 45¢ 50¢
(yes) no

4. 72¢
25¢ 50¢ 60¢ 65¢ 66¢ 67¢
yes (no)

Use with Grade 2, Chapter 4, Lesson 2, pages 123–124. (97)

Reteach

Counting Money

R 4-2 RETEACH

Count the coin with the greatest value first.

dime 10¢   nickel 5¢   penny 1¢

Count dimes by 10.   Count nickels by 5.   Count pennies by 1.
Find the total amount.

10 ¢ 20 ¢ 25 ¢ 30 ¢ 31 ¢ 32 ¢
Total 32 ¢

Count to find the total amount.

1.
10 ¢ 20 ¢ 30 ¢ 35 ¢ 36 ¢
Total 36 ¢

2.
25 ¢ 35 ¢ 40 ¢ 41 ¢ 42 ¢
Total 42 ¢

3.
25 ¢ 50 ¢ 60 ¢ 70 ¢ 80 ¢ 81 ¢

Use with Grade 2, Chapter 4, Lesson 2, pages 123–124. (98)

Enrich

Counting Money
Hidden Coins

E 4-2 ENRICH

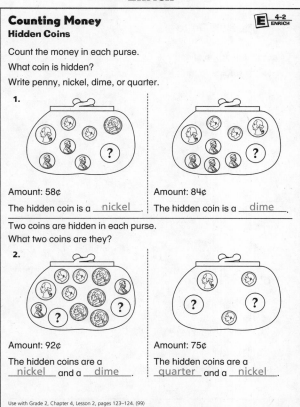

Count the money in each purse.
What coin is hidden?
Write penny, nickel, dime, or quarter.

1.
Amount: 58¢
The hidden coin is a nickel .

Amount: 84¢
The hidden coin is a dime .

Two coins are hidden in each purse.
What two coins are they?

2.
Amount: 92¢
The hidden coins are a nickel and a dime .

Amount: 75¢
The hidden coins are a quarter and a nickel .

Use with Grade 2, Chapter 4, Lesson 2, pages 123–124. (99)

Daily Homework

4-2 Counting Money

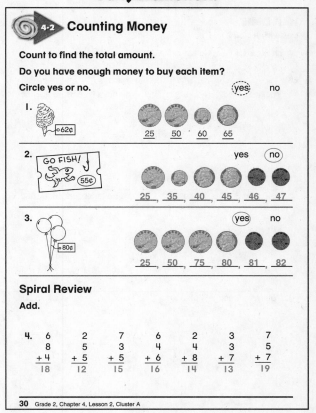

Count to find the total amount.
Do you have enough money to buy each item?
Circle yes or no.

(yes) no

1. 62¢
25 50 60 65

2. GO FISH! 55¢
25 35 40 45 46 47
yes (no)

3. 80¢
25 50 75 80 81 82
(yes) no

Spiral Review
Add.

4.	6	2	7	6	2	3	7
	8	5	3	4	4	3	5
	+4	+5	+5	+6	+8	+7	+7
	18	12	15	16	14	13	19

Chapter 4 ~ Lesson 3

Practice

Half Dollar

Count each group of coins.
Write the total amount.

1. 58 ¢   75 ¢

2. 81 ¢   87 ¢

Circle the coins for each amount.

3.

65¢   78¢

Reteach

Half Dollar

Find the total amount.

50 ¢   60 ¢   70 ¢   75 ¢   80 ¢

Total 80 ¢

Count each group of coins. Write the total amount.

1. 50 ¢   60 ¢   70 ¢   80 ¢   81 ¢

Total 81 ¢

2. 50 ¢   55 ¢   60 ¢   65 ¢   66 ¢

Total 66 ¢

3. 50 ¢   75 ¢   85 ¢   90 ¢

Total 90 ¢

Enrich

Half Dollar
Let's Make 50¢

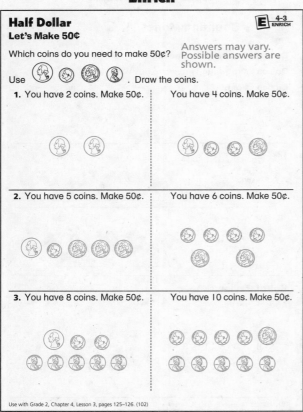

Which coins do you need to make 50¢?

Use [coins] . Draw the coins.

Answers may vary. Possible answers are shown.

1. You have 2 coins. Make 50¢.   You have 4 coins. Make 50¢.

2. You have 5 coins. Make 50¢.   You have 6 coins. Make 50¢.

3. You have 8 coins. Make 50¢.   You have 10 coins. Make 50¢.

Daily Homework

4-3 Half Dollar

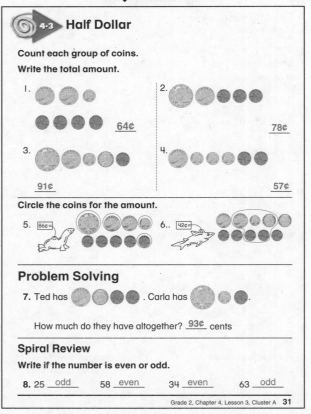

Count each group of coins.

Write the total amount.

1. 64¢   2. 78¢

3. 91¢   4. 57¢

Circle the coins for the amount.

5. 86¢   6. 42¢

Problem Solving

7. Ted has [coins] . Carla has [coins] .

How much do they have altogether? 93¢ cents

Spiral Review

Write if the number is even or odd.

8. 25 odd   58 even   34 even   63 odd

Chapter 4 ~ Lesson 4

Practice

Coins Used to Buy

Use the fewest number of coins to pay.
Draw the coins.

1. 🐱 36¢

2. 🐶 57¢

3. 🐸 70¢

4. 🐰 81¢

Reteach

Coins Used to Buy

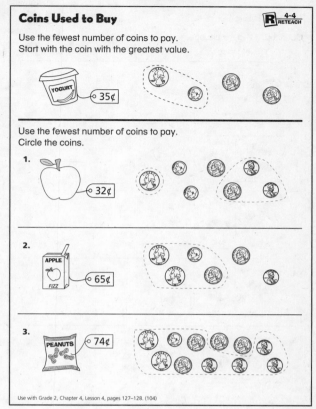

Use the fewest number of coins to pay.
Start with the coin with the greatest value.

YOGURT 35¢

Use the fewest number of coins to pay.
Circle the coins.

1. 🍎 32¢

2. APPLE FIZZ 65¢

3. PEANUTS 74¢

Enrich

Coins Used to Buy

Animal Fair Answers may vary. Possible answers are given.

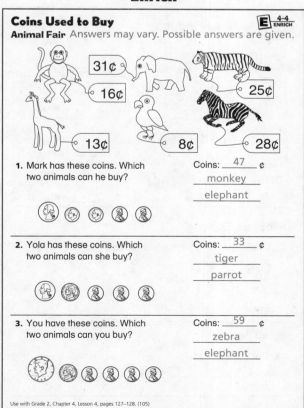

31¢   16¢   25¢   13¢   8¢   28¢

1. Mark has these coins. Which two animals can he buy?

Coins: ___47___ ¢
monkey
elephant

2. Yola has these coins. Which two animals can she buy?

Coins: ___33___ ¢
tiger
parrot

3. You have these coins. Which two animals can you buy?

Coins: ___59___ ¢
zebra
elephant

Daily Homework

4-4 Coins Used to Buy

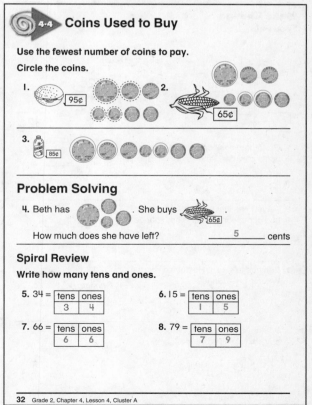

Use the fewest number of coins to pay.
Circle the coins.

1. 🍔 95¢

2. 🌽 65¢

3. 🍾 85¢

Problem Solving

4. Beth has ⬤⬤ ⬤⬤ She buys 🌽 65¢

How much does she have left? ___5___ cents

Spiral Review

Write how many tens and ones.

5. 34 =

tens	ones
3	4

6. 15 =

tens	ones
1	5

7. 66 =

tens	ones
6	6

8. 79 =

tens	ones
7	9

Chapter 4 ~ Lesson 5

Practice

Make Change

P 4-5 PRACTICE

Count up to find the change.

Ticket Price	You Pay	Your Change
1. FERRIS WHEEL ADMIT 27¢ ONE		_3_ ¢
2. GO-CARTS ADMIT 33¢ ONE		_2_ ¢
3. BALL TOSS ADMIT 49¢ ONE		_1_ ¢
4. ROLLER COASTER ADMIT 81¢ ONE		_4_ ¢
5. BOTTLE TOSS ADMIT 65¢ ONE		_5_ ¢

Use with Grade 2, Chapter 4, Lesson 5, pages 129–130. (106)

Reteach

Make Change

R 4-5 RETEACH

You have 40¢. You spend 37¢.
Count up from the cost.
Count until you reach what you pay.

Count up 1¢.	Count up 1¢.	Count up 1¢.
_38_ ¢	_39_ ¢	_40_ ¢

You get _3_ ¢ change.

Count up to find the change. Draw the coins.

	You Have	You Spend	Count up.	You get
1.	35¢	31¢		_4_ ¢
2.	76¢	75¢		_1_ ¢
3.	84¢	81¢		_3_ ¢

Use with Grade 2, Chapter 4, Lesson 5, pages 129–130. (107)

Enrich

Make Change
Food Fair

E 4-5 ENRICH

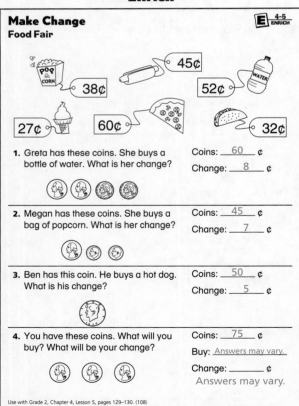

POPCORN 38¢   45¢   WATER 52¢
27¢   60¢   32¢

1. Greta has these coins. She buys a bottle of water. What is her change?

Coins: _60_ ¢
Change: _8_ ¢

2. Megan has these coins. She buys a bag of popcorn. What is her change?

Coins: _45_ ¢
Change: _7_ ¢

3. Ben has this coin. He buys a hot dog. What is his change?

Coins: _50_ ¢
Change: _5_ ¢

4. You have these coins. What will you buy? What will be your change?

Coins: _75_ ¢
Buy: _Answers may vary._
Change: _____ ¢
Answers may vary.

Use with Grade 2, Chapter 4, Lesson 5, pages 129–130. (108)

Daily Homework

4-5 Make Change

Count up to find the change.

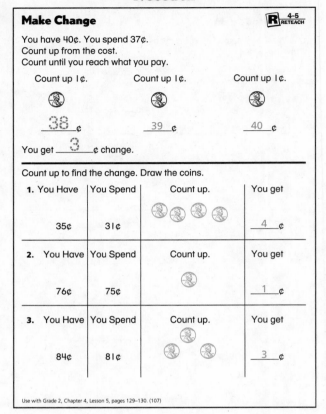

	Price	You pay	Change
1.	16¢		_4¢_ change
2.	77¢	50 25 5	_3¢_ change
3.	42¢	25 10 10	_3¢_ change

Problem Solving

4. Which set of coins has the greater value? Explain.

The first set. 95¢ > 90¢

Spiral Review

5. Skip count by fives.

5 10 _15_ _20_ 25 _30_ _35_ _40_

Grade 2, Chapter 4, Lesson 5, Cluster A **33**

Chapter 4 ~ Lesson 6

Practice

Problem Solving: Reading for Math
Cause and Effect

Marcus wants to buy a baseball mitt.

He helps his father clean out the garage.

His father gives Marcus 1 quarter, 3 dimes, and 5 pennies.

Answer each question.

1. How does Marcus help his father?
   <u>He helps clean out the garage.</u>

2. Why does Marcus help his father?
   <u>He wants to buy a baseball mitt.</u>

3. What does Marcus get for helping?
   <u>1 quarter, 3 dimes, and 5 pennies</u>

4. How much money does Marcus get?
   <u>60¢</u>

Use with Grade 2, Chapter 4, Lesson 6, pages 131–132. (109)

Practice

Problem Solving: Reading for Math
Cause and Effect

Kayla wants to buy some stickers.

She helps her neighbor.

She waters the garden.

She gets the mail.

Her neighbor gives Kayla 2 quarters, 1 dime, and 1 nickel.

Choose the best answer. Fill in the ◯.

1. What job does Kayla do?
   - Ⓐ Buy stickers.
   - Ⓑ Water the garden.
   - Ⓒ Mail letters.
   - Ⓓ Count money.

2. Why is Kayla helping her neighbor?
   - Ⓕ Her neighbor likes stickers.
   - Ⓖ Her mother told her to do that.
   - Ⓗ She wants to buy stickers.

3. What does Kayla get for helping?
   - Ⓐ 2 quarters and 3 dimes
   - Ⓑ 2 quarters, 1 dime, and 1 penny
   - Ⓒ 2 quarters, 1 dime, and 1 nickel
   - Ⓓ 2 stickers

4. How much money does Kayla get?
   - Ⓕ 70¢
   - Ⓖ 60¢
   - Ⓗ 40¢
   - Ⓙ 65¢

Use with Grade 2, Chapter 4, Lesson 6, pages 131–132. (110)

Practice

Problem Solving: Reading for Math
Cause and Effect

Kelly and Anna want to buy pizza.

They help their grandmother do the laundry.

Her grandmother gives Kelly 1 quarter and 3 nickels.

She gives Anna 4 dimes.

Choose the best answer. Fill in the ◯.

1. How do Kelly and Anna help their grandmother?
   - Ⓐ They make pizza.
   - Ⓑ They do laundry.
   - Ⓒ They wash dishes.
   - Ⓓ They buy pizza.

2. Why are Kelly and Anna helping their grandmother?
   - Ⓕ They want to buy pizza.
   - Ⓖ They like to do laundry.
   - Ⓗ They want to make pizza.
   - Ⓙ They have a lot of laundry.

Solve.

3. What does Kelly get for helping? <u>1 quarter and 3 nickels</u>

4. What does Anna get for helping? <u>4 dimes</u>

Use with Grade 2, Chapter 4, Lesson 6, pages 131–132. (111)

Daily Homework

4-6 Problem Solving: Reading for Math
Cause and Effect

Josh wants to go to the fair.

He helps the lady next door sweep the walk and put out the trash.

She gives Josh 1 quarter, 2 dimes, and 1 nickel.

1. How does Josh help the lady next door?
   <u>He sweeps the walk and puts out the trash.</u>

2. Why does Josh help the lady next door?
   <u>He wants to go to the Fair.</u>

3. What does Josh get for helping?
   <u>1 quarter, 2 dimes, and 1 nickel</u>

4. How much money does Josh get? <u>50¢</u>

Spiral Review

first

Follow each direction. Check students' work.

5. Color the third duck red.

6. Color the eighth duck yellow.

7. Color the tenth duck blue.

34 Grade 2, Chapter 4, Lesson 6, Cluster A

Chapter 4 ~ Lesson 7

Practice

Problem Solving: Strategy
Act It Out

Use coins. Work with a partner. Act it out.

1. How many dimes does it take to make 60¢?

__6__ dimes

2. How many nickels does it take to make 45¢?

__9__ nickels

3. Mai has quarters, dimes, and nickels. In how many ways can she buy a pencil that costs 35¢?

__6__ ways

4. Maggie has 2 quarters. She bought a sticker that costs 40¢. How much change should she get back?

__10__ ¢

5. Erik has quarters, dimes, and nickels. In how many ways can he buy an apple for 50¢?

__10__ ways

6. Sanjay has a half dollar and 3 dimes. He bought a bagel for 75¢. How much change should he get back?

__5__ ¢

Mixed Strategy Review

Solve.

7. There are 13 otters swimming in the river. 5 otters are sunning on the rocks. How many otters are there in all?

__18__ otters

8. Create a problem which you would act out to solve. Share it with others.

_____

_____

Reteach

Problem Solving: Strategy
Act It Out

Page 136, Problem 3

Darren has quarters, dimes, and nickels in a bag.

In how many ways can he buy a ticket for 25¢?

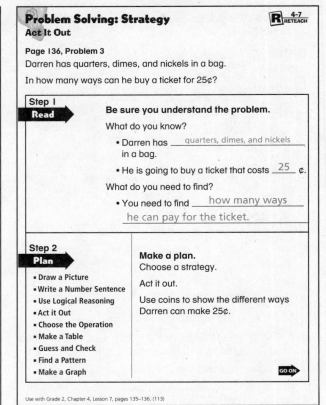

Step 1 Read — Be sure you understand the problem.

What do you know?

• Darren has __quarters, dimes, and nickels__ in a bag.

• He is going to buy a ticket that costs __25__ ¢.

What do you need to find?

• You need to find __how many ways he can pay for the ticket.__

Step 2 Plan — **Make a plan.**

Choose a strategy.

- Draw a Picture
- Write a Number Sentence
- Use Logical Reasoning
- **Act it Out**
- Choose the Operation
- Make a Table
- Guess and Check
- Find a Pattern
- Make a Graph

Act it out.

Use coins to show the different ways Darren can make 25¢.

GO ON

Reteach

Problem Solving: Strategy
Act It Out

Step 3 Solve — Carry out your plan.

• Draw the different ways Darren can make 25¢.

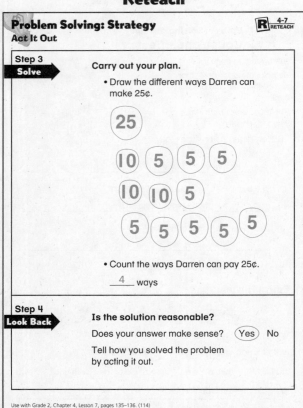

• Count the ways Darren can pay 25¢.

__4__ ways

Step 4 Look Back — Is the solution reasonable?

Does your answer make sense? (Yes) No

Tell how you solved the problem by acting it out.

Daily Homework

4-7 Problem Solving: Strategy
Act It Out

Use coins. Act it out.

1. Kate has quarters, dimes, and nickels. Show 3 ways she can buy an ice cream cone for 35¢. **Answers will vary.**

_____ quarters _____ dimes _____ nickels

_____ quarters _____ dimes _____ nickels

_____ quarters _____ dimes _____ nickels

2. Beth has 6 dimes. She bought a ticket for 55¢. How much change should she get back?

__5¢__

3. Pat has 2 quarters. He buys a raffle ticket for 40¢. How much change should he get back?

__10¢__

4. How many dimes make 90¢?

__9 dimes__

5. How many nickels make 65¢?

__13 nickels__

Spiral Review

Find each missing addend.

6. 9 + 8 = 17   7 + 7 = 14   6 + 6 = 12

7. 5 + 6 = 11   7 + 6 = 13   4 + 8 = 12

Chapter 4 ~ Lesson 8

Practice

Dollars and Cents

P 4-8 PRACTICE

Count the money.
Write the total amount.

1. Marie has money to spend at the Book Fair. How much does she have?

$ 1 . 54

Tyler is saving his money to buy a new kite. How much money does he have?

$ 4 . 88

2. Kitty has money to spend at the Game Day. How much does she have to spend?

$ 3 . 69

Sam is saving his money to buy some new blocks. How much does he have?

$ 2 . 52

Use with Grade 2, Chapter 4, Lesson 8, pages 137–138. (115)

Reteach

Dollars and Cents

R 4-8 RETEACH

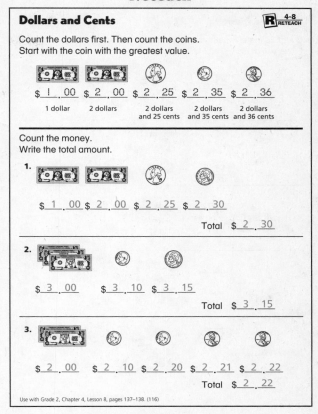

Count the dollars first. Then count the coins.
Start with the coin with the greatest value.

$ 1 . 00 $ 2 . 00 $ 2 . 25 $ 2 . 35 $ 2 . 36
1 dollar   2 dollars   2 dollars and 25 cents   2 dollars and 35 cents   2 dollars and 36 cents

Count the money.
Write the total amount.

1.

$ 1 . 00 $ 2 . 00 $ 2 . 25 $ 2 . 30

Total $ 2 . 30

2.

$ 3 . 00 $ 3 . 10 $ 3 . 15

Total $ 3 . 15

3.

$ 2 . 00 $ 2 . 10 $ 2 . 20 $ 2 . 21 $ 2 . 22

Total $ 2 . 22

Use with Grade 2, Chapter 4, Lesson 8, pages 137–138. (116)

Enrich

Dollars and Cents
What Can You Buy?

E 4-8 ENRICH

$2.15 $2.45 $2.95 $1.85

You have the bills and coins that are shown.
You get more money.

Find the total amount. Write what you can buy.

1.

You get 25¢ more.

Now you have $ 2.15 .

What can you buy?

boat

2.

You get 2 nickels more.

Now you have $ 2.95 .

What can you buy?

train

3.

You get 1 quarter more.

Now you have $ 1.85 .

What can you buy?

car

Use with Grade 2, Chapter 4, Lesson 8, pages 137–138. (117)

Daily Homework

4-8 Dollars and Cents

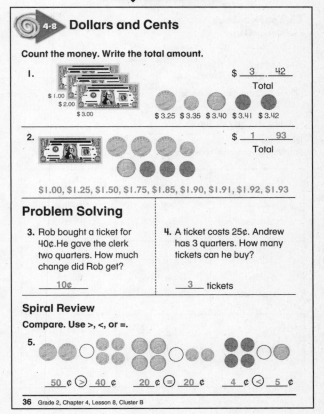

Count the money. Write the total amount.

1.

$1.00
$2.00
$3.00

$ 3 . 42
Total

$3.25 $3.35 $3.40 $3.41 $3.42

2.

$ 1 . 93
Total

$1.00, $1.25, $1.50, $1.75, $1.85, $1.90, $1.91, $1.92, $1.93

Problem Solving

3. Rob bought a ticket for 40¢. He gave the clerk two quarters. How much change did Rob get?

10¢

4. A ticket costs 25¢. Andrew has 3 quarters. How many tickets can he buy?

3 tickets

Spiral Review

Compare. Use >, <, or =.

5.

50 ¢ > 40 ¢   20 ¢ = 20 ¢   4 ¢ < 5 ¢

Chapter 4 ~ Lesson 9

Practice

Compare Money

P 4-9 PRACTICE

Count. Is there enough money to buy each item?
Circle yes or no.

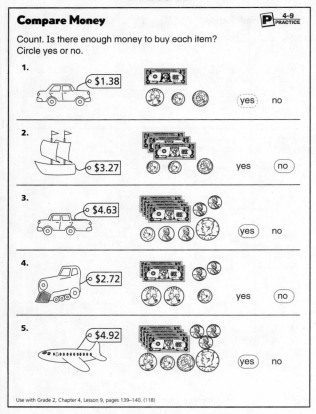

1. $1.38   (yes)   no

2. $3.27   yes   (no)

3. $4.63   (yes)   no

4. $2.72   yes   (no)

5. $4.92   (yes)   no

Use with Grade 2, Chapter 4, Lesson 9, pages 139–140. (118)

Reteach

Compare Money

R 4-9 RETEACH

Is there enough money to buy yogurt?
First, count the money you have.

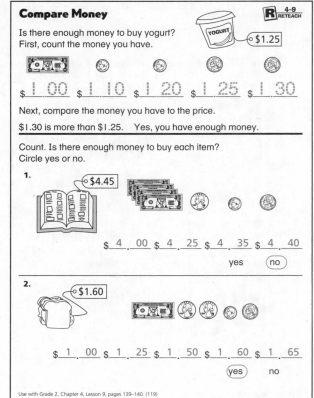

$1.00 $1.10 $1.20 $1.25 $1.30

Next, compare the money you have to the price.
$1.30 is more than $1.25.   Yes, you have enough money.

Count. Is there enough money to buy each item?
Circle yes or no.

1. $4.45

$4.00 $4.25 $4.35 $4.40   yes   (no)

2. $1.60

$1.00 $1.25 $1.50 $1.60 $1.65   (yes)   no

Use with Grade 2, Chapter 4, Lesson 9, pages 139–140. (119)

Enrich

Compare Money
The Money Game

E 4-9 ENRICH

You will need:
Play with a partner. Take turns.

- Drop the button on the gameboard.
- Show the amount with play money.
- Compare money amounts.

The player with more money gets a point.
The first player with 10 points wins.

1 dollar 1 quarter 2 dimes	1 dollar 2 quarters 5 pennies	2 dollars 4 dimes 1 nickel
2 dollars 5 nickels 10 pennies	1 dollar 1 half dollar 3 quarters	2 dollars 4 quarters 3 dimes
2 dollars 2 half dollars 5 nickels	1 dollar 3 dimes 6 nickels	2 dollars 5 dimes 8 nickels

Use with Grade 2, Chapter 4, Lesson 9, pages 139–140. (120)

Daily Homework

4-9 Compare Money

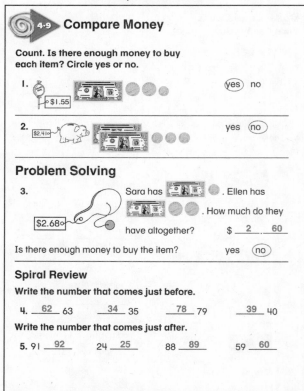

Count. Is there enough money to buy
each item? Circle yes or no.

1. $1.55   (yes)   no

2. $2.41   yes   (no)

Problem Solving

3. $2.68   Sara has _____ . Ellen has
_____ . How much do they
have altogether? $ 2.60

Is there enough money to buy the item?   yes   (no)

Spiral Review

Write the number that comes just before.

4. _62_ 63   _34_ 35   _78_ 79   _39_ 40

Write the number that comes just after.

5. 91 _92_   24 _25_   88 _89_   59 _60_

Chapter 4 ~ Lesson 10

Part A Worksheet

Problem Solving: Application
Plan a Fair Day!

Part A 4-10 WORKSHEET Decision Making

Cut out the tickets.

You have 99¢.

Decide which tickets you will buy.

Use coins to act it out.

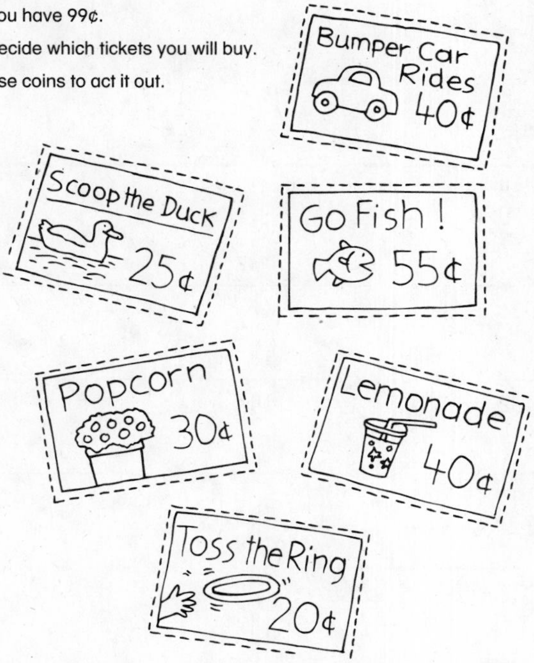

Bumper Car Rides 40¢
Scoop the Duck 25¢
Go Fish! 55¢
Popcorn 30¢
Lemonade 40¢
Toss the Ring 20¢

Use with Grade 2, Chapter 4, Lesson 10, pages 141–144. (121)

Part A Worksheet

Problem Solving: Application
Plan a Fair Day!

Part A 4-10 WORKSHEET Decision Making

1. What tickets did you buy? Answers may vary.

____

2. How much money did you spend?

____

3. What coins did you use to pay for your tickets?

____

4. What if you had $2.00?
   Which tickets would you buy?

____

   How much money would you spend?

____

Use with Grade 2, Chapter 4, Lesson 10, pages 141–144. (122)

Part B Worksheet

Problem Solving: Application
How Does a Seesaw Work?

Part B 4-10 WORKSHEET Math & Science

1. Describe what happened.
   When the pencil was taped to the table

____

   When the pencil was not taped to the table

____

2. When did the ruler balance?
   Answers may vary. Possible answer: When I moved the pencil

____

3. What else do you think you could have done to make the ruler balance?
   Answers may vary. Possible answer: Put the same number of pennies on each end of the ruler.

____

Use with Grade 2, Chapter 4, Lesson 10, pages 141–144. (123)

Chapter 5 ~ Lesson 1

Practice

Add Tens
P 5-1 PRACTICE

Add.

1. $43 + 20 = 63$ $50 + 27 = 77$ $35 + 30 = 65$

2. $18 + 40 = 58$ $51 + 10 = 61$ $60 + 14 = 74$

3.
62	24	40	13	30	50
+ 10	+ 30	+ 28	+ 70	+ 17	+ 20
72	54	68	83	47	70

4.
20	30	57	60	80	48
+ 49	+ 20	+ 30	+ 44	+ 11	+ 40
69	50	87	104	91	88

5.
35	20	30	40	36	17
+ 10	+ 53	+ 13	+ 50	+ 50	+ 30
45	73	43	90	86	47

6.
80	44	38	60	70	57
+ 10	+ 40	+ 20	+ 18	+ 23	+ 10
90	84	58	78	93	67

Problem Solving

7. There are 30 children in the second grade. There are 45 children in the third grade. How many children are there in all?

____75____ children

8. There are 27 children on a bus. There are 40 children on another bus. How many children are there in all?

____67____ children

Reteach

Add Tens
R 5-1 RETEACH

Find the sum.

$45 + 20 = 65$

Count on by tens to add.

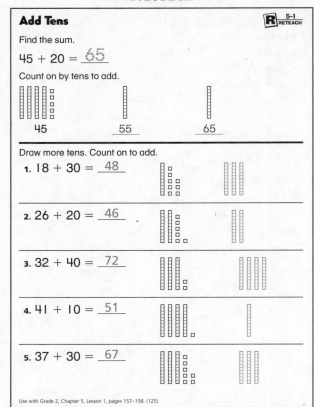

45   55   65

Draw more tens. Count on to add.

1. $18 + 30 = 48$

2. $26 + 20 = 46$

3. $32 + 40 = 72$

4. $41 + 10 = 51$

5. $37 + 30 = 67$

Enrich

Add Tens
Missing Tens
E 5-1 ENRICH

Circle the missing tens.

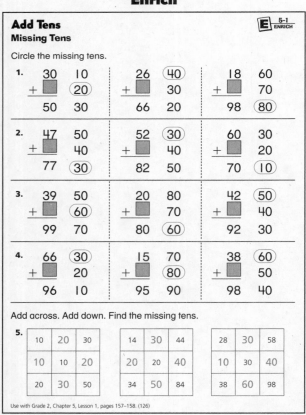

1.
30	10
+ ▢	(20)
50	30

26	(40)
+ ▢	30
66	20

18	60
+ ▢	70
98	(80)

2.
47	50
+ ▢	40
77	(30)

52	(30)
+ ▢	40
82	50

60	30
+ ▢	20
70	(10)

3.
39	50
+ ▢	(60)
99	70

20	80
+ ▢	70
80	(60)

42	(50)
+ ▢	40
92	30

4.
66	(30)
+ ▢	20
96	10

15	70
+ ▢	(80)
95	90

38	(60)
+ ▢	50
98	40

Add across. Add down. Find the missing tens.

5.
10	20	30
10	10	20
20	30	50

14	30	44
20	20	40
34	50	84

28	30	58
10	30	40
38	60	98

Daily Homework

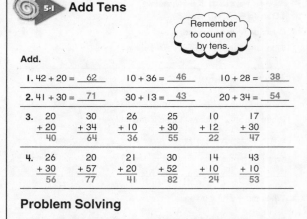

5-1 **Add Tens**

Remember to count on by tens.

Add.

1. $42 + 20 = 62$ $10 + 36 = 46$ $10 + 28 = 38$

2. $41 + 30 = 71$ $30 + 13 = 43$ $20 + 34 = 54$

3.
20	30	26	25	10	17
+ 20	+ 34	+ 10	+ 30	+ 12	+ 30
40	64	36	55	22	47

4.
26	20	21	30	14	43
+ 30	+ 57	+ 20	+ 52	+ 10	+ 10
56	77	41	82	24	53

Problem Solving

5. Fred has 38 nails. Sue has 20 nails. How many nails do they have in all?

____58____ nails

6. John has 24 nails. Liz has 10 more nails than John. How many nails does Liz have?

____34____ nails

Spiral Review

Skip count by tens.

7. 10 20 __30__ __40__ __50__ 60 __70__ __80__ 90

8. 13 23 __33__ __43__ 53 __63__ __73__ 83 __93__

Chapter 5 ~ Lesson 2

Practice

2-Digit Addition Without Regrouping

Add.

1.

tens	ones
2	3
+1	5
3	**8**

tens	ones
3	2
+2	7
5	9

tens	ones
1	5
+6	2
7	7

tens	ones
4	4
+1	5
5	9

2.
```
  17     24     63     26     55     73
+ 42   + 41   + 25   + 13   + 12   + 12
  59     65     88     39     67     85
```

3.
```
  44     31     28     53     32     27
+ 25   + 26   + 21   + 41   + 67   + 41
  69     57     49     94     99     68
```

4.
```
  34     52     33     23     26     13
+ 13   + 25   + 51   + 55   + 22   + 26
  47     77     84     78     48     39
```

5.
```
  11     47     58     67     25     34
+ 25   + 21   + 21   + 12   + 63   + 34
  36     68     79     79     88     68
```

Problem Solving

6. Jane has 34 marbles. Judy has 42 marbles. How many marbles do they have in all?

___76___ marbles

7. Mike has 56 red marbles. He has 13 blue marbles. How many marbles does he have in all?

___69___ marbles

Use with Grade 2, Chapter 5, Lesson 2, pages 161–162. (127)

Reteach

2-Digit Addition Without Regrouping

Find the sum.

Add 16 + 23 = ___39___

First add the ones.

Tens	Ones
1	6
+2	3
	9

Then add the tens.

Tens	Ones
1	6
+2	3
3	9

Circle the ones. Circle the tens. Add.

1.
Tens	Ones
4	3
+2	6
6	9

2.
Tens	Ones
5	4
+3	2
8	6

Add.

3.
Tens	Ones
5	4
+3	2
8	6

Tens	Ones
5	5
+3	3
8	8

Tens	Ones
4	7
+5	2
9	9

Tens	Ones
7	1
+2	6
9	7

4.
Tens	Ones
6	2
+2	5
8	7

Tens	Ones
3	5
+4	4
7	9

Tens	Ones
3	7
+5	0
8	7

Tens	Ones
6	4
+3	4
9	8

Use with Grade 2, Chapter 5, Lesson 2, pages 161–162. (128)

Enrich

2-Digit Addition Without Regrouping
Addition Puzzles

Use the numbers in the boxes to write two different addition sentences.

You may use a number more than once.

1.
15	34	57
23	38	

23 + 15 = 38

34 + 23 = 57

2.
47	16	42
58	31	

42 + 16 = 58

16 + 31 = 47

3.
79	77	15
39	40	62

40 + 39 = 79

62 + 15 = 77

4.
25	34	71
82	59	11

11 + 71 = 82

34 + 25 = 59

5.
35	39	19
52	20	87

35 + 52 = 87

20 + 19 = 39

Use with Grade 2, Chapter 5, Lesson 2, pages 161–162. (129)

Daily Homework

5-2 2-Digit Addition Without Regrouping

Add.

1.

tens	ones
2	3
+5	2
7	5

tens	ones
6	1
+	8
6	9

tens	ones
4	2
+1	5
5	7

tens	ones
6	4
+2	2
8	6

2.
```
  31     23     42     53     12     34
+  5   +  4   +  6   + 22   + 37   + 64
  36     27     48     75     49     98
```

3.
```
  28     71     35     51     52     21
+ 51   + 11   +  3   + 25   +  5   + 68
  79     82     38     76     57     89
```

Solve.

4. José made 24 sandwiches. Chris made 12 sandwiches. How many sandwiches did they make all together? ___36___ sandwiches

5. Ann made 15 glasses of lemonade. Jenna made 13 glasses of lemonade. How many glasses of lemonade in all? ___28___ glasses

Spiral Review

Write each number in expanded form.

6. 42 ___40 + 2___   27 ___20 + 7___   53 ___50 + 3___   66 ___60 + 6___

Grade 2, Chapter 5, Lesson 2, Cluster A **39**

Chapter 5 ~ Lesson 3

Practice

Decide When to Regroup

Use tens and ones models and a workmat.

	Add.	Do you need to regroup?	How many in all?
1.	27 + 6	(yes) no	33
2.	32 + 7	yes (no)	39
3.	61 + 9	(yes) no	70
4.	47 + 5	(yes) no	52
5.	72 + 6	yes (no)	78
6.	54 + 9	(yes) no	63
7.	84 + 5	yes (no)	89
8.	16 + 8	(yes) no	24

Problem Solving

9. Sam has 93 duck stamps. Lee gives him 4 more. How many stamps does he have in all?

____97____ stamps

10. Sara has 36 beads. Jamie gives her 9 more. How many beads does she have in all?

____45____ beads

Use with Grade 2, Chapter 5, Lesson 3, pages 163–164. (130)

Reteach

Decide When to Regroup

Find the sum.

Add 18 + 7 = __25__

Regroup when you have 10 ones.

Can you regroup?   Regroup 10 ones as 1 ten.

(yes)   no

Add. Can you regroup? Circle 10 ones.

1. 24 + 7 = __31__   36 + 8 = __44__

(yes)   no   (yes)   no

2. 17 + 9 = __26__   44 + 5 = __49__

(yes)   no   yes   (no)

3. 32 + 6 = __38__   25 + 5 = __30__

yes   (no)   (yes)   no

Use with Grade 2, Chapter 5, Lesson 3, pages 163–164. (131)

Enrich

Decide When to Regroup
Find the Secret Path

Add. Color the additions for which you need to regroup.

Find the path through the maze.

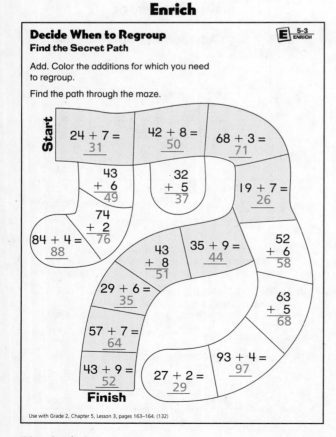

Start

24 + 7 = 31   42 + 8 = 50   68 + 3 = 71

43 + 6 = 49   32 + 5 = 37   19 + 7 = 26

74 + 2 = 76

84 + 4 = 88   43 + 8 = 51   35 + 9 = 44   52 + 6 = 58

29 + 6 = 35   63 + 5 = 68

57 + 7 = 64   93 + 4 = 97

43 + 9 = 52   27 + 2 = 29

Finish

Use with Grade 2, Chapter 5, Lesson 3, pages 163–164. (132)

Daily Homework

5-3 Decide When to Regroup

Use ▭▭▭▭ and ▫.

Regroup when you need to.

	Add.	Do you need to regroup?	How many in all?
1.	53 + 6	yes (no)	59
2.	46 + 5	(yes) no	51
3.	78 + 4	(yes) no	82
4.	25 + 3	yes (no)	28
5.	57 + 1	yes (no)	58
6.	39 + 2	(yes) no	41

Problem Solving

Find the answer.

7. Becky puts 14 pieces of candy in a jar. Jack adds 8 more pieces. How many pieces of candy all together? ____22____ pieces

Spiral Review

Count each group of coins.

8.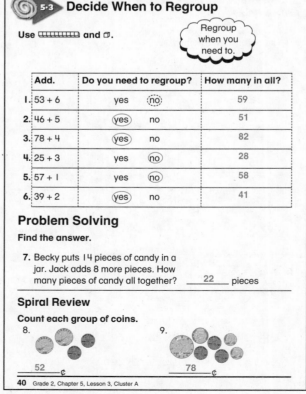

____52____ ¢

9.

____78____ ¢

40   Grade 2, Chapter 5, Lesson 3, Cluster A

© McGraw-Hill School Division

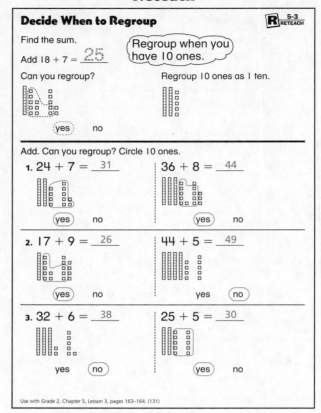

44   Grade 2

Chapter 5 ~ Lesson 4

Practice

2-Digit Addition
P 5-4 PRACTICE

Add. You can use tens and ones models.

1.

Tens	Ones
[1]	
3	5
+2	5
6	0

Tens	Ones
[1]	
4	3
+	8
5	1

Tens	Ones
	[1]
1	5
+5	9
7	4

Tens	Ones
[1]	
2	9
+1	8
4	7

2.

Tens	Ones
[1]	
5	6
+3	5
9	1

Tens	Ones
[ ]	
2	7
+2	8
5	5

Tens	Ones
[ ]	
1	4
+3	3
4	7

Tens	Ones
[1]	
3	7
+4	6
8	3

3.

Tens	Ones
[1]	
2	3
+	8
3	1

Tens	Ones
[ ]	
5	4
+2	2
7	6

Tens	Ones
[1]	
4	6
+1	9
6	5

Tens	Ones
[1]	
1	9
+3	4
5	3

Problem Solving

4. Jenny sells 32 cups of lemonade. Bruce sells 17 cups. How many cups do they sell in all?

___49___ cups

5. There are 45 red cups for lemonade. There are 27 blue cups. How many cups are there in all?

___72___ cups

Use with Grade 2, Chapter 5, Lesson 4, pages 165–166. (133)

Reteach

2-Digit Addition
R 5-4 RETEACH

Find the sum.

Add 26 + 18 = _____

Add the ones.

Regroup 10 ones as 1 ten. Add the tens.

Tens	Ones
[1]	
2	6
+1	8

Tens	Ones
1	
2	6
+1	8
	4

Add. Use models and a tens and ones workmat.

1.

Tens	Ones
[1]	
5	6
+2	9
8	5

Tens	Ones
[1]	
4	4
+3	6
8	0

Tens	Ones
[1]	
2	7
+6	5
9	2

Tens	Ones
[1]	
4	8
+4	6
9	4

2.

Tens	Ones
[1]	
3	5
+3	8
7	3

Tens	Ones
[1]	
4	3
+2	9
7	2

Tens	Ones
[1]	
4	7
+3	4
8	1

Tens	Ones
[1]	
5	4
+3	8
9	2

Use with Grade 2, Chapter 5, Lesson 4, pages 165–166. (134)

Enrich

2-Digit Addition
E 5-4 ENRICH

Addition Race to 10

Play with a partner. Take turns.

- Drop a coin on the gameboard two times.
- Add the numbers on a separate sheet of paper.

Scoring Chart	
Name	Points

The person with the greater sum gets 1 point.

The person who gets 10 points first wins the game.

14	37	52	38
25	46	17	21
43	33	28	9
7	11	42	30
65	27	92	86

Use with Grade 2, Chapter 5, Lesson 4, pages 165–166. (135)

Daily Homework

5·4 2-Digit Addition

Decide if you need to regroup.

Add.

1.

tens	ones
[1]	
2	6
+1	5
4	1

tens	ones
[ ]	
4	5
+2	3
6	8

tens	ones
[ ]	
2	1
+6	8
8	9

tens	ones
[1]	
7	3
+	8
8	1

2.

tens	ones
[1]	
1	2
+4	9
6	1

tens	ones
[1]	
1	8
+	6
2	4

tens	ones
[1]	
3	4
+	9
4	3

tens	ones
[1]	
5	6
+1	7
7	3

3.

tens	ones
[1]	
3	7
+1	3
5	0

tens	ones
[1]	
7	9
+	7
8	6

tens	ones
[ ]	
2	4
+3	5
5	9

tens	ones
[ ]	
5	3
+4	4
9	7

Solve.

4. Jenna makes a pile of 35 bricks. Joe makes a pile of 47 bricks. How many bricks do Jenna and Joe have altogether? ___82___ bricks

Spiral Review

Add.

5.

10	23	30	39	65	60
+40	+50	+31	+10	+20	+38
50	73	61	49	85	98

Chapter 5 ~ Lesson 5

Practice

MORE 2-Digit Addition
P 5-5 PRACTICE

Add. You can use tens and ones models.

1.

Tens	Ones
☐	
3	1
+3	5
6	6

Tens	Ones
1	
5	9
+1	5
7	4

Tens	Ones
1	
3	3
+	8
4	1

Tens	Ones
1	
3	8
+4	8
8	6

2.

Tens	Ones
1	
4	2
+	9
5	1

Tens	Ones
☐	
2	2
+1	7
3	9

Tens	Ones
1	
4	4
+2	8
7	2

Tens	Ones
1	
6	7
+1	8
8	5

3.

Tens	Ones
1	
2	9
+2	8
5	7

Tens	Ones
1	
6	3
+2	8
9	1

Tens	Ones
1	
4	7
+3	9
8	6

Tens	Ones
☐	
4	1
+3	2
7	3

Problem Solving

4. There are 38 crayons in a box. Sally gets 27 more crayons. How many crayons are there now?

___65___ crayons

5. One coloring book has 32 pages. Another coloring book has 48 pages. How many pages are there in all?

___80___ pages

Reteach

MORE 2-Digit Addition
R 5-5 RETEACH

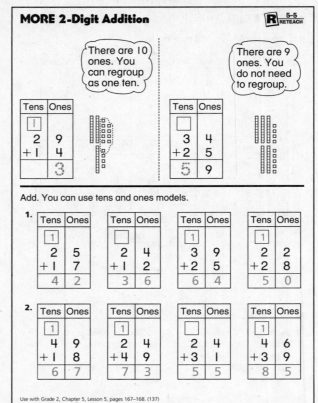

There are 10 ones. You can regroup as one ten.

There are 9 ones. You do not need to regroup.

Tens	Ones
1	
2	9
+1	4
	3

Tens	Ones
☐	
3	4
+2	5
5	9

Add. You can use tens and ones models.

1.

Tens	Ones
1	
2	5
+1	7
4	2

Tens	Ones
☐	
2	4
+1	2
3	6

Tens	Ones
1	
3	9
+2	5
6	4

Tens	Ones
1	
2	2
+2	8
5	0

2.

Tens	Ones
1	
4	9
+1	8
6	7

Tens	Ones
1	
2	4
+4	9
7	3

Tens	Ones
☐	
2	4
+3	1
5	5

Tens	Ones
1	
4	6
+3	9
8	5

Enrich

MORE 2-Digit Addition
E 5-5 ENRICH

What's My Rule?

Each row of numbers is in a pattern.

Find the next number in the pattern.

Circle the rule.

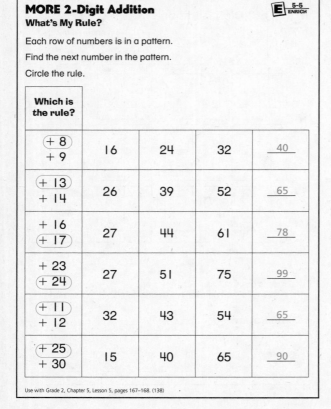

Which is the rule?				
(+ 8) + 9	16	24	32	_40_
(+ 13) + 14	26	39	52	_65_
+ 16 (+ 17)	27	44	61	_78_
+ 23 (+ 24)	27	51	75	_99_
(+ 11) + 12	32	43	54	_65_
(+ 25) + 30	15	40	65	_90_

Daily Homework

5-5 More 2-Digit Addition

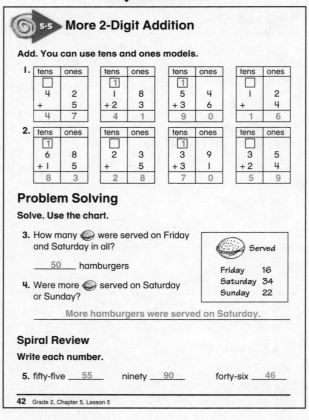

Add. You can use tens and ones models.

1.

tens	ones
☐	
4	2
+	5
4	7

tens	ones
1	
1	8
+2	3
4	1

tens	ones
1	
5	4
+3	6
9	0

tens	ones
☐	
1	2
+	4
1	6

2.

tens	ones
1	
6	8
+1	5
8	3

tens	ones
☐	
2	3
+	5
2	8

tens	ones
1	
3	9
+3	1
7	0

tens	ones
☐	
3	5
+2	4
5	9

Problem Solving

Solve. Use the chart.

3. How many 🍔 were served on Friday and Saturday in all?

___50___ hamburgers

🍔	Served
Friday	16
Saturday	34
Sunday	22

4. Were more 🍔 served on Saturday or Sunday?

___More hamburgers were served on Saturday.___

Spiral Review

Write each number.

5. fifty-five ___55___   ninety ___90___   forty-six ___46___

Chapter 5 ~ Lesson 6

Practice

Practice 2-Digit Addition

Add. You can use tens and ones models.

1.

Tens	Ones
1	
4	3
+	9
5	2

Tens	Ones
1	
6	4
+	7
7	1

Tens	Ones
1	
5	8
+	8
6	6

Tens	Ones
4	5
+	4
4	9

2.

Tens	Ones
1	
7	2
+1	8
9	0

Tens	Ones
1	
4	4
+3	7
8	1

Tens	Ones
2	1
+2	8
4	9

Tens	Ones
1	
5	4
+1	9
7	3

Rewrite. Then add.

3. 36 + 22

$$\begin{array}{r} 36 \\ + 22 \\ \hline 58 \end{array}$$

29 + 13

$$\begin{array}{r} 29 \\ + 13 \\ \hline 42 \end{array}$$

42 + 28

$$\begin{array}{r} 42 \\ + 28 \\ \hline 70 \end{array}$$

Problem Solving

4. Adam puts 57 stickers in a book. Samantha puts 24 stickers in the book. How many stickers are in the book now?

___81___ stickers

5. Rita has 49 marbles. Paco has 36 marbles. How many marbles do they have in all?

___85___ marbles

Use with Grade 2, Chapter 5, Lesson 6, pages 169–170. (139)

Reteach

Practice 2-Digit Addition
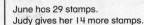

June has 29 stamps. Judy gives her 14 more stamps.

How many stamps does June have now?

Find the sum.

29 + 14 = ___43___

June has 43 stamps now.

Add the ones. Regroup.

Tens	Ones
1	
2	9
+1	4
	3

Add the tens.

Tens	Ones
1	
2	9
+1	4
4	3

Add. You can use tens and ones models.

1.

Tens	Ones
1	
3	7
+2	7
6	4

Tens	Ones
1	
3	5
+1	5
5	0

Tens	Ones
4	8
+2	5
7	3

Tens	Ones
1	4
+2	3
3	7

2.

Tens	Ones
1	
1	9
+6	8
8	7

Tens	Ones
3	6
+4	3
7	9

Tens	Ones
1	
5	4
+2	7
8	1

Tens	Ones
1	
3	8
+2	9
6	7

Use with Grade 2, Chapter 5, Lesson 6, pages 169–170. (140)

Enrich

Practice 2-Digit Addition
Missing Number Riddles

Find the missing number.

1. I have a 9 in the ones place. When you add 26 to me, you get 45. What number am I?

$$\begin{array}{r} 19 \\ + 26 \\ \hline 45 \end{array}$$

___19___

2. I have a 2 in the tens place. When you add 18 to me, you get 39. What number am I?

___21___

I have a 5 in the ones place. When you add 30 to me, you get 55. What number am I?

___25___

3. My tens digit and my ones digit are the same number. When you add 42 to me, you get 75. What number am I?

___33___

My ones digit is 5 greater than my tens digit. When you add 16 to me, you get 43. What number am I?

___27___

4. My tens digit is 3 fewer than my ones digit. When you add 52 to me, you get 66. What number am I?

___14___

My tens digit and my ones digit are even numbers. When you add 33 to me, you get 77. What number am I?

___44___

5. Write your own missing number riddle. Solve it. Then give it to a classmate to solve.

_____

Answers may vary.

_____

_____

Use with Grade 2, Chapter 5, Lesson 6, pages 169–170. (141)

Daily Homework

5-6 Practice 2-Digit Addition

Add. You can use tens and ones models.

1.

$$\begin{array}{r} 1 \\ 27 \\ + 33 \\ \hline 60 \end{array}$$

$$\begin{array}{r} \\ 15 \\ + 24 \\ \hline 39 \end{array}$$

$$\begin{array}{r} \\ 41 \\ + 4 \\ \hline 45 \end{array}$$

$$\begin{array}{r} 1 \\ 58 \\ + 13 \\ \hline 71 \end{array}$$

2.

$$\begin{array}{r} \\ 13 \\ + 6 \\ \hline 19 \end{array}$$

$$\begin{array}{r} 1 \\ 39 \\ + 5 \\ \hline 44 \end{array}$$

$$\begin{array}{r} 1 \\ 29 \\ + 12 \\ \hline 41 \end{array}$$

$$\begin{array}{r} \\ 26 \\ + 31 \\ \hline 57 \end{array}$$

Rewrite. Then add.

3. 32 + 26

$$\begin{array}{r} 32 \\ + 26 \\ \hline 58 \end{array}$$

48 + 17

$$\begin{array}{r} 48 \\ + 17 \\ \hline 65 \end{array}$$

55 + 35

$$\begin{array}{r} 55 \\ + 35 \\ \hline 90 \end{array}$$

Solve.

4. Myra plants 45 flowers in front of the house. Jeff plants 25 flowers in back of the house. How many flowers do they plant all together?

___70___ flowers

Spiral Review

Circle the coins that show the amount.

5. 72¢

6. 45¢

Grade 2, Chapter 5, Lesson 6, Cluster A **43**

© McGraw-Hill School Division

Grade 2 **47**

Practice

Problem Solving: Reading for Math
Important and Unimportant Information

The second grade at Bryant School went to the theater.

They saw "The Velveteen Rabbit."

36 children rode on a school bus.

22 children rode in vans.

6 parents went with the children.

How many children went to the theater?

Does the information help you to solve the problem? Circle yes or no.

1. The class saw "The Velveteen Rabbit."   yes   (no)
2. 36 children rode on a school bus.   (yes)   no
3. 22 children rode in vans.   (yes)   no
4. 6 parents went with the children.   yes   (no)
5. Solve the problem. Write a number sentence.

$$36 + 22 = 58 \text{ children}$$

Use with Grade 2, Chapter 5, Lesson 7, pages 171–172. (142)

Practice

Problem Solving: Reading for Math
Important and Unimportant Information

Milo and Betsy are in the second grade.

They live on the same block.

5 apartment buildings and 2 stores are on that block.

There are 21 apartments in Milo's apartment building.

There are 18 apartments in Betsy's apartment building.

How many apartments are in Milo's and Betsy's buildings altogether?

Choose the best answer. Fill in the ◯.

1. Which information would help you solve the problem?
   - Ⓐ Milo and Betsy live on the same block.
   - Ⓑ 5 apartment buildings are on the block.
   - Ⓒ There are 21 apartments in Milo's apartment building.

2. Which information would help you solve the problem?
   - Ⓕ 2 stores are on the block.
   - Ⓖ There are 18 apartments in Betsy's apartment building.
   - Ⓗ Milo and Betsy are in the second grade.

3. Which number sentence could you write to solve the problem?
   - Ⓐ 7 + 18 = 25
   - Ⓑ 21 + 5 = 26
   - Ⓒ 21 + 18 = 39

4. How many apartments are in Milo's and Betsy's buildings altogether?
   - Ⓕ 7
   - Ⓖ 39
   - Ⓗ 29
   - Ⓙ 21

Use with Grade 2, Chapter 5, Lesson 7, pages 171–172. (143)

Practice

Problem Solving: Reading for Math
Important and Unimportant Information

Maria and Ellie are friends.
They collect dolls from around the world.
They keep the dolls on 2 shelves in their bedrooms.
Maria has 16 dolls in her collection.
Ellie has 13 dolls in her collection.
Altogether, Maria and Ellie have dolls from 12 different countries.

How many dolls do Maria and Ellie have in all?

Choose the best answer. Fill in the ◯.

1. Which information would help you solve the problem?
   - Ⓐ Maria and Ellie collect dolls from around the world.
   - Ⓑ Maria and Ellie have dolls from 12 different countries.
   - Ⓒ Ellie has 13 dolls in her collection.

2. Which information would help you solve the problem?
   - Ⓕ Maria and Ellie are friends.
   - Ⓖ Maria has 16 dolls in her collection.
   - Ⓗ Maria and Ellie keep the dolls on 2 shelves in their bedrooms.

Solve.

3. Solve the problem. Write a number sentence. Then label the parts of the number sentence.

16	+	13	=	29
addend	plus sign	addend	equal sign	sum

Use with Grade 2, Chapter 5, Lesson 7, pages 171–172. (144)

Daily Homework

5-7

Problem Solving: Reading for Math
Important and Unimportant Information

10 children visit the zoo. The children see animals that are awake at night. They see 15 bats. They see 16 owls. It is very dark!

How many animals do the children see?

1. Does the information help you to solve the problem? Circle yes or no.

   10 children visit the zoo.   yes   (no)

   They see 15 bats.   (yes)   no

   They see 16 owls.   (yes)   no

   It is very dark!   yes   (no)

2. Solve the problem. Write a number sentence.

   Answers will vary. 15 + 16 = 31

Spiral Review

Add.

3. 15 + 20 = __35__ | 33 + 30 = __63__ | 27 + 10 = __37__

Chapter 5 ~ Lesson 8

Practice

© McGraw-Hill School Division

Problem Solving: Strategy
Draw a Picture P 5-8 PRACTICE

Draw a picture. Solve. Check students' drawings.

1. 14 children are swimming in the deep end of the pool. 22 children are swimming in the shallow end of the pool. How many children are in the pool?

___36___ children

2. 15 children in Marti's class ride the bus to school. The other 12 children walk. How many children are in Marti's class?

___27___ children

3. Jed has 15 players on his soccer team. The other team has 14 players. How many players are at the game?

___29___ players

Mixed Strategy Review

Solve.

4. Grace has 2 quarters and 1 dime. She bought a charm that costs 55¢. How much change should she get back?

___5___ ¢

5. Create a problem which you would draw a picture to solve. Share it with others.

_____

_____

Use with Grade 2, Chapter 5, Lesson 8, pages 175–176. (145)

Reteach

Problem Solving: Strategy
Draw a Picture R 5-8 RETEACH

Page 176, Problem 3

16 children take the first bus to the movies.

18 children take the second bus.

How many children are on the two buses?

_____ children

Step 1
Read ▶

Be sure you understand the problem.

What do you know?

- ___16___ children take the first bus.
- ___18___ children take the second bus.

What do you need to find?

- You need to find ___how many children___ ___are on the two buses.___

Step 2
Plan ▶

- Draw a Picture
- Write a Number Sentence
- Use Logical Reasoning
- Act it Out
- Choose the Operation
- Make a Table
- Guess and Check
- Find a Pattern
- Make a Graph

Make a plan.
Choose a strategy.

Draw a picture.

Draw tens and ones to show children.

Use the picture to solve the problem.

Use with Grade 2, Chapter 5, Lesson 8, pages 175–176. (146)

Reteach

Problem Solving: Strategy
Draw a Picture R 5-8 RETEACH

Step 3
Solve ▶

Carry out your plan.

- You know that ___16___ children rode the first bus.
- You know that ___18___ children rode the second bus.
- Draw tens and ones to show the children on the two buses.

- How many children do the tens and ones show?

___34___ children

Step 4
Look Back ▶

Is the solution reasonable?

Does your answer make sense? (Yes) No

Did you answer the question? (Yes) No

Use with Grade 2, Chapter 5, Lesson 8, pages 175–176. (147)

Daily Homework

5-8 **Problem Solving: Strategy**
Draw a Picture

Draw a picture. Solve.

1. 10 children gave their reports on Tuesday. 5 children gave their reports on Wednesday. How many children gave reports in all?

___15___ children

2. 15 children read a book called *Arthur's Eyes*. 8 children read a book called *Charlotte's Web*. How many children read books?

___23___ children

3. 11 children will bring their lunches to school. 7 children will buy their lunch. How many children will eat lunch all together?

___18___ children

Workspace

Drawings may vary.

Spiral Review

Add.

4.

tens	ones
[1]	
1	8
+ 2	7
4	5

tens	ones
3	3
+ 4	6
7	9

tens	ones
□	
5	2
+ 3	4
8	6

tens	ones
[1]	
8	5
+	8
9	3

Grade 2, Chapter 5, Lesson 8, Cluster B **45**

Chapter 5 ~ Lesson 9

Practice

Algebra: Check Addition

Add. Check by adding in a different order.

1.
```
  27      15      48       2      18      37
+ 15    + 27    +  2    + 48    + 37    + 18
  42      42      50      50      55      55
```

2.
```
  62       9      41      37      36      37
+  9    + 62    + 37    + 41    + 37    + 36
  71      71      78      78      73      73
```

3.
```
  52      26      67       9      39      17
+ 26    + 52    +  9    + 67    + 17    + 39
  78      78      76      76      56      56
```

4.
```
  53       8      71      18      68       6
+  8    + 53    + 18    + 71    +  6    + 68
  61      61      89      89      74      74
```

5.
```
  69      21      77      18      66      25
+ 21    + 69    + 18    + 77    + 25    + 66
  90      90      95      95      91      91
```

Problem Solving

6. There are 35 girls in the park. There are 47 boys in the park. How many children are in the park?

___82___ children

7. There are 16 houses on Elm Street. There are 27 houses on Oak Street. How many houses are there in all?

___43___ houses

Reteach

Algebra: Check Addition

You can add numbers in a different order to check addition.

```
  28              14
+ 14            + 28
  42              42
```

The sums are the same.

Add. Check by adding in a different order.

1.
```
  34      19      15      31      46       5
+ 19    + 34    + 31    + 15    +  5    + 46
  53      53      46      46      51      51
```

2.
```
  52      29      48      16      27      35
+ 29    + 52    + 16    + 48    + 35    + 27
  81      81      64      64      62      62
```

3.
```
  18       4      24      22      53      37
+  4    + 18    + 22    + 24    + 37    + 53
  22      22      46      46      90      90
```

Enrich

Algebra: Check Addition

Number Pairs

Circle two pairs of numbers with the same sum.

Then find all sums.

1. 27 + 54 _81_   18 + 47 _65_   (55 + 21) _76_

   (21 + 55) _76_   54 + 37 _91_   37 + 18 _55_

2. (34 + 61) _95_   45 + 16 _61_   62 + 11 _73_

   16 + 35 _51_   11 + 52 _63_   (61 + 34) _95_

3. (29 + 46) _75_   64 + 28 _92_   44 + 29 _73_

   18 + 64 _82_   (46 + 29) _75_   36 + 44 _80_

4. 27 + 19 _46_   (39 + 38) _77_   19 + 29 _48_

   (38 + 39) _77_   45 + 37 _82_   37 + 54 _91_

How do you know the number pairs have the same sum?

The addends are the same, but in a different order.

Daily Homework

5-9 Check Addition

Add. Check by adding in a different order.

1.
```
  43      25      25      62      33      49
+ 25    + 43    + 62    + 25    + 49    + 33
  68      68      87      87      82      82
```

2.
```
   6      42      21      49      52      36
+ 42    +  6    + 49    + 21    + 36    + 52
  48      48      70      70      88      88
```

3.
```
   9      39      44      13      13      38
+ 39    +  9    + 13    + 44    + 38    + 13
  48      48      57      57      51      51
```

Solve. Use the chart. Check by adding in a different order.

4. Which two children sold the most cookies?

___Matt and Kate___

How many boxes did these two children sell in all?

___97___ boxes

Cookies Sold	
Gayle	39 boxes
Joy	26 boxes
Keith	25 boxes
Matt	43 boxes
Kate	54 boxes

Spiral Review

Compare. Use >, <, or =.

5. 83 (>) 76   45 (=) 45   29 (<) 31   6 (<) 10

Chapter 5 ~ Lesson 10

Practice

Estimate Sums

Add. Estimate to see if your answer is reasonable.

1.
$$54 + 15 = 69 \quad 50 + 20 = 70$$
$$34 + 37 = 71 \quad 30 + 40 = 70$$
$$24 + 19 = 43 \quad 20 + 20 = 40$$

2.
$$17 + 17 = 34 \quad 20 + 20 = 40$$
$$58 + 29 = 87 \quad 60 + 30 = 90$$
$$32 + 41 = 73 \quad 30 + 40 = 70$$

3.
$$48 + 26 = 74 \quad 50 + 30 = 80$$
$$29 + 14 = 43 \quad 30 + 10 = 40$$
$$67 + 22 = 89 \quad 70 + 20 = 90$$

4.
$$16 + 67 = 83 \quad 20 + 70 = 90$$
$$46 + 19 = 65 \quad 50 + 20 = 70$$
$$37 + 27 = 64 \quad 40 + 30 = 70$$

5.
$$18 + 23 = 41 \quad 20 + 20 = 40$$
$$72 + 16 = 88 \quad 70 + 20 = 90$$
$$39 + 22 = 61 \quad 40 + 20 = 60$$

Problem Solving

6. There are 33 adults at the Swim Club. There are 57 children at the Swim Club. How many people are at the Swim Club?

___90___ people

7. Sasha swims for 45 minutes in the morning. She swims for 38 minutes in the afternoon. For how many minutes does Sasha swim?

___83___ minutes

Use with Grade 2, Chapter 5, Lesson 10, pages 179–180. (151)

Reteach

Estimate Sums

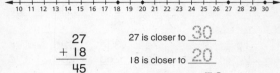

You can estimate to check addition.
A number line can help you estimate.

10 11 12 13 14 15 16 17 18 19 20 21 22 23 24 25 26 27 28 29 30

$$27 + 18 = 45$$

27 is closer to ___30___

18 is closer to ___20___

27 + 18 is about ___50___

45 is close to 50. The answer is reasonable.

Add. Estimate to see if the answer is reasonable.

1.
$$18 + 18 = 36 \quad 20 + 20 = 40$$
$$38 + 49 = 87 \quad 40 + 50 = 90$$
$$32 + 41 = 73 \quad 30 + 40 = 70$$

2.
$$48 + 33 = 81 \quad 50 + 30 = 80$$
$$24 + 32 = 56 \quad 20 + 30 = 50$$
$$22 + 68 = 90 \quad 20 + 70 = 90$$

3.
$$47 + 19 = 66 \quad 50 + 20 = 70$$
$$56 + 32 = 88 \quad 60 + 30 = 90$$
$$47 + 37 = 84 \quad 50 + 40 = 90$$

4.
$$34 + 38 = 72 \quad 30 + 40 = 70$$
$$34 + 37 = 71 \quad 30 + 40 = 70$$
$$44 + 19 = 63 \quad 40 + 20 = 60$$

Use with Grade 2, Chapter 5, Lesson 10, pages 179–180. (152)

Enrich

Estimate Sums
Recycling Day

Mr. Marvin's class collected bottles for recycling.

The chart shows how many bottles each child collected.
Estimate how many bottles each pair collected.

Jackson 34	Marie 49	Jamal 52	Keesha 18
Kenny 51	Paco 27	Paula 38	Maura 43

1. About how many bottles did Jackson and Jamal collect?

$$30 + 50 = 80$$

about ___80___ bottles

About how many bottles did Marie and Maura collect?

$$50 + 40 = 90$$

about ___90___ bottles

2. About how many bottles did Keesha and Kenny collect?

$$20 + 50 = 70$$

about ___70___ bottles

About how many bottles did Paula and Paco collect?

$$40 + 30 = 70$$

about ___70___ bottles

Three of the students collected about 100 bottles.
Who are the three students?

<u>Answers may vary. Possible answers: Jackson, Paco,</u>
<u>Maura; Jamal, Keesha, Paco</u>

Use with Grade 2, Chapter 5, Lesson 10, pages 179–180. (153)

Daily Homework

5-10 Estimate Sums

Add. Estimate to see if your answer is reasonable.

1.
$$51 + 28 = 79 \quad 50 + 30 = 80$$
$$29 + 32 = 61 \quad 30 + 30 = 60$$
$$31 + 28 = 59 \quad 30 + 30 = 60$$

2.
$$22 + 49 = 71 \quad 20 + 50 = 70$$
$$13 + 27 = 40 \quad 10 + 30 = 40$$
$$62 + 17 = 79 \quad 60 + 20 = 80$$

3.
$$57 + 29 = 86 \quad 60 + 30 = 90$$
$$38 + 49 = 87 \quad 40 + 50 = 90$$
$$41 + 48 = 89 \quad 40 + 50 = 90$$

Problem Solving

Solve. Estimate to see if your answer is reasonable.

4. Lisa spends 21 minutes on math homework and 18 minutes on spelling homework. How much time does she spend on homework in all?

___39___ minutes

5. Becky's class takes 49 books out of the library. Barry's class takes out 37 books. How many books do the two classes take out in all?

___86___ books

Spiral Review

Write the number that comes just after.

6. 34 | 35   47 | 48   83 | 84   22 | 23

Grade 2, Chapter 5, Lesson 10, Cluster B **47**

Chapter 5 ~ Lesson 11

Practice

Add Money Amounts

P 5-11 PRACTICE

Add.

1.
  13¢   44¢   25¢   63¢   47¢   18¢
+ 19¢ + 37¢ + 25¢ + 21¢ + 28¢ + 28¢
  32¢   81¢   50¢   84¢   75¢   46¢

2.
  51¢   35¢   87¢   38¢   42¢   59¢
+ 29¢ + 20¢ + 9¢ + 26¢ + 28¢ + 19¢
  80¢   55¢   96¢   64¢   70¢   78¢

3.
  16¢   54¢   38¢   79¢   14¢   24¢
+ 66¢ + 27¢ + 16¢ + 6¢ + 29¢ + 44¢
  82¢   81¢   54¢   85¢   43¢   68¢

4.
  47¢   26¢   38¢   59¢   32¢   13¢
+ 47¢ + 33¢ + 49¢ + 8¢ + 38¢ + 79¢
  94¢   59¢   87¢   67¢   70¢   92¢

5.
  34¢   25¢   73¢   28¢   83¢   46¢
+ 43¢ + 15¢ + 18¢ + 28¢ + 5¢ + 33¢
  77¢   40¢   91¢   56¢   88¢   79¢

Problem Solving

6. Randy has 24¢. He gets 67¢ more. How much money does Randy have in all?   91¢

7. Jasmine has 49¢. She gets 17¢ more. How much money does Jasmine have in all?   66¢

Use with Grade 2, Chapter 5, Lesson 11, pages 181–182. (154)

Reteach

Add Money Amounts

R 5-11 RETEACH

Adding money is the same as adding tens and ones.
Find the total amount.

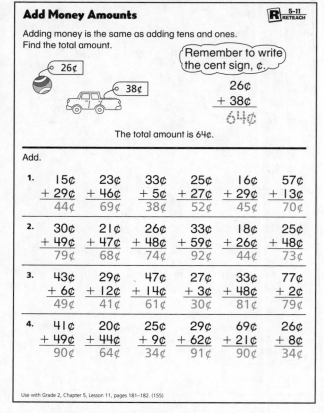

Remember to write the cent sign, ¢.

  26¢
+ 38¢
  64¢

The total amount is 64¢.

Add.

1.
  15¢   23¢   33¢   25¢   16¢   57¢
+ 29¢ + 46¢ + 5¢ + 27¢ + 29¢ + 13¢
  44¢   69¢   38¢   52¢   45¢   70¢

2.
  30¢   21¢   26¢   33¢   18¢   25¢
+ 49¢ + 47¢ + 48¢ + 59¢ + 26¢ + 48¢
  79¢   68¢   74¢   92¢   44¢   73¢

3.
  43¢   29¢   47¢   27¢   33¢   77¢
+ 6¢ + 12¢ + 14¢ + 3¢ + 48¢ + 2¢
  49¢   41¢   61¢   30¢   81¢   79¢

4.
  41¢   20¢   25¢   29¢   69¢   26¢
+ 49¢ + 44¢ + 9¢ + 62¢ + 21¢ + 8¢
  90¢   64¢   34¢   91¢   90¢   34¢

Use with Grade 2, Chapter 5, Lesson 11, pages 181–182. (155)

Enrich

Add Money Amounts
Which Toy Can You Buy?

E 5-11 ENRICH

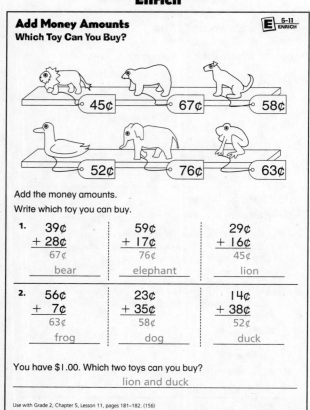

45¢   67¢   58¢

52¢   76¢   63¢

Add the money amounts.
Write which toy you can buy.

1.
  39¢
+ 28¢
  67¢
bear

  59¢
+ 17¢
  76¢
elephant

  29¢
+ 16¢
  45¢
lion

2.
  56¢
+ 7¢
  63¢
frog

  23¢
+ 35¢
  58¢
dog

  14¢
+ 38¢
  52¢
duck

You have $1.00. Which two toys can you buy?
  lion and duck

Use with Grade 2, Chapter 5, Lesson 11, pages 181–182. (156)

Daily Homework

5-11 Add Money Amounts

Add.

1.
  65¢   48¢   13¢   22¢   41¢   65¢
+ 8¢ + 38¢ + 44¢ + 35¢ + 8¢ + 6¢
  72¢   86¢   57¢   57¢   49¢   71¢

2.
  53¢   11¢   24¢   32¢   14¢   25¢
+ 15¢ + 16¢ + 9¢ + 47¢ + 58¢ + 38¢
  68¢   27¢   33¢   79¢   72¢   63¢

3.
  26¢   23¢   49¢   17¢   37¢   33¢
+ 36¢ + 12¢ + 26¢ + 13¢ + 8¢ + 28¢
  62¢   35¢   75¢   30¢   45¢   61¢

Problem Solving

Solve.

4. Keisha buys 2 charms for 25¢ each. How much does she spend in all?   50¢

Spiral Review

Add.

6.
  8   8   9   6   9   6
  4   7   9   4   5   5
+ 2 + 3 + 1 + 7 + 1 + 5
 14 18 19 17 15 16

Chapter 5 ~ Lesson 12

Practice

Three Addends

Add. You can use tens and ones models.

1.
23	41	37	13	25	17
14	32	18	24	37	40
+ 29	+ 16	+ 25	+ 4	+ 14	+ 33
66	89	80	41	76	90

2.
8	36	55	11	35	24
20	28	13	63	16	2
+ 13	+ 31	+ 14	+ 24	+ 34	+ 36
41	95	82	98	85	62

3.
14	52	44	19	24	35
18	20	16	68	3	12
+ 13	+ 11	+ 22	+ 12	+ 25	+ 47
45	83	82	99	52	94

4.
21	37	14	62	43	36
18	13	45	11	15	21
+ 21	+ 27	+ 3	+ 23	+ 22	+ 41
60	77	62	96	80	98

Problem Solving

5. There are 34 children in first grade. There are 27 children in second grade. There are 31 children in third grade. How many children are there in all?

__92__ children

6. Brian collects 24 bundles of newspapers. Marie collects 17 bundles. Ellie collects 22 bundles. How many bundles of newspapers do the children collect in all?

__63__ bundles

Reteach

Three Addends

You can use addition strategies to help you add three addends.

Look for doubles.

| 24 |
| 14 |→ 8
| + 32 |
| 70 |

Look for a ten.

| 37 |
| 11 |→ 10
| + 33 |
| 81 |

Add.

1.
14	42	28	29	24	47
24	27	0	42	11	11
+ 13	+ 12	+ 13	+ 21	+ 26	+ 12
51	81	41	92	61	70

2.
17	23	45	6	10	23
30	26	13	24	58	16
+ 13	+ 46	+ 15	+ 40	+ 23	+ 33
60	95	73	70	91	72

3.
32	13	55	19	37	21
18	36	20	41	17	17
+ 1	+ 46	+ 15	+ 13	+ 32	+ 3
51	95	90	73	86	41

Enrich

Three Addends

Target Practice

Play with a partner. Take turns.

• Drop a coin on the target below.

• Add the three numbers in the section where the coin lands.

• Play three rounds.

Add up the three sums on your paper. That number is your score.

The player with the greater number of points is the winner.

Daily Homework

5-12 Three Addends

Add. You can use tens and ones models.

1.
25	32	38	56	25	4
18	22	8	21	12	77
+ 35	+ 14	+ 13	+ 2	+ 45	+ 17
78	68	59	79	82	98

2.
17	22	37	22	28	29
2	19	23	43	30	10
+ 34	+ 25	+ 26	+ 32	+ 21	+ 39
57	66	86	97	79	78

Problem Solving

Solve. Use the chart.

3. Which 3 colors got the most votes?
__blue, red, purple__

How many votes did these colors get in all?
__68__ votes

Grade 2 Favorite Colors	
blue	31 votes
red	22 votes
purple	15 votes
green	14 votes
yellow	6 votes
orange	2 votes

4. Which 3 colors got the fewest votes? __green, yellow, orange__

How many votes did these colors get in all? __22__ votes

Spiral Review

Subtract.

5.
18	13	16	17	14	15
− 9	− 7	− 8	− 9	− 8	− 9
9	6	8	8	6	6

Chapter 5 ~ Lesson 13

Part A Worksheet

Problem Solving: Application

Part A 5-13 WORKSHEET Decision Making

Plan a Bus Route

Plan a bus route from your home to school.

Draw your home in one of the boxes below.

Draw your school in another box.

Draw places that you would pass on your route in the other boxes.

Cut out the boxes.

Paste them on a sheet of paper.

Then draw the streets to show your route.

Check students' drawings

Use with Grade 2, Chapter 5, Lesson 13, pages 185–186. (160)

Part A Worksheet

Problem Solving: Application

Part A 5-13 WORKSHEET Decision Making

Plan a Bus Route

1. Why did you plan the bus route that you did?

____

____

____

2. How long is your route?

_____ blocks _____ miles

3. What if you could plan another bus route?

How would you change it?

____

____

____

____

Answers may vary.

Use with Grade 2, Chapter 5, Lesson 13, pages 185–186. (161)

Part B Worksheet

Problem Solving: Application

Part B 5-13 WORKSHEET Math & Science

What Do You See in a Tree?

1. Record the number of different trees you see around your school. Answers may vary.

Number of Different Trees

2. How are the trees alike?

____

____

3. How are the trees different?

____

____

4. Why do you think trees have leaves?

____

____

Use with Grade 2, Chapter 5, Lesson 13, pages 187–188. (162)

Chapter 6 ~ Lesson 1

Practice

Subtract Tens

Count back by tens to subtract.

1. $73 - 20 = \underline{53}$ $60 - 30 = \underline{30}$ $50 - 30 = \underline{20}$

2. $66 - 40 = \underline{26}$ $92 - 10 = \underline{82}$ $70 - 20 = \underline{50}$

3.
85	59	80	43	90	30
− 10	− 30	− 20	− 10	− 40	− 20
75	29	60	33	50	10

4.
22	90	43	64	60	87
− 10	− 20	− 20	− 40	− 50	− 30
12	70	23	24	10	57

5.
71	40	65	80	41	63
− 10	− 30	− 20	− 50	− 10	− 40
61	10	45	30	31	23

6.
50	68	76	40	97	55
− 20	− 50	− 20	− 20	− 60	− 10
30	18	56	20	37	45

Problem Solving

7. Lin collects 82 leaves. She gives 50 leaves to her friend. How many leaves does Lin have left?

   $\underline{32}$ leaves

Mandy collects 47 leaves. She uses 20 leaves to make a picture. How many leaves does Mandy have left?

   $\underline{27}$ leaves

Use with Grade 2, Chapter 6, Lesson 1, pages 201–202. (163)

Reteach

Subtract Tens

Find the difference.

Subtract $59 - 20 = \underline{39}$

Count back by tens to subtract.

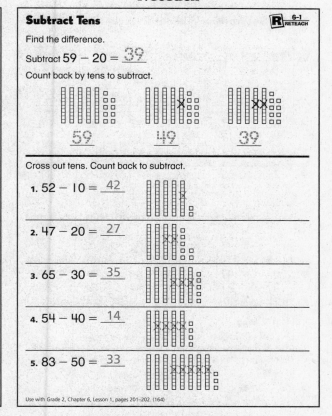

   $\underline{59}$ $\underline{49}$ $\underline{39}$

Cross out tens. Count back to subtract.

1. $52 - 10 = \underline{42}$

2. $47 - 20 = \underline{27}$

3. $65 - 30 = \underline{35}$

4. $54 - 40 = \underline{14}$

5. $83 - 50 = \underline{33}$

Use with Grade 2, Chapter 6, Lesson 1, pages 201–202. (164)

Enrich

Subtract Tens
Riddle

How do you keep a 🌡 from falling?

Subtract. Match each difference to the letter in the box. Write the letter on the line below the difference. Answer the riddle.

8	9	15	17	21	23	28
P	O	E	D	A	N	I
30	32	44	49	54	56	60
U	T	S	G	L	R	B

90	74	85		41
− 60	− 30	− 70		− 20
30	44	15		21
U	S	E		A

64	82	66	99	93	89
− 20	− 50	− 10	− 90	− 70	− 40
44	32	56	9	23	49
S	T	R	O	N	G

96	39	98	25		51	73	97
− 40	− 30	− 90	− 10		− 30	− 50	− 80
56	9	8	15		21	23	17
R	O	P	E		A	N	D

61		83	91	78	94
− 40		− 60	− 70	− 50	− 40
21		23	21	28	54
A		N	A	I	L

Use with Grade 2, Chapter 6, Lesson 1, pages 201–202. (165)

Daily Homework

6-1 Subtract Tens

Remember to count back by tens.

Subtract.

1. $86 - 30 = \underline{56}$ $92 - 20 = \underline{72}$ $47 - 20 = \underline{27}$

2. $84 - 20 = \underline{64}$ $61 - 10 = \underline{51}$ $38 - 30 = \underline{8}$

3.
53	93	30	78	52	38
− 30	− 10	− 20	− 10	− 30	− 20
23	83	10	68	22	18

4.
77	35	81	49	87	89
− 30	− 20	− 10	− 30	− 20	− 10
47	15	71	19	67	79

Solve.

5. 54 people wait in line for movie tickets. 20 people buy tickets and go inside. How many people are left in the ticket line? $\underline{34}$ people

6. Linda has 36 bags of popcorn. She sells 20 bags of popcorn. How many bags are left? $\underline{16}$ bags

Spiral Review

Count up to find the change.

Ticket Price	You Pay	Change

7. 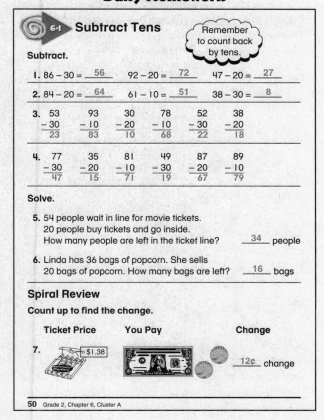 $1.38 $\underline{12¢}$ change

Chapter 6 ~ Lesson 2

Practice

2-Digit Subtraction Without Regrouping

P | 6-2 PRACTICE

Subtract.

1.

Tens	Ones
3	3
− 1	2
2	1

Tens	Ones
4	8
− 2	5
2	3

Tens	Ones
7	4
− 6	2
1	2

Tens	Ones
5	9
− 2	1
3	8

2.
68	37	88	47	93	38
− 42	− 17	− 31	− 13	− 21	− 17
26	20	57	34	72	21

3.
71	59	26	75	99	27
− 41	− 48	− 21	− 62	− 92	− 17
30	11	5	13	7	10

4.
52	67	89	58	71	46
− 21	− 15	− 19	− 55	− 40	− 26
31	52	70	3	31	20

5.
93	47	82	54	77	38
− 42	− 21	− 21	− 41	− 33	− 34
51	26	61	13	44	4

Problem Solving

6. Ling picks 57 apples. She uses 32 apples to make a pie. How many apples does Ling have left?

_25_ apples

Rob picks 72 flowers. He uses 40 flowers to make a wreath. How many flowers does Rob have left?

_32_ flowers

Reteach

2-Digit Subtraction Without Regrouping

R | 6-2 RETEACH

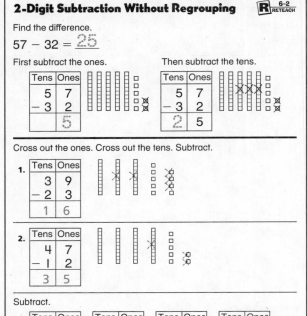

Find the difference.

$57 - 32 = 25$

First subtract the ones.

Tens	Ones
5	7
− 3	2
	5

Then subtract the tens.

Tens	Ones
5	7
− 3	2
2	5

Cross out the ones. Cross out the tens. Subtract.

1.
Tens	Ones
3	9
− 2	3
1	6

2.
Tens	Ones
4	7
− 1	2
3	5

Subtract.

3.
Tens	Ones
5	3
− 3	2
2	1

Tens	Ones
2	9
− 1	6
1	3

Tens	Ones
5	6
−	5
5	1

Tens	Ones
7	7
− 3	4
4	3

Enrich

2-Digit Subtraction Without Regrouping
Race to Subtract

E | 6-2 ENRICH

Cut out the cards at the bottom of the page.
Mix them up. Put them facedown on a table.
To play:
- Take turns.
- Pick a card. Subtract.
- If your answer is correct, move the number of spaces shown in the circle.

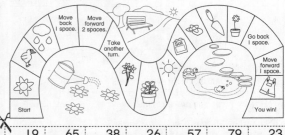

19	65	38	26	57	79	23
− 14	− 62	− 36	− 25	− 53	− 78	− 3
① 5	① 3	① 2	① 1	① 4	① 1	① 20

53	38	65	27	59	24	97
− 31	− 8	− 34	− 5	− 57	− 13	− 66
② 22	② 30	② 31	② 22	② 2	② 11	② 31

83	88	97	99	98	67	88
− 23	− 47	− 6	− 75	− 44	− 64	− 11
③ 60	③ 41	③ 91	③ 24	③ 54	③ 3	③ 77

Daily Homework

6-2 2-Digit Subtraction Without Regrouping

Subtract.

1.
tens	ones
3	5
2	1
1	4

tens	ones
8	9
4	2
4	7

tens	ones
6	6
6	3
	3

2.
75	22	93	64	86	59
− 60	− 11	− 2	− 31	− 54	− 7
15	11	91	33	32	52

3.
58	59	66	57	94	88
− 7	− 17	− 12	− 43	− 72	− 67
51	42	54	14	22	21

4.
56	97	79	76	68	87
− 2	− 32	− 11	− 4	− 15	− 3
54	65	68	72	53	84

Solve.

5. 47 people are on the bus. 25 people get off at the first stop. How many people are left on the bus?

_22_ people

Spiral Review

Add.

6.
53	29	56	45	38	79
+ 27	+ 55	+ 43	+ 14	+ 35	+ 13
80	84	99	59	73	92

Chapter 6 ~ Lesson 3

Practice

Decide When to Regroup

P 6-3 PRACTICE

Use models and tens and ones workmat.

	Subtract.	Do you need to regroup?	How many are left?
1.	54 − 6	(yes) no	48
2.	32 − 7	(yes) no	25
3.	82 − 8	(yes) no	74
4.	47 − 5	yes (no)	42
5.	63 − 6	(yes) no	57
6.	91 − 3	(yes) no	88
7.	32 − 4	(yes) no	28
8.	79 − 2	yes (no)	77
9.	54 − 7	(yes) no	47
10.	38 − 9	(yes) no	29

Problem Solving

11. Sam baked 41 cookies. He ate 4 cookies for his snack. How many cookies are left?

__37__ cookies

Sam and his family ate 9 more of the cookies for dinner. How many cookies are left now?

__28__ cookies

Use with Grade 2, Chapter 6, Lesson 3, pages 207–208. (169)

Reteach

Decide When to Regroup

R 6-3 RETEACH

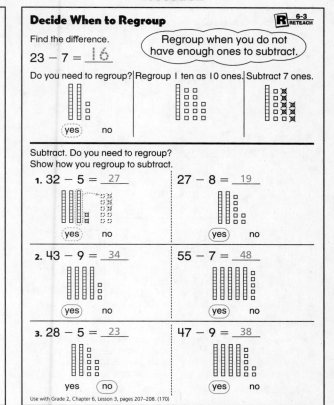

Find the difference.

$23 - 7 = \underline{16}$

Regroup when you do not have enough ones to subtract.

Do you need to regroup? | Regroup 1 ten as 10 ones. | Subtract 7 ones.

(yes) no

Subtract. Do you need to regroup? Show how you regroup to subtract.

1. $32 - 5 = \underline{27}$ (yes) no $27 - 8 = \underline{19}$ (yes) no

2. $43 - 9 = \underline{34}$ (yes) no $55 - 7 = \underline{48}$ (yes) no

3. $28 - 5 = \underline{23}$ yes (no) $47 - 9 = \underline{38}$ (yes) no

Use with Grade 2, Chapter 6, Lesson 3, pages 207–208. (170)

Enrich

Decide When to Regroup
A Regrouping Game

E 6-3 ENRICH

Play with a partner. Take turns.

- Drop a counter on the game board. Subtract.
- Score one point if you need to regroup.
- Score one point for a correct answer.

The first player to reach 10 points is the winner.

Scoring Chart	
Name	Points

57 − 9 R; 48	24 − 6 R; 18	37 − 5 32	88 − 3 85
45 − 7 R; 38	67 − 4 63	39 − 6 33	80 − 5 R; 75
18 − 2 16	27 − 8 R; 19	46 − 7 R; 39	53 − 1 52
55 − 6 R; 49	79 − 4 75	92 − 8 R; 84	66 − 6 60
97 − 3 94	62 − 9 R; 53	31 − 6 R; 25	72 − 5 R; 67

With your partner, write a rule that tells when you need to regroup.

__Possible answer: You need to regroup when there are not enough ones to subtract.__

Use with Grade 2, Chapter 6, Lesson 3, pages 207–208. (171)

Daily Homework

6-3 Decide When to Regroup

	Subtract	Do you need to regroup?	How many are left?
1.	68 − 9	(yes) no	59
2.	45 − 3	yes (no)	42
3.	77 − 5	yes (no)	72
4.	94 − 6	(yes) no	88
5.	52 − 4	(yes) no	48
6.	39 − 7	yes (no)	32

Problem Solving

7. Marc works in the pet store. He has 36 birds to sell. People buy 8 birds. How many birds are left? __28__ birds

8. Marc has 24 boxes of bird seed. He sells 3 boxes of bird seed. How many boxes of bird seed are left? __21__ boxes

Spiral Review

Complete each number sentence. Use + or − .

9. $13 \ominus 5 = 8$ $8 \oplus 4 = 12$ $9 \oplus 2 = 11$

10. $17 \ominus 9 = 8$ $9 \oplus 6 = 15$ $15 \ominus 8 = 7$

Chapter 6 ~ Lesson 4

Practice

2-Digit Subtraction

Subtract. Use models or the tens and ones workmat.

1.

Tens	Ones
4̶	1̶5̶
5	5
−2	7
2	8

Tens	Ones
7	1̶3̶
8̶	3̶
−	5
7	8

Tens	Ones
2	1̶6̶
3̶	6̶
−1	9
1	7

Tens	Ones
8	1̶0̶
9̶	0̶
−4	8
4	2

2.

Tens	Ones
4	3
−3	1
1	2

Tens	Ones
5	1̶2̶
6̶	2̶
−2	8
3	4

Tens	Ones
6	1̶8̶
7̶	8̶
−2	9
4	9

Tens	Ones
8	1̶1̶
9̶	1̶
−2	4
6	7

3.

Tens	Ones
4	7
−1	3
3	4

Tens	Ones
4	1̶2̶
5̶	2̶
−3	6
1	6

Tens	Ones
6	1̶0̶
7̶	0̶
−2	1
4	9

Tens	Ones
8	1̶3̶
9̶	3̶
−	8
8	5

Problem Solving

4. There are 73 children on a playground. 27 of the children go inside. How many children are left?

___46___ children

There are 41 children on the bus. 35 children are wearing hats. How many children aren't wearing hats?

___6___ children

Reteach

2-Digit Subtraction

Find the difference.

$34 - 18 = \underline{16}$

Can you subtract 8 ones?	Regroup 1 ten as 10 ones. Subtract the ones.	Subtract the tens.

(yes) no

Tens	Ones
3	4
−1	8

Tens	Ones
2̶	1̶4̶
3̶	4̶
−1	8
	6

Tens	Ones
2̶	1̶4̶
3̶	4̶
−1	8
1	6

Subtract. Use models or the tens and ones workmat.

1.

Tens	Ones
1	1̶3̶
2̶	3̶
−	9
1	4

Tens	Ones
2	1̶6̶
3̶	6̶
−1	9
1	7

Tens	Ones
3	1̶1̶
4̶	1̶
−2	5
1	6

Tens	Ones
4	1̶8̶
5̶	8̶
−2	9
2	9

2.

Tens	Ones
3	1̶6̶
4̶	6̶
−2	7
1	9

Tens	Ones
4	1̶2̶
5̶	2̶
−1	6
3	6

Tens	Ones
2	1̶7̶
3̶	7̶
−1	9
1	8

Tens	Ones
5	1̶5̶
6̶	5̶
−4	8
1	7

Enrich

2-Digit Subtraction
Secret Code

Subtract.

Then write the differences in order from least to greatest in the boxes below.

Write the letters on the lines. Read the secret message.

$$\begin{array}{cc} 53 \\ -37 \\ \hline 16 \end{array} W \quad \begin{array}{cc} 64 \\ -19 \\ \hline 45 \end{array} R \quad \begin{array}{cc} 44 \\ -8 \\ \hline 36 \end{array} R \quad \begin{array}{cc} 71 \\ -49 \\ \hline 22 \end{array} H \quad \begin{array}{cc} 43 \\ -38 \\ \hline 5 \end{array} I \quad \begin{array}{cc} 92 \\ -48 \\ \hline 44 \end{array} G$$

$$\begin{array}{cc} 75 \\ -18 \\ \hline 57 \end{array} P \quad \begin{array}{cc} 31 \\ -6 \\ \hline 25 \end{array} W \quad \begin{array}{cc} 71 \\ -19 \\ \hline 52 \end{array} U \quad \begin{array}{cc} 24 \\ -15 \\ \hline 9 \end{array} K \quad \begin{array}{cc} 65 \\ -17 \\ \hline 48 \end{array} O \quad \begin{array}{cc} 81 \\ -68 \\ \hline 13 \end{array} N$$

$$\begin{array}{cc} 93 \\ -79 \\ \hline 14 \end{array} O \quad \begin{array}{cc} 51 \\ -18 \\ \hline 33 \end{array} O \quad \begin{array}{cc} 82 \\ -59 \\ \hline 23 \end{array} O \quad \begin{array}{cc} 55 \\ -18 \\ \hline 37 \end{array} E \quad \begin{array}{cc} 56 \\ -28 \\ \hline 28 \end{array} T$$

5	9	13	14	16		22	23	25
I	K	N	O	W		H	O	W

28	33		36	37	44	45	48	52	57
T	O		R	E	G	R	O	U	P

Daily Homework

6-4 2-Digit Subtraction

Subtract. You can use tens and ones models.

1.

tens	ones
3	1
−1	1
2	0

tens	ones
3	1̶1̶
4̶	1̶
−1	2
2	9

tens	ones
5	6
−1	4
4	2

tens	ones
5	1̶6̶
6̶	6̶
−1	7
4	9

2.

tens	ones
3	1̶5̶
4̶	5̶
−1	8
2	7

tens	ones
9	8
−	5
9	3

tens	ones
8	1̶2̶
9̶	2̶
−4	6
4	6

tens	ones
2	1̶6̶
3̶	6̶
−1	7
1	9

3.

tens	ones
7	8
−3	5
4	3

tens	ones
6	1̶8̶
7̶	8̶
−3	9
3	9

tens	ones
3	1̶3̶
4̶	3̶
−3	8
3	5

tens	ones
2	1̶2̶
3̶	2̶
−2	8
4	

Solve.

4. Jan counts 35 birds. 18 are robins. How many birds are not robins? ___17___ birds

5. The second graders have a pet fair. 25 pets are shown. 3 pets are hamsters. How many are not hamsters? ___22___ pets

Spiral Review

Add. Estimate to see if your answer is reasonable.

6.	33	30	52	50	49	50	19	20
	+18	+20	+27	+30	+21	+20	+31	+30
	51	50	79	80	70	70	50	50

Chapter 6 ~ Lesson 5

Practice

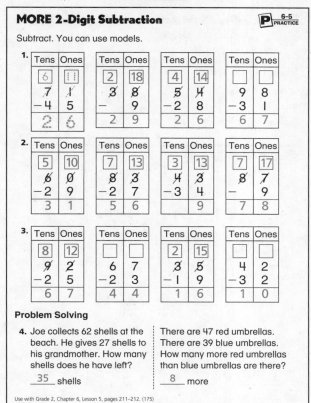

MORE 2-Digit Subtraction P 6-5 PRACTICE

Subtract. You can use models.

1.

Tens	Ones
6	11
7	1
−4	5
2	6

Tens	Ones
2	18
3	8
−	9
2	9

Tens	Ones
4	14
5	4
−2	8
2	6

Tens	Ones
9	8
−3	1
6	7

2.

Tens	Ones
5	10
6	0
−2	9
3	1

Tens	Ones
7	13
8	3
−2	7
5	6

Tens	Ones
3	13
4	3
−3	4
	9

Tens	Ones
7	17
8	7
−	9
7	8

3.

Tens	Ones
8	12
9	2
−2	5
6	7

Tens	Ones
6	7
−2	3
4	4

Tens	Ones
2	15
3	5
−1	9
1	6

Tens	Ones
4	2
−3	2
1	0

Problem Solving

4. Joe collects 62 shells at the beach. He gives 27 shells to his grandmother. How many shells does he have left?

___35___ shells

There are 47 red umbrellas. There are 39 blue umbrellas. How many more red umbrellas than blue umbrellas are there?

___8___ more

Use with Grade 2, Chapter 6, Lesson 5, pages 211–212. (175)

Reteach

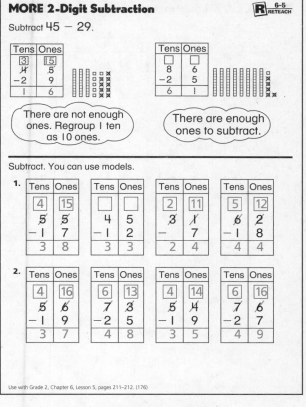

MORE 2-Digit Subtraction R 6-5 RETEACH

Subtract 45 − 29.

Tens	Ones
3	15
4	5
−2	9
1	6

There are not enough ones. Regroup 1 ten as 10 ones.

Tens	Ones
8	6
−2	5
6	1

There are enough ones to subtract.

Subtract. You can use models.

1.

Tens	Ones
4	15
5	5
−1	7
3	8

Tens	Ones
4	5
−1	2
3	3

Tens	Ones
2	11
3	1
−	7
2	4

Tens	Ones
5	12
6	2
−1	8
4	4

2.

Tens	Ones
4	16
5	6
−1	9
3	7

Tens	Ones
6	13
7	3
−2	5
4	8

Tens	Ones
4	14
5	4
−1	9
3	5

Tens	Ones
6	16
7	6
−2	7
4	9

Use with Grade 2, Chapter 6, Lesson 5, pages 211–212. (176)

Enrich

MORE 2-Digit Subtraction E 6-5 ENRICH

Find Your Way

Subtract. Follow the differences from greatest to least.

Trace the path from Start to the Fountain.

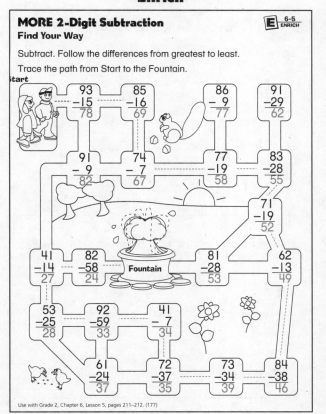

Start

93 −15 = 78   85 −16 = 69   86 − 9 = 77   91 −29 = 62

91 − 9 = 82   74 − 7 = 67   77 −19 = 58   83 −28 = 55

71 −19 = 52

41 −14 = 27   82 −58 = 24   Fountain   81 −28 = 53   62 −13 = 49

53 −25 = 28   92 −59 = 33   41 − 7 = 34

61 −24 = 37   72 −37 = 35   73 −34 = 39   84 −38 = 46

Use with Grade 2, Chapter 6, Lesson 5, pages 211–212. (177)

Daily Homework

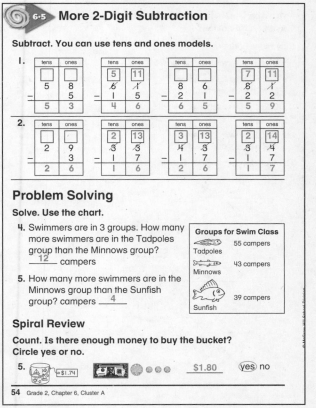

6-5 **More 2-Digit Subtraction**

Subtract. You can use tens and ones models.

1.

tens	ones
5	8
−	5
5	3

tens	ones
5	11
6	1
−1	5
4	6

tens	ones
8	6
−2	1
6	5

tens	ones
7	11
8	1
−2	2
5	9

2.

tens	ones
2	9
−	3
2	6

tens	ones
2	13
3	3
−1	7
1	6

tens	ones
3	13
4	3
−1	7
2	6

tens	ones
2	14
3	4
−1	7
1	7

Problem Solving

Solve. Use the chart.

4. Swimmers are in 3 groups. How many more swimmers are in the Tadpoles group than the Minnows group? ___12___ campers

5. How many more swimmers are in the Minnows group than the Sunfish group? campers ___4___

Groups for Swim Class	
Tadpoles	55 campers
Minnows	43 campers
Sunfish	39 campers

Spiral Review

Count. Is there enough money to buy the bucket? Circle yes or no.

5. $1.74 $1.80   **yes** no

54 Grade 2, Chapter 6, Cluster A

Chapter 6 ~ Lesson 6

Practice

Practice 2-Digit Subtraction
P 6-6 PRACTICE

Subtract. You can use models.

1.

Tens	Ones
3	13
4̶	3̶
−	9
3	4

Tens	Ones
8	12
9̶	2̶
−4	7
4	5

Tens	Ones
5	14
6̶	4̶
−4	7
1	7

Tens	Ones
8	8
−3	8
5	0

2.

Tens	Ones
6	12
7̶	2̶
−1	6
5	6

Tens	Ones
3	17
4̶	7̶
−3	9
	8

Tens	Ones
3	15
4̶	5̶
−2	7
1	8

Tens	Ones
8	11
9̶	1̶
−2	5
6	6

3.

Tens	Ones
7	14
8̶	4̶
−1	5
6	9

Tens	Ones
2	16
3̶	6̶
−1	8
1	8

Tens	Ones
6	9
−4	7
2	2

Tens	Ones
4	17
5̶	7̶
−	8
4	9

Rewrite. Then subtract.

4. 62 − 48 = ■

$$\begin{array}{r} 62 \\ -\ 48 \\ \hline 14 \end{array}$$

84 − 39 = ■

$$\begin{array}{r} 84 \\ -\ 39 \\ \hline 45 \end{array}$$

Reteach

Practice 2-Digit Subtraction
R 6-6 RETEACH

Therese has 55 stamps. She gives 29 stamps to Nan. How many stamps does Therese have now?

Find the difference.

55 − 29 = 26

Therese has 26 stamps now.

Subtract the ones. Subtract the tens. Regroup.

Tens	Ones
4	15
5̶	5̶
−2	9
	6

Tens	Ones
4	15
5̶	5̶
−2	9
2	6

Subtract. You can use models.

1.

Tens	Ones
4	11
5̶	1̶
−2	7
2	4

Tens	Ones
3	16
4̶	6̶
−2	7
1	9

Tens	Ones
8	5
−3	5
5	0

Tens	Ones
6	18
7̶	8̶
−2	9
4	9

2.

Tens	Ones
5	12
6̶	2̶
−2	8
3	4

Tens	Ones
4	17
5̶	7̶
−2	8
2	9

Tens	Ones
9	9
−1	3
8	6

Tens	Ones
2	14
3̶	4̶
−2	7
	7

Enrich

Practice 2-Digit Subtraction
E 6-6 ENRICH

Target Subtraction

Play with a partner.

- Drop a coin twice on the target.
- Subtract the lesser number from the greater number.
- Compare your answer with your partner's.
- The player with the greater answer gets one point.

The first player who gets 10 points is the winner.

Scoring Chart	
Name	Points

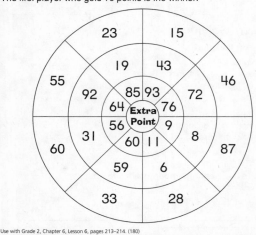

Daily Homework

6·6 Practice 2-Digit Subtraction

Subtract. You can use tens and ones models.

1.

5 13			2 14	7 17		3 11
6̶3̶	75	3̶4̶	8̶7̶	55	4̶1̶
−37	−22	−16	−78	− 3	−23
2 6	53	18	9	52	18

2.

		7 14		5 14	4 17
77	59	8̶4̶	99	6̶4̶	5̶7̶
−45	− 7	−29	−38	−39	− 9
3 2	52	55	61	25	48

3.

8 11		8 12	5 15		8 14
9̶1̶	68	9̶2̶	6̶5̶	74	9̶4̶
−49	−36	−56	− 8	−31	−19
4 2	32	36	57	43	7 5

Solve.

4. Jim's team scores 58 points. Eve's team scores 65 points. By how many points does Eve's team win?

____7____ points

Spiral Review

Write as tens and ones. Then write in expanded form.

6. 74 = __7__ tens __4__ ones = __70__ + __4__

7. 93 = __9__ tens __3__ ones = __90__ + __3__

8. 85 = __8__ tens __5__ ones = __80__ + __5__

Chapter 6 ~ Lesson 7

Practice

Problem Solving: Reading for Math
Steps in a Process

P 6-7 PRACTICE
Reading Skill

Rick and his father are getting food ready for a picnic.
First, they mix the lemonade. Next, they bake 40 cookies.
Then they wash 16 apples. Finally, they make 20 sandwiches.

Solve.

1. What do Rick and his father do first?
_____mix lemonade_____

2. What do they do next? _____bake 40 cookies_____

3. What do they do after that? _____wash 16 apples_____

4. What do Rick and his father do last? ___make 20 sandwiches___

5. Write a subtraction problem about the story.
_____Problems may vary._____

Use with Grade 2, Chapter 6, Lesson 7, pages 215–216. (181)

Practice

Problem Solving: Reading for Math
Steps in a Process

P 6-7 PRACTICE
Math Skills Test Prep

Marina and her mother go to the
farmer's market.
First, they buy 8 ears of corn.
Next, they buy 10 apples.
Then they buy 6 tomatoes.
Finally, they eat 2 of the apples.

Choose the best answer. Fill in the ◯.

1. What do Marina and her mother do first?
- Ⓐ Buy 6 tomatoes.
- Ⓑ Buy 8 ears of corn.
- Ⓒ Eat 2 apples.
- Ⓓ Buy 10 apples.

2. What do Marina and her mother do next?
- Ⓕ Buy 10 apples.
- Ⓖ Eat 2 apples.
- Ⓗ Buy 6 tomatoes.
- Ⓙ Buy 8 ears of corn.

3. What do Marina and her mother do last?
- Ⓐ Buy 8 ears of corn.
- Ⓑ Buy 10 apples.
- Ⓒ Eat 2 apples.
- Ⓓ Buy 6 tomatoes.

4. How many apples do Marina and her mother have left?
- Ⓕ 7
- Ⓗ 12
- Ⓖ 8
- Ⓙ 9

Use with Grade 2, Chapter 6, Lesson 7, pages 215–216. (182)

Practice

Problem Solving: Reading for Math
Steps in a Process

P 6-7 PRACTICE
Math Skills Test Prep

Ben is collecting shells at the beach.
First, he rinses the sand out of his pail.
Next, he picks up 14 clam shells.
Then, he picks up 2 sand dollars.
Finally, he finds 25 snail shells.

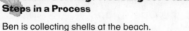

Choose the best answer. Fill in the ◯.

1. What does Ben do first?
- Ⓐ He picks up 14 clam shells.
- Ⓑ He picks up 2 sand dollars.
- Ⓒ He rinses his pail.
- Ⓓ He finds 25 snail shells.

2. What does Ben do next?
- Ⓕ He finds 25 snail shells.
- Ⓖ He picks up 14 clam shells.
- Ⓗ He picks up 2 sand dollars.
- Ⓙ He rinses his pail.

Solve.

3. What does Ben do after that?
_____He picks up 2 sand dollars._____

4. What does Ben do last?
_____He finds 25 snail shells._____

5. Write a subtraction problem about the story.
_____Problems may vary._____

Use with Grade 2, Chapter 6, Lesson 7, pages 215–216. (183)

Daily Homework

6-7 **Problem Solving: Reading for Math**
Steps in a Process
Answer each question.

Ella and Bert work in the garden on
Monday. First, they pick 24 tomatoes.
Next, they pick 15 peppers. After that,
they rinse the dirt off the tomatoes and
peppers. Finally, they put the tomatoes
and peppers in baskets.

1. What do Ella and Bert do first? ___pick tomatoes___

2. What do they do next? ___pick peppers___

3. What do they do after that? ___rinse peppers and tomatoes___

4. What did they do last? ___put peppers and tomatoes in baskets___

5. Write a subtraction problem about the story. _____
_____Problems may vary._____

Spiral Review

What could the next number be? Find the pattern.

6. 77 67 57 47 __37__   43 33 23 13 __3__

56 Grade 2, Chapter 6, Cluster A

Chapter 6 ~ Lesson 8

Practice

P 6-8 PRACTICE

Problem Solving: Strategy
Choose the Operation

Circle add or subtract. Solve.

1. 21 children are playing tag. 5 children are watching. How many more children are playing tag than watching?

add (subtract)

___16___ children

2. Jamie picked 32 strawberries. Alex picked 40 raspberries. How many berries did they pick in all?

(add) subtract

___72___ berries

3. There are 10 boys and 12 girls in the tap-dance class. How many children are in the tap-dance class?

(add) subtract

___22___ children

4. Ian has 28 pretzels. He gave all but 6 of them to his sister. How many pretzels did Ian give to his sister?

add (subtract)

___22___ pretzels

Mixed Strategy Review

Solve.

5. Eve is making up a dance. She leaps, slides, turns, freezes, leaps, slides, turns, freezes, leaps. What move comes next?

___slide___

6. Create a problem for which you would choose the operation to solve. Share it with others.

_____

_____

Reteach

R 6-8 RETEACH

Problem Solving: Strategy
Choose the Operation

Page 220, Problem 4

Last fall the children planted 31 tulip bulbs. All but 3 bulbs came up in the spring. How many tulip bulbs came up?

add   subtract   _____ tulip bulbs

| Step 1 Read | Be sure you understand the problem. |

What do you know?

• The children planted ___31___ tulip bulbs.

• ___3___ tulip bulbs did not come up.

What do you need to find?

• You need to find __how many tulip bulbs__ __came up__

| Step 2 Plan | Make a plan. |

Choose a strategy.

- Draw a Picture
- Write a Number Sentence
- Use Logical Reasoning
- Act it Out
- Choose the Operation
- Make a Table
- Guess and Check
- Find a Pattern
- Make a Graph

Choose the operation.

Subtract the number of bulbs that did not come up from the number of bulbs that were planted.

Reteach

R 6-8 RETEACH

Problem Solving: Strategy
Choose the Operation

| Step 3 Solve | Carry out your plan. |

• Write a subtraction sentence.

___31 − 3 = 28___

___28___ tulip bulbs

| Step 4 Look Back | Is the solution reasonable? |

Does your answer make sense?   (Yes)   No

Did you answer the question?   (Yes)   No

Daily Homework

 6-8

Problem Solving Strategy:
Choose the Operation

Circle add or subtract. Solve.

1. 10 children go to the library. 8 more children join them. How many children are in the library altogether?

(add) subtract

___10 + 8 = 18___

___18___ children

2. 16 children read picture books. 9 read chapter books. How many more read picture books?

add (subtract)

___16 − 9 = 7___

___7___ children

3. Ms. Lee's class reads 27 books. Mr. Brown's class 34. How many books do they read in all?

(add) subtract

___27 + 34 = 61___

___61___ books

4. Students take 45 books out of the library. 23 are returned. How many have not been returned?

add (subtract)

___45 − 23 = 22___

___22___ books

Spiral Review

Complete each fact family.

5. $8 + 2 = $ ___10___ $9 + 8 = $ ___17___   ___7___ $+ 4 = 11$

$2 + 8 = $ ___10___ $8 + 9 = $ ___17___ $4 \oplus 7 = 11$

$10 − $ ___2___ $ = 8$ $17 \ominus 9 = 8$ ___11___ $− 7 = 4$

___10___ $− 8 = 2$ $17 − $ ___8___ $ = 9$ $11 − $ ___4___ $ = 7$

Chapter 6 ~ Lesson 9

Practice

Algebra: Check Subtraction
P 6-9 PRACTICE

Subtract. Check by adding.

1.
$$\begin{array}{r} 37 \\ -15 \\ \hline 22 \end{array}\qquad \begin{array}{r} 22 \\ +15 \\ \hline 37 \end{array}\qquad \begin{array}{r} 67 \\ -48 \\ \hline 19 \end{array}\qquad \begin{array}{r} 19 \\ +48 \\ \hline 67 \end{array}\qquad \begin{array}{r} 52 \\ -36 \\ \hline 16 \end{array}\qquad \begin{array}{r} 16 \\ +36 \\ \hline 52 \end{array}$$

2.
$$\begin{array}{r} 48 \\ -18 \\ \hline 30 \end{array}\qquad \begin{array}{r} 30 \\ +18 \\ \hline 48 \end{array}\qquad \begin{array}{r} 73 \\ -7 \\ \hline 66 \end{array}\qquad \begin{array}{r} 66 \\ +7 \\ \hline 73 \end{array}\qquad \begin{array}{r} 82 \\ -68 \\ \hline 14 \end{array}\qquad \begin{array}{r} 14 \\ +68 \\ \hline 82 \end{array}$$

3.
$$\begin{array}{r} 91 \\ -45 \\ \hline 46 \end{array}\qquad \begin{array}{r} 46 \\ +45 \\ \hline 91 \end{array}\qquad \begin{array}{r} 35 \\ -17 \\ \hline 18 \end{array}\qquad \begin{array}{r} 18 \\ +17 \\ \hline 35 \end{array}\qquad \begin{array}{r} 77 \\ -41 \\ \hline 36 \end{array}\qquad \begin{array}{r} 36 \\ +41 \\ \hline 77 \end{array}$$

4.
$$\begin{array}{r} 56 \\ -28 \\ \hline 28 \end{array}\qquad \begin{array}{r} 28 \\ +28 \\ \hline 56 \end{array}\qquad \begin{array}{r} 42 \\ -19 \\ \hline 23 \end{array}\qquad \begin{array}{r} 23 \\ +19 \\ \hline 42 \end{array}\qquad \begin{array}{r} 37 \\ -9 \\ \hline 28 \end{array}\qquad \begin{array}{r} 28 \\ +9 \\ \hline 37 \end{array}$$

5.
$$\begin{array}{r} 69 \\ -45 \\ \hline 24 \end{array}\qquad \begin{array}{r} 24 \\ +45 \\ \hline 69 \end{array}\qquad \begin{array}{r} 85 \\ -39 \\ \hline 46 \end{array}\qquad \begin{array}{r} 46 \\ +39 \\ \hline 85 \end{array}\qquad \begin{array}{r} 62 \\ -23 \\ \hline 39 \end{array}\qquad \begin{array}{r} 39 \\ +23 \\ \hline 62 \end{array}$$

Problem Solving

6. There are 46 girls ice skating. There are 67 boys ice skating. How many more boys than girls are ice skating?

   __21__ more boys

   There are 81 people hiking in the woods. 57 people leave the woods. How many people are still hiking?

   __24__ people

Reteach

Algebra: Check Subtraction
R 6-9 RETEACH

You can add to check subtraction.

> Add the answer to what you subtracted.

Subtract.
$$\begin{array}{r} 37 \\ -12 \\ \hline 25 \end{array}$$

Add to check.
$$\begin{array}{r} 25 \\ +12 \\ \hline 37 \end{array}$$

Subtract. Check by adding.

1.
$$\begin{array}{r} 65 \\ -21 \\ \hline 44 \end{array}\qquad \begin{array}{r} 44 \\ +21 \\ \hline 65 \end{array}\qquad \begin{array}{r} 37 \\ -14 \\ \hline 23 \end{array}\qquad \begin{array}{r} 23 \\ +14 \\ \hline 37 \end{array}\qquad \begin{array}{r} 43 \\ -25 \\ \hline 18 \end{array}\qquad \begin{array}{r} 18 \\ +25 \\ \hline 43 \end{array}$$

2.
$$\begin{array}{r} 71 \\ -7 \\ \hline 64 \end{array}\qquad \begin{array}{r} 64 \\ +7 \\ \hline 71 \end{array}\qquad \begin{array}{r} 54 \\ -36 \\ \hline 18 \end{array}\qquad \begin{array}{r} 18 \\ +36 \\ \hline 54 \end{array}\qquad \begin{array}{r} 81 \\ -34 \\ \hline 47 \end{array}\qquad \begin{array}{r} 47 \\ +34 \\ \hline 81 \end{array}$$

3.
$$\begin{array}{r} 95 \\ -23 \\ \hline 72 \end{array}\qquad \begin{array}{r} 72 \\ +23 \\ \hline 95 \end{array}\qquad \begin{array}{r} 63 \\ -9 \\ \hline 54 \end{array}\qquad \begin{array}{r} 54 \\ +9 \\ \hline 63 \end{array}\qquad \begin{array}{r} 48 \\ -19 \\ \hline 29 \end{array}\qquad \begin{array}{r} 29 \\ +19 \\ \hline 48 \end{array}$$

Enrich

Algebra: Check Subtraction
E 6-9 ENRICH

The Birdwatching Club

Birds Spotted in One Month

Blue Jays	Sparrows	Robins	Cardinals	Wrens
61	45	37	52	18

Solve and check your answer.

	Subtract	Check
1. How many more cardinals did the club see than sparrows? __7__ cardinals	$\begin{array}{r} 52 \\ -45 \\ \hline 7 \end{array}$	$\begin{array}{r} 7 \\ +45 \\ \hline 52 \end{array}$
2. How many more blue jays did the club see than robins? __24__ blue jays	$\begin{array}{r} 61 \\ -37 \\ \hline 24 \end{array}$	$\begin{array}{r} 24 \\ +37 \\ \hline 61 \end{array}$
3. How many fewer wrens did the club see than cardinals? __34__ wrens	$\begin{array}{r} 52 \\ -18 \\ \hline 34 \end{array}$	$\begin{array}{r} 34 \\ +18 \\ \hline 52 \end{array}$
4. The next month, the club spotted 25 blue jays. How many fewer blue jays were spotted than the month before? __36__ blue jays	$\begin{array}{r} 61 \\ -25 \\ \hline 36 \end{array}$	$\begin{array}{r} 36 \\ +25 \\ \hline 61 \end{array}$

Daily Homework

6-9 Check Subtraction

Subtract. Check by adding.

1.
$$\begin{array}{r} 86 \\ -44 \\ \hline 42 \end{array}\qquad \begin{array}{r} 42 \\ +44 \\ \hline 86 \end{array}\qquad \begin{array}{r} 83 \\ -69 \\ \hline 14 \end{array}\qquad \begin{array}{r} 14 \\ +69 \\ \hline 83 \end{array}\qquad \begin{array}{r} 72 \\ -48 \\ \hline 24 \end{array}\qquad \begin{array}{r} 24 \\ +48 \\ \hline 72 \end{array}\qquad \begin{array}{r} 35 \\ -17 \\ \hline 18 \end{array}\qquad \begin{array}{r} 18 \\ +17 \\ \hline 35 \end{array}$$

2.
$$\begin{array}{r} 62 \\ -26 \\ \hline 36 \end{array}\qquad \begin{array}{r} 36 \\ +26 \\ \hline 62 \end{array}\qquad \begin{array}{r} 95 \\ -13 \\ \hline 82 \end{array}\qquad \begin{array}{r} 82 \\ +13 \\ \hline 95 \end{array}\qquad \begin{array}{r} 96 \\ -79 \\ \hline 17 \end{array}\qquad \begin{array}{r} 17 \\ +79 \\ \hline 96 \end{array}\qquad \begin{array}{r} 61 \\ -43 \\ \hline 18 \end{array}\qquad \begin{array}{r} 18 \\ +43 \\ \hline 61 \end{array}$$

3.
$$\begin{array}{r} 81 \\ -32 \\ \hline 49 \end{array}\qquad \begin{array}{r} 49 \\ +32 \\ \hline 81 \end{array}\qquad \begin{array}{r} 54 \\ -28 \\ \hline 26 \end{array}\qquad \begin{array}{r} 26 \\ +28 \\ \hline 54 \end{array}\qquad \begin{array}{r} 82 \\ -21 \\ \hline 61 \end{array}\qquad \begin{array}{r} 61 \\ +21 \\ \hline 82 \end{array}\qquad \begin{array}{r} 42 \\ -27 \\ \hline 15 \end{array}\qquad \begin{array}{r} 15 \\ +27 \\ \hline 42 \end{array}$$

Solve. Use the chart. Check by adding.

4. How many more books does Ezra read than Kathy?

   __7__ books

5. How many more books does Kathy read than Mike?

   __14__ books

Reading Club

Ezra	92 books
Kathy	85 books
Mike	71 books

Spiral Review

Add.

6.
$$\begin{array}{r} 16 \\ 34 \\ +23 \\ \hline 73 \end{array}\qquad \begin{array}{r} 23 \\ 23 \\ +12 \\ \hline 58 \end{array}\qquad \begin{array}{r} 22 \\ 47 \\ +13 \\ \hline 82 \end{array}\qquad \begin{array}{r} 27 \\ 21 \\ +31 \\ \hline 79 \end{array}\qquad \begin{array}{r} 45 \\ 24 \\ +25 \\ \hline 94 \end{array}\qquad \begin{array}{r} 37 \\ 12 \\ +28 \\ \hline 77 \end{array}$$

Chapter 6 ~ Lesson 10

Practice

Estimate Differences

P 6-10 PRACTICE

Subtract. Estimate to see if your answer is reasonable.

1. 74   70   63   60   86   90
   −16 −20   −21 −20   −59 −60
    58   50   42   40   27   30

2. 54   50   92   90   44   40
   −17 −20   −26 −30   −14 −10
    37   30   66   60   30   30

3. 76   80   82   80   67   70
   −27 −30   −37 −40   −29 −30
    49   50   45   40   38   40

4. 38   40   54   50   87   90
   −29 −30   −19 −20   −24 −20
     9   10   35   30   63   70

5. 64   60   91   90   49   50
   −16 −20   −73 −70   −13 −10
    48   40   18   20   36   40

Problem Solving

6. There are 72 baskets of apples for sale. 37 baskets of apples are sold. How many baskets of apples are left?

   __35__ baskets

Melanie picks 52 baskets of strawberries. Greg picks 28 baskets. How many more baskets does Melanie pick?

   __24__ more baskets

Use with Grade 2, Chapter 6, Lesson 10, pages 223–224. (190)

Reteach

Estimate Differences

R 6-10 RETEACH

You can estimate to check subtraction.
A number line can help you estimate.

20 21 22 23 24 25 26 27 28 29 30 31 32 33 34 35 36 37 38 39 40

   37   37 is close to 40   40
  −21   21 is close to 20   −20
   16   37 − 21 is about 20   20

16 is close to 20. The answer is reasonable.

Subtract. Estimate to see if your answer is reasonable.

1. 64   60   39   40   86   90
   −19 −20   −12 −10   −59 −60
    45   40   27   30   27   30

2. 57   60   32   30   72   70
   −27 −30   −16 −20   −22 −20
    30   30   16   10   50   50

3. 26   30   82   80   47   50
   − 7 −10   −37 −40   −29 −30
    19   20   45   40   18   20

4. 92   90   76   80   87   90
   −29 −30   −19 −20   −24 −20
    63   60   57   60   63   70

Use with Grade 2, Chapter 6, Lesson 10, pages 223–224. (191)

Enrich

Estimate Differences
Find the Butterfly

E 6-10 ENRICH

Estimate each difference.
Color estimates of 10 through 50 (orange).
Color estimates of 60 through 90 (yellow).

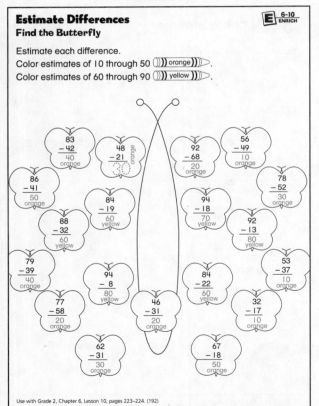

Use with Grade 2, Chapter 6, Lesson 10, pages 223–224. (192)

Daily Homework

6-10 Estimate Differences

Subtract. Estimate to see if your answer is reasonable.

1. 29   30   31   30   92   90   88   90
   −18 −20   −12 −10   −22 −20   −29 −30
    11   10   19   20   70   70   59   60

2. 51   50   89   90   79   80   82   80
   −22 −20   −32 −30   −21 −20   −28 −30
    29   30   57   60   58   60   54   50

3. 77   80   36   40   64   60   73   70
   −18 −20   −19 −20   −16 −20   −59 −60
    59   60   17   20   48   40   14   10

Problem Solving

Solve. Estimate to see if your answer is reasonable.

4. Janelle collects 22 newspapers for recycling. Erin collects 19 newspapers. How many more newspapers does Janelle collect than Erin?

   __3__ newspapers

5. Eric collects 48 bottles and cans. 31 are bottles. How many are cans?

   __17__ cans

Spiral Review

Add or subtract.

7. 25   33   26   61   53   46
   −16   +49   +32   −28   + 7   +39
     9   82   58   33   60   85

Chapter 6 ~ Lesson 11

Practice

Subtract Money Amounts

Subtract.

1.
47¢	92¢	32¢	45¢	81¢	90¢
− 19¢	− 27¢	− 15¢	− 9¢	− 28¢	− 55¢
28¢	65¢	17¢	36¢	53¢	35¢

2.
57¢	74¢	87¢	41¢	25¢	59¢
− 16¢	− 30¢	− 8¢	− 36¢	− 9¢	− 19¢
41¢	44¢	79¢	5¢	16¢	40¢

3.
83¢	67¢	65¢	71¢	47¢	50¢
− 56¢	− 31¢	− 16¢	− 6¢	− 17¢	− 44¢
27¢	36¢	49¢	65¢	30¢	6¢

4.
99¢	42¢	28¢	67¢	44¢	73¢
− 26¢	− 28¢	− 19¢	− 6¢	− 18¢	− 25¢
73¢	14¢	9¢	61¢	26¢	48¢

5.
55¢	81¢	60¢	35¢	33¢	76¢
− 43¢	− 15¢	− 25¢	− 28¢	− 5¢	− 33¢
12¢	66¢	35¢	7¢	28¢	43¢

Problem Solving

6. Marco has 56¢. He spends 17¢. How much money does Marco have left?

_39_ ¢

Shawna has 88¢. She spends 44¢. How much money does Shawna have left?

_44_ ¢

Reteach

Subtract Money Amounts

Subtracting money is the same as subtracting tens and ones.
April has 21¢.
How much more money does she need to buy the jump rope?

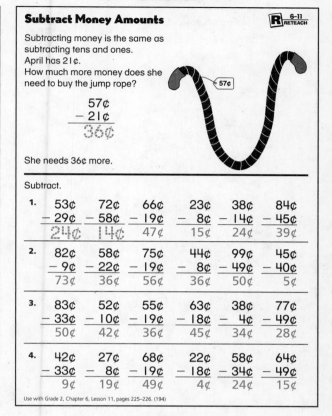

57¢
− 21¢
36¢

She needs 36¢ more.

Subtract.

1.
53¢	72¢	66¢	23¢	38¢	84¢
− 29¢	− 58¢	− 19¢	− 8¢	− 14¢	− 45¢
24¢	14¢	47¢	15¢	24¢	39¢

2.
82¢	58¢	75¢	44¢	99¢	45¢
− 9¢	− 22¢	− 19¢	− 8¢	− 49¢	− 40¢
73¢	36¢	56¢	36¢	50¢	5¢

3.
83¢	52¢	55¢	63¢	38¢	77¢
− 33¢	− 10¢	− 19¢	− 18¢	− 4¢	− 49¢
50¢	42¢	36¢	45¢	34¢	28¢

4.
42¢	27¢	68¢	22¢	58¢	64¢
− 33¢	− 8¢	− 19¢	− 18¢	− 34¢	− 49¢
9¢	19¢	49¢	4¢	24¢	15¢

Enrich

Subtract Money Amounts
What's for Lunch?

You have some money. You buy three things for lunch.

Write what you order for lunch and how much it costs.

Write how much money you have left after you buy each thing.

Answers may vary. Possible answers are shown.

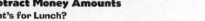 35¢ soup   48¢ sandwich   12¢ apple

 21¢ milk   16¢ juice   27¢ salad

1.
I have 99¢.
I buy ___sandwich___ .
It costs _48¢_ .
I have _51¢_ left.
So, I buy ___salad___ .
It costs _27¢_ .
I now have _24¢_
So, I buy ___milk___ .
It costs _21¢_ .
I end up with _3¢_ .

2.
I have 96¢.
I buy ___soup___ .
It costs _35¢_ .
I have _61¢_ left.
So, I buy ___salad___ .
It costs _27¢_ .
I now have _34¢_
So, I buy ___juice___ .
It costs _16¢_ .
I end up with _18¢_ .

Daily Homework

6-11 Subtract Money Amounts

Subtract. Remember to write the ¢ sign.

1.
63¢	98¢	87¢	68¢	54¢	38¢
− 45¢	− 88¢	− 34¢	− 23¢	− 47¢	− 17¢
18¢	10¢	53¢	45¢	7¢	21¢

2.
26¢	76¢	58¢	74¢	49¢	26¢
− 18¢	− 38¢	− 39¢	− 15¢	− 42¢	− 7¢
8¢	38¢	19¢	59¢	7¢	19¢

3.
52¢	34¢	73¢	84¢	29¢	68¢
− 41¢	− 7¢	− 68¢	− 23¢	− 18¢	− 49¢
11¢	27¢	5¢	61¢	11¢	19¢

4.
64¢	14¢	96¢	83¢	44¢	82¢
− 18¢	− 11¢	− 47¢	− 38¢	− 23¢	− 72¢
46¢	3¢	49¢	45¢	21¢	10¢

Problem Solving

5. Kitty buys an apple for 37¢. She gives the clerk 50¢. She gets back 15¢ change. Is this correct? Why or why not?

___It is not correct. Kitty gets back 13¢.___

6. Tray buys a pear for 63¢. He gives the clerk 75¢. How much change does he receive?   _12¢_

Spiral Review

Complete each number sentence. Use + or −.

7. 19 ⊖ 5 = 14   6 ⊕ 4 = 10   9 ⊕ 8 = 17   16 ⊖ 7 = 9

Chapter 6 ~ Lesson 12

Part A Worksheet

Problem Solving: Application
Plant a Garden

Plan a garden.

You have 99¢.

Choose the seeds you will buy.

Sweet Peas 50¢
Strawberries 65¢
Carrots 25¢
Zinnias 60¢
Melons 10¢
Sunflowers 75¢
Daisies 30¢
Beans 40¢

Use with Grade 2, Chapter 6, Lesson 12, pages 227–228. (196)

Part A Worksheet

Problem Solving: Application
Plant a Garden

1. Which seeds did you buy?
   Answers may vary.

2. How much did you spend? Answers may vary.
   Show your work.

3. How much do you have left? Answers may vary.
   Show your work.

4. What if you only had 75¢?
   What would you buy?
   Answers may vary.
   How much would you spend? Answers may vary.

Use with Grade 2, Chapter 6, Lesson 12, pages 227–228. (197)

Part B Worksheet

Problem Solving: Application
Why Is Weather Important?

1. Record the weather you observe for 5 days.

	Monday	Tuesday	Wednesday	Thursday	Friday
Morning					
Afternoon					

2. What changes happened in the weather?
   _____
   _____

3. How did the temperature change?
   _____
   _____

4. What do you think the weather will be like tomorrow?
   Tell why you think that.
   _____
   _____

Answers may vary.

Use with Grade 2, Chapter 6, Lesson 12, pages 229–230. (198)

Chapter 7 ~ Lesson 1

Practice

Time to the Hour and Half Hour

P 7-1 PRACTICE

Write each time.

1.

2:00   2:30   7:00   7:30

2.

1:00   1:30   3:00   10:00

Draw the minute hand to show each time.

3. 4:30

4. 8:00

Use with Grade 2, Chapter 7, Lesson 1, pages 243–244. (199)

Reteach

Time to the Hour and Half Hour

R 7-1 RETEACH

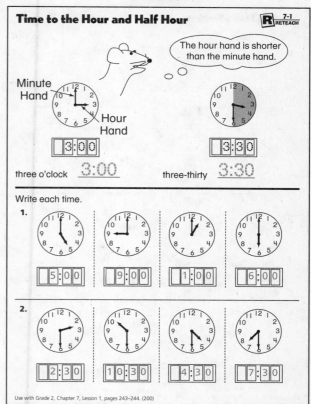

The hour hand is shorter than the minute hand.

Minute Hand

Hour Hand

3:00   three o'clock   3:00

3:30   three-thirty   3:30

Write each time.

1.

5:00   9:00   1:00   6:00

2.

2:30   10:30   4:30   7:30

Use with Grade 2, Chapter 7, Lesson 1, pages 243–244. (200)

Enrich

Time to the Hour and Half Hour
Time Patterns

E 7-1 ENRICH

What time will most likely be next in the pattern?

Draw the clock hands on the clock. Write the time.

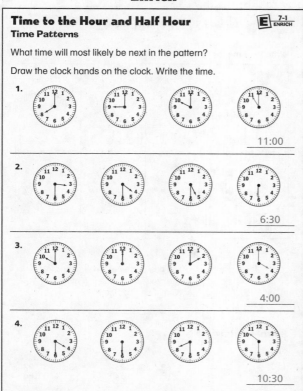

1.   11:00

2.   6:30

3.   4:00

4.   10:30

Use with Grade 2, Chapter 7, Lesson 1, pages 243–244. (201)

Daily Homework

7-1 Time to the Hour and Half Hour

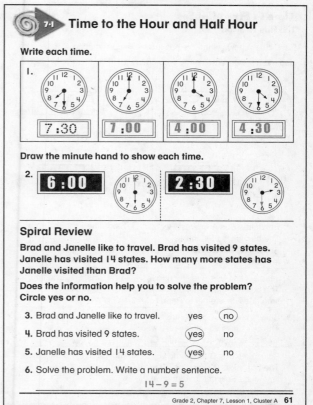

Write each time.

1.   7:30   7:00   4:00   4:30

Draw the minute hand to show each time.

2.   6:00   2:30

Spiral Review

Brad and Janelle like to travel. Brad has visited 9 states. Janelle has visited 14 states. How many more states has Janelle visited than Brad?

Does the information help you to solve the problem? Circle yes or no.

3. Brad and Janelle like to travel.   yes   (no)

4. Brad has visited 9 states.   (yes)   no

5. Janelle has visited 14 states.   (yes)   no

6. Solve the problem. Write a number sentence.

14 – 9 = 5

Grade 2, Chapter 7, Lesson 1, Cluster A   61

Chapter 7 ~ Lesson 2

Practice

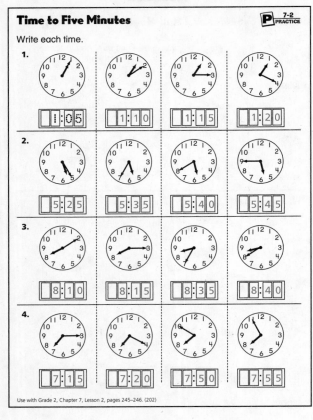

Time to Five Minutes

Write each time.

1. `1:05` `1:10` `1:15` `1:20`

2. `5:25` `5:35` `5:40` `5:45`

3. `8:10` `8:15` `8:35` `8:40`

4. `7:15` `7:20` `7:50` `7:55`

Use with Grade 2, Chapter 7, Lesson 2, pages 245–246. (202)

Reteach

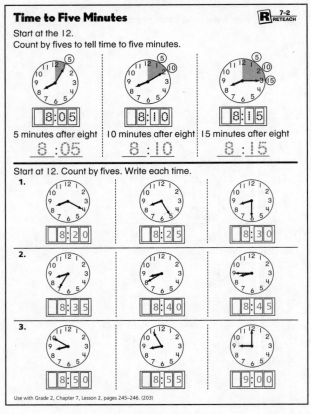

Time to Five Minutes

Start at the 12.
Count by fives to tell time to five minutes.

`8:05` `8:10` `8:15`

5 minutes after eight | 10 minutes after eight | 15 minutes after eight

8 : 05   8 : 10   8 : 15

Start at 12. Count by fives. Write each time.

1. `8:20` `8:25` `8:30`

2. `8:35` `8:40` `8:45`

3. `8:50` `8:55` `9:00`

Use with Grade 2, Chapter 7, Lesson 2, pages 245–246. (203)

Enrich

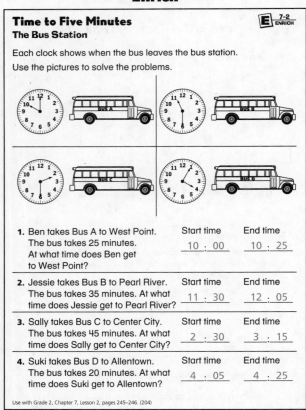

Time to Five Minutes

The Bus Station

Each clock shows when the bus leaves the bus station.
Use the pictures to solve the problems.

	Start time	End time
1. Ben takes Bus A to West Point. The bus takes 25 minutes. At what time does Ben get to West Point?	10 : 00	10 : 25
2. Jessie takes Bus B to Pearl River. The bus takes 35 minutes. At what time does Jessie get to Pearl River?	11 : 30	12 : 05
3. Sally takes Bus C to Center City. The bus takes 45 minutes. At what time does Sally get to Center City?	2 : 30	3 : 15
4. Suki takes Bus D to Allentown. The bus takes 20 minutes. At what time does Suki get to Allentown?	4 : 05	4 : 25

Use with Grade 2, Chapter 7, Lesson 2, pages 245–246. (204)

Daily Homework

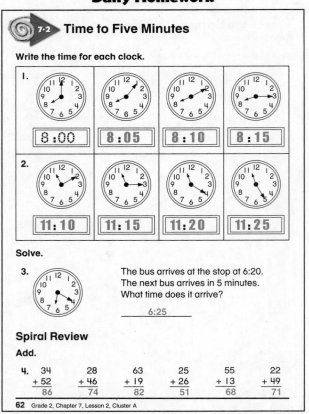

7-2 Time to Five Minutes

Write the time for each clock.

1. `8:00` `8:05` `8:10` `8:15`

2. `11:10` `11:15` `11:20` `11:25`

Solve.

3. The bus arrives at the stop at 6:20. The next bus arrives in 5 minutes. What time does it arrive?

6:25

Spiral Review

Add.

4.	34	28	63	25	55	22
	+ 52	+ 46	+ 19	+ 26	+ 13	+ 49
	86	74	82	51	68	71

Chapter 7 ~ Lesson 3

Practice

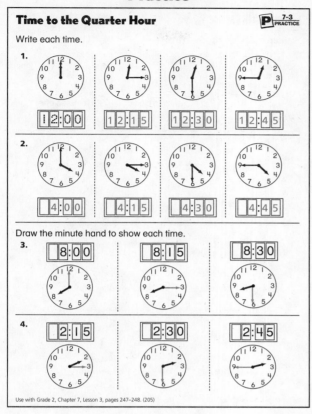

Time to the Quarter Hour P 7-3 PRACTICE

Write each time.

1. 12:00   12:15   12:30   12:45

2. 4:00   4:15   4:30   4:45

Draw the minute hand to show each time.

3. 8:00   8:15   8:30

4. 2:15   2:30   2:45

Use with Grade 2, Chapter 7, Lesson 3, pages 247–248. (205)

Reteach

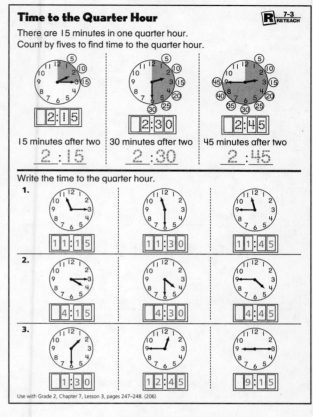

Time to the Quarter Hour R 7-3 RETEACH

There are 15 minutes in one quarter hour.
Count by fives to find time to the quarter hour.

2:15   2:30   2:45

15 minutes after two   30 minutes after two   45 minutes after two

2:15   2:30   2:45

Write the time to the quarter hour.

1. 11:15   11:30   11:45

2. 4:15   4:30   4:45

3. 1:30   12:45   9:15

Use with Grade 2, Chapter 7, Lesson 3, pages 247–248. (206)

Enrich

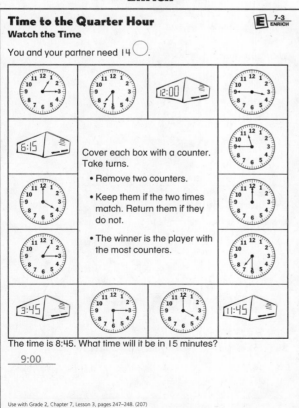

Time to the Quarter Hour E 7-3 ENRICH
Watch the Time

You and your partner need 14 ◯.

12:00

6:15

3:45   11:45

Cover each box with a counter.
Take turns.

• Remove two counters.

• Keep them if the two times match. Return them if they do not.

• The winner is the player with the most counters.

The time is 8:45. What time will it be in 15 minutes?

___9:00___

Use with Grade 2, Chapter 7, Lesson 3, pages 247–248. (207)

Daily Homework

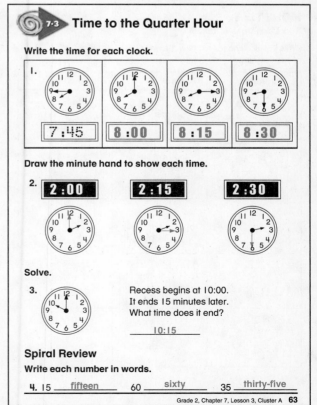

7-3 **Time to the Quarter Hour**

Write the time for each clock.

1. 7:45   8:00   8:15   8:30

Draw the minute hand to show each time.

2. 2:00   2:15   2:30

Solve.

3. Recess begins at 10:00.
It ends 15 minutes later.
What time does it end?

___10:15___

Spiral Review
Write each number in words.

4. 15 ___fifteen___   60 ___sixty___   35 ___thirty-five___

Chapter 7 ~ Lesson 4

Practice

MORE Time

Write each time.

1.
7 : 15
15 minutes after 7

10 : 45
45 minutes after 10

2.
6 : 05
5 minutes after 6

9 : 50
50 minutes after 9

3.
8 : 10
10 minutes after 8

2 : 40
40 minutes after 2

4.
1 : 30
30 minutes after 1

4 : 55
55 minutes after 4

Use with Grade 2, Chapter 7, Lesson 4, pages 249–250. (208)

Reteach

MORE Time

You can read time in more than one way.

Remember to count by fives to tell time to five minutes.

seven o'clock
7 : 00

20 minutes after 7
7 : 20

Write each time two ways.

1.
35 minutes after 2
2 : 35

15 minutes after 9
9 : 15

2.
10 minutes after 11
11 : 10

25 minutes after 4
4 : 25

3.
45 minutes after 3
3 : 45

55 minutes after 5
5 : 55

Use with Grade 2, Chapter 7, Lesson 4, pages 249–250. (209)

Enrich

MORE Time

How Long Does It Take?

Answers may vary. Possible answers are given.

Draw the clock hands to show the end time of each activity.

Start time	Activity	End time
		7:03
		3:10
		3:00
		5:05
		6:30

Use with Grade 2, Chapter 7, Lesson 4, pages 249–250. (210)

Daily Homework

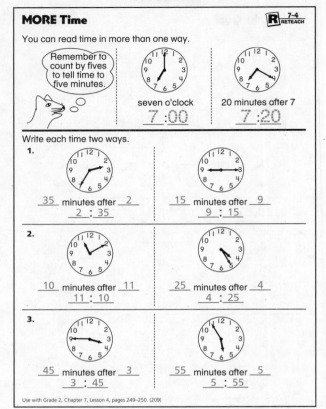

7-4 More Time

Write each time.

1.
10 : 15
quarter after
10

5 : 40
40 minutes after 5
20 minutes before 6

Problem Solving

Draw hour and minute hands to show each time.

2.

| 8:22 | 4:01 | 10:17 | 5:52 |

Spiral Review

Subtract. Estimate to see if your answer is reasonable.

3.
88	90
− 41	− 40
47	50

82	80
− 23	− 20
59	60

61	60
− 17	− 20
44	40

Chapter 7 ~ Lesson 5

Practice

Problem Solving: Reading for Math
Sequence of Events

A Tea Party
Please join me at half past 3.
We'll play before we drink our tea.
That will happen at a quarter to 4.
At 4:15, my brother Luke
will come home and read us a book.
When he's done, we'll say good-bye.
I expect that to be at
10 minutes before 5!

Answer each question.

1. At what time does the tea party begin?
   _____3:30_____

2. At what time will the children drink their tea?
   Write the time in two ways.
   3:45, quarter to 4, 15 minutes before 4,
   or 45 minutes after 3

3. Will the children listen to a story or play first? ____play____

4. At what time does the tea party end? _____4:50_____

Use with Grade 2, Chapter 7, Lesson 5, pages 251–252. (211)

Practice

Problem Solving: Reading for Math
Sequence of Events

At 6:30 Megan gets up.
By quarter after 8,
she's off to school.
She's back at home at
20 minutes to 4.
Soccer practice starts at
quarter to 6.
Don't come home late.
Bedtime is at 8!

Choose the best answer. Fill in the ○.

1. At what time does Megan leave for school?
   Ⓐ 8:00
   Ⓑ 8:45
   Ⓒ 8:15
   Ⓓ 7:45

2. At what time does Megan get home from school?
   Ⓕ 3:40
   Ⓖ 4:20
   Ⓗ quarter to 4
   Ⓙ 4:40

3. What does Megan do at 8:00?
   Ⓐ Go to school.
   Ⓑ Get up.
   Ⓒ Go to soccer practice.
   Ⓓ Go to bed.

4. Which of these things does Megan do first?
   Ⓕ Go to soccer practice.
   Ⓖ Go to school.
   Ⓗ Go to bed.

Use with Grade 2, Chapter 7, Lesson 5, pages 251–252. (212)

Practice

Problem Solving: Reading for Math
Sequence of Events

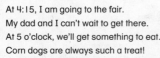

At 4:15, I am going to the fair.
My dad and I can't wait to get there.
At 5 o'clock, we'll get something to eat.
Corn dogs are always such a treat!
At 20 minutes after 6, we'll look at the animals:
cows, sheep, goats, and even some camels.
One more thing before we go home…
at 8:45, we'll take a bumper-car drive.

Choose the best answer. Fill in the ○.

1. At what time is the boy going to the fair?
   Ⓐ quarter to 4
   Ⓑ 15 minutes before 4
   Ⓒ quarter to 5
   Ⓓ quarter after 4

2. What is the first thing the boy will do at the fair?
   Ⓕ Get something to eat.
   Ⓖ Drive a bumper car.
   Ⓗ Look at animals.
   Ⓙ Go home.

Solve.

3. When will the boy and his father ride the bumper cars?
   Write the time in two ways.
   8:45, 45 minutes after 8, quarter to 9,
   or 15 minutes before 9

4. When will the boy and his father look at the animals?
   Write the time in two ways.
   20 minutes after 6, 6:20, or 40 minutes before 7

Use with Grade 2, Chapter 7, Lesson 5, pages 251–252. (213)

Daily Homework

7·5 Problem Solving: Reading for Math
Sequence of Events

Dear Jill,
You will love camp! We get up at 8:30.
Swim lessons are at quarter
to 11. Lunch is at 20 minutes after 12.
My favorite thing is the campfire at
7:00 each night.
Love,
Debra

Solve.

1. What time do the campers wake up?
   ____8:30____

2. At what time do swim lessons begin? Write the time 3 ways.
   10:45, 45 minutes after 10, 15 minutes before 11

3. When is lunch? ____12:20____

4. What happens at 7:00? ____campfire____

Spiral Review

Count to find the total amount.
Use >, <, or = to complete the sentence.

5.

$1.85 ⊜ $1.85

79¢ ⊙< 93¢

Grade 2, Chapter 7, Lesson 5, Cluster A **65**

Chapter 7 ~ Lesson 6

Practice

Problem Solving: Strategy
Act It Out

Use a clock to act it out. Solve.

1. Each child in the ballet class dances. Each dance takes 5 minutes. How long will it take 7 children to dance?

_____ 35 minutes _____

2. It takes Ramesh 20 minutes to make a card. How long will it take him to make 3 cards?

_____ 60 minutes or 1 hour _____

3. It takes Dana 15 minutes to make a bracelet. How long will it take her to make 4 bracelets?

_____ 60 minutes or 1 hour _____

4. It takes Sara 30 minutes to bake a batch of cupcakes. How long will it take her to bake 2 batches?

_____ 60 minutes or 1 hour _____

5. It takes Ryan 10 minutes to walk to his friend Jamal's house. How long wll it take him to walk there and back?

_____ 20 minutes _____

6. It takes Marc 15 minutes to paint a shelf. How long will it take him to paint 3 shelves?

_____ 45 minutes _____

Mixed Strategy Review

Solve.

7. 23 children are skating at the ice rink. 15 children are sitting in the bleachers watching. How many children are at the ice rink?

_____ 38 children _____

8. Create a problem which you would act out to solve. Share it with others.

_____

_____

Reteach

Problem Solving: Strategy
Act It Out

Page 256, Problem 4

The puppets tell jokes.
Each joke is 5 minutes long.
How many minutes will it take to tell 2 jokes?

Step 1 **Read**	**Be sure you understand the problem.**

What do you know?

- Each joke is __5__ minutes long.
- The puppets tell __2__ jokes.

What do you need to find?

- You need to find __how long it takes to__ __tell 2 jokes.__

Step 2 **Plan**	**Make a plan.**

Choose a strategy.

- Draw a Picture
- Write a Number Sentence
- Use Logical Reasoning
- Act it Out
- Choose the Operation
- Make a Table
- Guess and Check
- Find a Pattern
- Make a Graph

Act it out.

Use a clock to show the time it takes to tell the jokes.

Reteach

Problem Solving: Strategy
Act It Out

Step 3 **Solve**	**Carry out your plan.**

Use the clock to act out how long it takes to tell each joke.
You know that each joke is __5__ minutes long.
You know that the puppets tell __2__ jokes.

- Show the time it takes to tell the first joke.

Now show the time it takes to tell the second joke.

- Count the minutes you showed in all.

How many minutes does it take to tell 2 jokes? __10__ minutes

Step 4 **Look Back**	**Is the solution reasonable?**

Does your answer make sense? (Yes) No

Tell how you solved the problem by acting it out.

Daily Homework

7-6 **Problem Solving: Strategy**
Act It Out

Use a clock to act it out. Solve.

1. It takes a half hour to walk from Kate's house to the Children's Museum. How long does it take to walk there and back?

_____ 1 hour or 60 minutes _____

2. It takes 15 minutes to see each part of the museum. How long does it take to see 3 parts?

_____ 45 minutes _____

3. The museum has a sing-along. It takes 20 minutes. How long would 3 sing-alongs take?

_____ 1 hour or 60 minutes _____

4. Bill listens to tapes at the museum. Each tape is 5 minutes long. How long does it take to listen to 2 tapes?

_____ 10 minutes _____

5. Amy makes a stick puppet in 20 minutes. How long would it take to make 2 puppets?

_____ 40 minutes _____

6. Marie watches 3 movies at the museum. Each is 20 minutes long. How long does it take to watch all 3 movies?

_____ 1 hour or 60 minutes _____

Spiral Review

Skip count by threes.

7. 3 __6__ 9 __12__ __15__ 18 __21__ __24__

Skip count by fives.

8. 5 10 __15__ __20__ __25__ 30 __35__ __40__

Chapter 7 ~ Lesson 7

Practice

Elapsed Time [P] 7-7 PRACTICE

Write each start time and end time.
Then write how many hours passed.

1.

2 : 00   4 : 00

Make a costume.   2 hours passed.

2.

5 : 00   8 : 00

Act out the play.   3 hours passed.

Draw the clock hands to show the end time.

3.   I hour and 30 minutes later

4.   2 hours later

Reteach

Elapsed Time [R] 7-7 RETEACH

Count the hours on the clock to see how much time has passed.

Start time   End time
3 :00   5 :00   2 hours passed.

1.

Start time   End time
8 : 00   9 : 00   1 hour passed.

2.

Start time   End time
1 : 00   4 : 00   3 hours passed.

3.

Start time   End time
10 : 00   12 : 00   2 hours passed.

Enrich

Elapsed Time [E] 7-7 ENRICH

A Day at the Play

The Brown family takes a bus trip to see a play.

Answer each question.

Then complete their schedule.

Bus leaves	Bus arrives	Lunch time	Lunch ends	Play starts
11:00	12 : 00	12:15	1 : 15	2:00
Play ends	Arrive at bus stop	Bus leaves	Bus arrives	Arrive home
4 : 00	4:15	4 : 30	5:30	6 : 00

1. The bus arrives 15 minutes before lunch time. At what time does the bus arrive?   12 : 00

2. Lunch ends 45 minutes before the play starts. At what time does lunch end?   1 : 15

3. The play lasts for 2 hours. At what time does the play end?   4 : 00

4. The bus leaves to go home 15 minutes after the Brown family arrives at the bus stop. At what time does the bus leave?   4 : 30

5. It takes the Brown family one-half hour to walk home after the bus arrives. At what time do they get home?   6 : 00

Daily Homework

7-7 Elapsed Time

Complete the table.

I.		Start time	End time	Elapsed time
Watch a movie.		4 : 00	6 : 00	2 hours

Draw the clock hands to show the elapsed time.

2.   2 hours later

Spiral Review

Write the time for each clock.

3.

11:45   2:15   4:30   12:00

Chapter 7 ~ Lesson 8

Practice

Calendar

P 7-8 PRACTICE

Use the calendar to answer each question.

2001

	JANUARY					
S	M	T	W	T	F	S
		1	2	3	4	5	6

JANUARY
S M T W T F S
1 2 3 4 5 6
7 8 9 10 11 12 13
14 15 16 17 18 19 20
21 22 23 24 25 26 27
28 29 30 31

APRIL
S M T W T F S
1 2 3 4 5 6 7
8 9 10 11 12 13 14
15 16 17 18 19 20 21
22 23 24 25 26 27 28
29 30

FEBRUARY
S M T W T F S
1 2 3
4 5 6 7 8 9 10
11 12 13 14 15 16 17
18 19 20 21 22 23 24
25 26 27 28

MAY
S M T W T F S
1 2 3 4 5
6 7 8 9 10 11 12
13 14 15 16 17 18 19
20 21 22 23 24 25 26
27 28 29 30 31

MARCH
S M T W T F S
1 2 3
4 5 6 7 8 9 10
11 12 13 14 15 16 17
18 19 20 21 22 23 24
25 26 27 28 29 30 31

JUNE
S M T W T F S
1 2
3 4 5 6 7 8 9
10 11 12 13 14 15 16
17 18 19 20 21 22 23
24 25 26 27 28 29 30

1. On what day of the week does May begin? __Tuesday__

2. How many days are there between January 27 and February 12?
   __15__ days

3. School is closed from March 19 through the 22. How many days is school closed?
   __4__ days

4. Which months have 30 days in this calendar?
   __April and June__

5. The month just after April is __May__.

Use with Grade 2, Chapter 7, Lesson 8, pages 259–260. (220)

Reteach

Calendar

R 7-8 RETEACH

A calendar month has days and weeks.
The month of August has 31 days.

			August			
Sunday	Monday	Tuesday	Wednesday	Thursday	Friday	Saturday
			1	2	3	4
5	6	7	8	9	10	11
12	13	14	15	16	17	18
19	20	21	22	23	24	25
26	27	28	29	30	31	

Use the calendar to answer each question.

1. How many full weeks are in the month of August? __3__ weeks

2. On what day of the week does August begin? __Wednesday__

3. The day just after Monday is __Tuesday__.

4. On which day of the week is August 25? __Saturday__

5. What is the date of the second Sunday in August? __August 12__

6. How many days are there between August 13 and 20?
   __6__ days

A calendar year has 12 months.

January	February	March	April	May	June
July	August	September	October	November	December

7. The month just before August is __July__.

Use with Grade 2, Chapter 7, Lesson 8, pages 259–260. (221)

Enrich

Calendar

E 7-8 ENRICH

Let's Look at November!

November starts on a Friday. It has 30 days.
Fill in the calendar for November.

Sunday	Monday	Tuesday	Wednesday	Thursday	Friday	Saturday
					1	2
3	4	5	6	7	8	9
10	11	12	13	14	15	16
17	18	19	20	21	22	23
24	25	26	27	28	29	30

1. How many Fridays are there in November?
   Draw tally marks to show how many.

2. How many Mondays are there in November?
   Draw tally marks to show how many. ||||

3. Are there more Mondays or Fridays in November? __Fridays__

4. October is the month before November.
   On what day of the week does October end? __Thursday__

5. December is the month after November.
   On what day of the week does December start? __Sunday__

6. Thanksgiving is on November 28.
   School is closed for Thanksgiving and the day after. For how many days is school open in November? __19 days__

Use with Grade 2, Chapter 7, Lesson 8, pages 259–260. (222)

Daily Homework

7-8 Calendar

| January 2002 | February 2002 | March 2002 | April 2002 |

January 2002
S M T W T F S
1 2 3 4 5
6 7 8 9 10 11 12
13 14 15 16 17 18 19
20 21 22 23 24 25 26
27 28 29 30 31

February 2002
S M T W T F S
1 2
3 4 5 6 7 8 9
10 11 12 13 14 15 16
17 18 19 20 21 22 23
24 25 26 27 28

March 2002
S M T W T F S
1 2
3 4 5 6 7 8 9
10 11 12 13 14 15 16
17 18 19 20 21 22 23
24 25 26 27 28 29 30
31

April 2002
S M T W T F S
1 2 3 4 5 6
7 8 9 10 11 12 13
14 15 16 17 18 19 20
21 22 23 24 25 26 27
28 29 30

Use the calendar to answer each question.

1. How many days are there between February 14 and February 25? __10__ days

2. What day of the week is January 1? __Tuesday__

3. What month is just before April? __March__

4. What is the date of the third Wednesday in March? __March 20__

Problem Solving

5. Today is April 20. Anna's party is April 27. How many days until her party? __7__ days

Spiral Review

Draw the minute hand to show each time.

7.

| 8:15 | 10:30 | 3:45 |

© McGraw-Hill School Division

Chapter 7 ~ Lesson 9

Part A Worksheet

Problem Solving: Application
Plan a Puppet Show

Part A 7-9 WORKSHEET
Decision Making

Plan your puppet show.

It should last one hour.

Cut out each puppet-show act.

Choose the acts.

Put the acts in order.

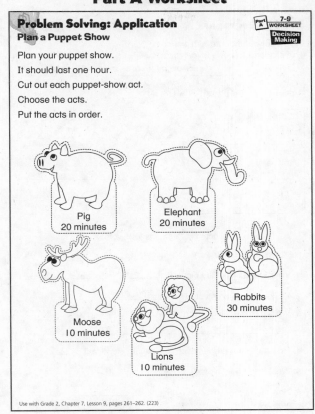

Pig
20 minutes

Elephant
20 minutes

Moose
10 minutes

Lions
10 minutes

Rabbits
30 minutes

Use with Grade 2, Chapter 7, Lesson 9, pages 261–262. (223)

Part A Worksheet

Problem Solving: Application
Plan a Puppet Show

Part A 7-9 WORKSHEET
Decision Making

1. List the acts in your puppet show. Check students' work.

Puppet Show	
Act	**Minutes**

2. How long will your show last? _60 minutes or 1 hour_

   Tell how you know.

   Answers may vary.

3. What if the show lasted for one and a half hours?
   Show the new schedule.

Puppet Show	
Act	**Minutes**

Use with Grade 2, Chapter 7, Lesson 9, pages 261–262. (224)

Part B Worksheet

Problem Solving: Application
How Long Is Your Shadow?

Part B 7-9 WORKSHEET
Math & Science

1. Compare your strings.
   Write *shortest* and *longest* beside the times.

Time	String Length

2. How did your shadow change during the day?
   Answers may vary. Possible answer: It got longer;
   then it got shorter again.

3. What if you measured your shadow
   again at 4 o'clock?
   How long do you think it would be?
   Answers may vary. Possible answer: It was shorter
   than it was at 3:00.

Use with Grade 2, Chapter 7, Lesson 9, pages 263–264. (225)

Chapter 8 ~ Lesson 1

Practice

Read Pictographs

Use the pictograph. Answer each question.

Favorite Books

Space Raiders	📖📖📖📖📖📖📖📖📖📖
Beneath the Sea	📖📖📖
House in the Woods	📖📖📖📖📖📖
Puppet Street	📖📖📖📖📖📖📖📖📖📖

Each 📖 stands for 2 votes.

1. How many children voted
   for House in the Woods? __12__

2. How many more children voted
   for Puppet Street than Beneath the Sea? __14__

3. How many children voted for
   Space Raiders and Puppet Street? __40__

4. Which book got the least number of votes? _Beneath the Sea_

5. How many children voted? __60__

Reteach

Read Pictographs

Pictographs show data with pictures.
This pictograph shows favorite flavors.

Favorite Flavors

Vanilla	👤👤👤👤👤
Chocolate	👤👤👤👤👤👤👤👤
Strawberry	👤👤👤
Blueberry	👤

Each 👤 stands for 1 vote.

Use the pictograph. Answer each question.

1. What is the title of the pictograph? _Favorite Flavors_

2. How many children voted? __17__

3. What picture is used to show the data?
   Children may draw or write stick figure.

4. How many votes does each little picture stand for? __1__

5. What flavor got 5 votes? _vanilla_

6. How many votes did chocolate get? __8__

Enrich

Read Pictographs
Make a Pictograph

Mr. Johnson's class took a vote on their favorite TV shows.
Each child had one vote.

Jungle World	Space Kids	Ranger Rob	My Friend Spot
9	11	5	8

Use the information to make a pictograph.

Our Favorite TV Shows

Jungle World	👤👤👤👤👤👤👤👤👤
Space Kids	👤👤👤👤👤👤👤👤👤👤👤
Ranger Rob	👤👤👤👤👤
My Friend Spot	👤👤👤👤👤👤👤👤

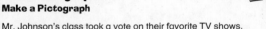

Each 👤 stands for one vote.

Use the pictograph to answer each question.

1. How many more children like Jungle World than
   Ranger Rob? __4__

2. How many more children like Space Kids than My
   Friend Spot? __3__

3. What if each 👤 stands for 2 votes. How many 👤
   would be drawn for My Friend Spot? Tell why.
   4; Answers may vary. Possible answer: There are 8 drawings
   for My Friend Spot, and 8 makes 4 groups of 2.

Daily Homework

Read Pictographs

Use the pictograph. Answer each question.

Second Graders' Favorite Foods

🍕	🍴🍴🍴🍴🍴🍴🍴
🍲	🍴🍴🍴🍴🍴
🍔	🍴🍴🍴🍴
🌮	🍴🍴🍴
🥗	🍴🍴

1 🍴 = 2 votes

1. How many votes does each 🍴 stand
   for? __2__ votes

2. How many children voted? __42__ children

3. How many children voted for pizza? __14__ children

4. How many more children voted for pizza
   than burgers? __6__ children

Problem Solving

5. What if each 🍴 stands for 5 votes. How many
   children voted for tacos? __15__ children

Spiral Review

Add.	Do you need to regroup?	How many in all?
6. 46 + 11	yes (no)	57
7. 58 + 33	(yes) no	91

Chapter 8 ~ Lesson 2

Practice

Tally Marks and Charts

Hannah took a survey.
She asked her friends about their favorite jungle animals.
Complete the chart.
Use data from the chart to answer each question.

Animal	Votes
elephant	⪢
lion	⫴⫴⫴ |||
zebra	||||
monkey	⫴⫴⫴ ⫴⫴⫴	
giraffe	⫴⫴⫴ ||||

1. Which animal got 8 votes? _____lion_____

2. Which animal got the most votes? _____monkey_____

3. Which animal got the least votes? _____zebra_____

4. How many more children like lions than elephants? _____3_____

5. How many more children like monkeys than zebras? _____7_____

6. How many children like zebras and lions? _____12_____

7. How many children voted in this chart? _____37_____

Use with Grade 2, Chapter 8, Lesson 2, pages 279–280. (229)

Reteach

Tally Marks and Charts

A **survey** is when people vote about something.

Tally marks look like this. ⫴⫴⫴

People use **charts** to record tally marks.

Favorite Hobbies

Sewing	|||
Building Models	⫴⫴⫴ ||
Painting	⫴⫴⫴	
Playing Music	⫴⫴⫴ ⫴⫴⫴	

Answer each question.

1. What is the title of the tally chart? _____Favorite Hobbies_____

2. How many hobbies are shown in the tally chart? _____4_____

3. How many tally marks did sewing get? _____3_____

4. How many tally marks did painting get? _____6_____

5. Which hobby was chosen the most? _____playing music_____

Use with Grade 2, Chapter 8, Lesson 2, pages 279–280. (230)

Enrich

Tally Marks and Charts
Our Favorite Colors

Take a class vote on everyone's favorite color.
Make a tally mark for each vote. Each classmate gets
one vote. Answers may vary.

Red	Blue	Yellow	Green	Orange	Purple

Use the chart to make a pictograph.
Draw one ♥ for each vote.

Our Favorite Colors

Red	
Blue	
Yellow	
Green	
Orange	
Purple	

Each ♥ stands for one classmate.

Use your graph to answer each question. Answers may vary.

1. Which color got the most votes? _____

2. Which color got the least votes? _____

3. How many more children liked green the best? _____

4. Write a question about the graph. Then answer it. _____

Use with Grade 2, Chapter 8, Lesson 2, pages 279–280. (231)

Daily Homework

8-2 Tally Marks and Charts

Becca took a survey. She asked her classmates what they
like about their best friends.

1. Which answer was chosen 5 times?

   _____Funny_____

2. Which answer was chosen the most?

   _____Understanding_____

What I Like About My Best Friend

Understanding	⫴⫴⫴ ||
Likes the things I like	⫴⫴⫴	
Funny	⫴⫴⫴
Good at sports	||||
Plays fair	|||
Shares	||

3. Which answer was chosen the fewest times? _____Shares_____

4. How many students did Becca ask? _____27_____ students

5. How many students chose "Plays fair" and "Shares"?

   _____5_____ students

6. How many more students chose "Understanding" than

   "Good at sports"? _____3_____ students

Spiral Review

Add. Check by adding in a different order.

7.
$$\begin{array}{c} 24 \\ +37 \\ \hline 61 \end{array} \quad \begin{array}{c} 37 \\ +24 \\ \hline 61 \end{array} \qquad \begin{array}{c} 38 \\ +56 \\ \hline 94 \end{array} \quad \begin{array}{c} 56 \\ +38 \\ \hline 94 \end{array} \qquad \begin{array}{c} 11 \\ +44 \\ \hline 55 \end{array} \quad \begin{array}{c} 44 \\ +11 \\ \hline 55 \end{array}$$

Chapter 8 ~ Lesson 3

Practice

Bar Graphs

This chart show favorite birds.

Our Favorite Birds	
Robin	11
Blue Jay	5
Swan	4
Parrot	8

Use the totals to complete the bar graph.
Color one space to show each vote.

Our Favorite Birds

Bird: Robin, Blue Jay, Swan, Parrot

Number of Votes: 0 1 2 3 4 5 6 7 8 9 10 11 12

Use data from the graph to answer each question.

1. Which bird got the most votes? _____ robin

2. How many more children like parrots than swans? _____ 4

3. How many blue jays does the graph show? _____ 5

4. How many children voted in all? _____ 28

Use with Grade 2, Chapter 8, Lesson 3, pages 281–282. (232)

Reteach

Bar Graphs

Bar graphs use bars to show data.
This bar graph shows favorite fruits.

Favorite Fruits

Fruit: Apples, Bananas, Oranges, Pears

Number of Votes: 0 1 2 3 4 5 6 7 8

Use the bar graph. Answer each question.

1. What is the title of this bar graph? _____ Favorite Fruits

2. How many fruits are shown in the bar graph? _____ 4

3. Which fruit has the longest bar? _____ apples

4. Which fruit has the shortest bar? _____ pears

5. How many votes did bananas get? _____ 4

Use with Grade 2, Chapter 8, Lesson 3, pages 281–282. (233)

Enrich

Bar Graphs

Favorite Pets

Solve each riddle to find out how many votes each pet got.

Then make a bar graph. Write a title for the graph.

1. Dogs got 8 votes in all. Cats got 3 more votes than dogs.   Cats got _____ 11 votes.

2. Birds got 4 fewer votes than cats.   Birds got _____ 7 votes.

3. Turtles got 3 fewer votes than birds.   Turtles got _____ 4 votes.

4. Fish got 2 more votes than turtles.   Fish got _____ 6 votes.

Possible title: Favorite Pets

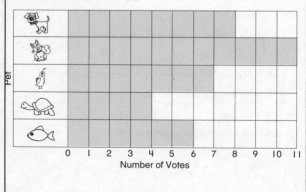

Pet

Number of Votes: 0 1 2 3 4 5 6 7 8 9 10 11

Use with Grade 2, Chapter 8, Lesson 3, pages 281–282. (234)

Daily Homework

8-3 Bar Graphs

Use the totals to complete the bar graph.
Color one space to show each vote.

Pool, Nature Trail, Theme Park, Museum, Playground

0 1 2 3 4 5 6 7 8 9 10

Children's Favorite Activities

pool 2
nature trail 3
theme park 6
museum 4
playground 8

Use data from the graph to answer each question.

1. Which place did the greatest number of children vote for? _____ playground

2. How many places does the graph show? _____ 5 places

3. How many children voted in all? _____ 23 children

4. How many more children voted for the museum than for the pool? _____ 2 children

Spiral Review

Write each number.

5. forty-eight _____ 48   twenty-one _____ 21   sixty _____ 60

6. seventy-six _____ 76   fifty-two _____ 52   seventeen _____ 17

Chapter 8 ~ Lesson 4

Practice

Carrie collected this data from her friends.

Have a Cat | Have a Dog

Megan
David
Amber
Julia
John
Kim
Leon

Corey
Eric
Lee
Emily

Rico
Grace
Kate
Lily
Kevin

Answer each question.

1. How many children have cats and dogs? __4__ children

2. How many children have dogs? __9__ children

3. How many children have a cat or a dog? __16__ children

4. How many children have cats but not dogs? __7__ children

5. Would more children rather have a cat or a dog? Explain your thinking.
   Possible answer: More children would rather have a cat. I compared how many children have each kind of pet.

Use with Grade 2, Chapter 8, Lesson 4, pages 283–284. (235)

Practice

Cal collected this data from his friends.

Like Pizza | Like Tacos

Sam
Laura
Nick

Nina
Brooke
Alex
Mario
Jeff
Yoko

Tina
Ming

Choose the best answer. Fill in the ○.

1. How many children like pizza and tacos?
   Ⓐ 11   Ⓒ 3
   Ⓑ 5   Ⓓ 6

2. How many children like pizza?
   Ⓕ 9   Ⓗ 3
   Ⓖ 6   Ⓙ 8

3. How many children like tacos but not pizza?
   Ⓐ 6   Ⓒ 3
   Ⓑ 2   Ⓓ 8

4. How many children like pizza or tacos?
   Ⓕ 5   Ⓗ 11
   Ⓖ 6   Ⓙ 3

Use with Grade 2, Chapter 8, Lesson 4, pages 283–284. (236)

Practice

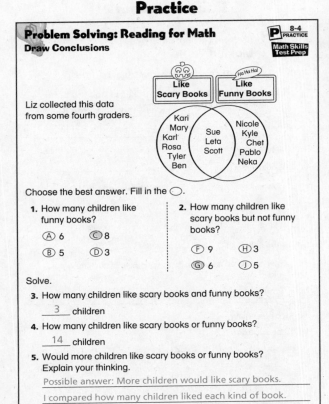

Liz collected this data from some fourth graders.

Like Scary Books | Like Funny Books

Kari
Mary
Karl
Rosa
Tyler
Ben

Sue
Leta
Scott

Nicole
Kyle
Chet
Pablo
Neka

Choose the best answer. Fill in the ○.

1. How many children like funny books?
   Ⓐ 6   Ⓒ 8
   Ⓑ 5   Ⓓ 3

2. How many children like scary books but not funny books?
   Ⓕ 9   Ⓗ 3
   Ⓖ 6   Ⓙ 5

Solve.

3. How many children like scary books and funny books?
   __3__ children

4. How many children like scary books or funny books?
   __14__ children

5. Would more children like scary books or funny books? Explain your thinking.
   Possible answer: More children would like scary books.
   I compared how many children liked each kind of book.

Use with Grade 2, Chapter 8, Lesson 4, pages 283–284. (237)

Daily Homework

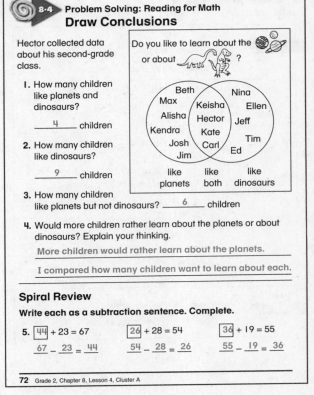

Hector collected data about his second-grade class.

Do you like to learn about the 🪐 or about 🦕 ?

Beth
Max
Alisha
Kendra
Josh
Jim

Keisha
Hector
Kate
Carl

Nina
Ellen
Jeff
Tim
Ed

like planets | like both | like dinosaurs

1. How many children like planets and dinosaurs?
   __4__ children

2. How many children like dinosaurs?
   __9__ children

3. How many children like planets but not dinosaurs? __6__ children

4. Would more children rather learn about the planets or about dinosaurs? Explain your thinking.
   More children would rather learn about the planets.
   I compared how many children want to learn about each.

Spiral Review
Write each as a subtraction sentence. Complete.

5. $\boxed{44} + 23 = 67$ $\boxed{26} + 28 = 54$ $\boxed{36} + 19 = 55$
   $67 - 23 = 44$ $54 - 28 = 26$ $55 - 19 = 36$

Chapter 8 ~ Lesson 5

Practice

Make a Table

Casey has been reading each day in November. On the first day, Casey read 10 pages. On the second day, Casey read 17 pages. On the third day, Casey read 12 pages, and on the fourth day, Casey read 15 pages.

Use data from the story to make a table. Use your table to answer each question.

Casey's November Reading				
Day	1	2	3	4
How many pages read	10	17	12	15

1. How many pages did Casey read during day 3?

___12___ pages

2. During which day did Casey read the most pages?

Day ___2___

3. How many pages did Casey read in the second and third days?

___29___ pages

4. How many more pages did Casey read in the fourth day than in the first day?

___5___ pages

Mixed Strategy Review

Solve.

5. Mona made 25 sugar cookies. She made 21 oatmeal cookies. How many more sugar cookies than oatmeal cookies did Mona make?

___4___ sugar cookies

6. Create a problem for which you would make a table to solve. Share it with others.

_____

_____

Use with Grade 2, Chapter 8, Lesson 5, pages 287–288. (238)

Reteach

Make a Table

Page 288, Problem 1

Mrs. Marshall's second grade class is holding a book drive. They collected 10 books in January and 12 in February. In March they collected another 10. In April they collected 22, and in May they collected 20.

Make a table and use the table to answer the question.
During which month were the most books collected?

Step 1 Read	Be sure you understand the problem.
	What do you know?
	• The second grade collected books for ___5___ months.
	What do you need to find?
	• You need to find ___which month the___ ___most books were collected.___

Step 2 Plan	Make a plan.
• Draw a Picture	Choose a strategy.
• Write a Number Sentence	Make a table.
• Use Logical Reasoning	
• Act it Out	Use the data in the table to help
• Choose the Operation	you solve the problem.
• Make a Table	
• Guess and Check	
• Find a Pattern	
• Make a Graph	

Use with Grade 2, Chapter 8, Lesson 5, pages 287–288. (239)

Reteach

Make a Table

Step 3 Solve	Carry out your plan.
	• Make the table.

Second Grade Book Collection				
Month	Jan.	Feb.	March	April	May
How many books collected	10	12	10	22	20

The first row in the table shows the ___months___.

The second row in the table shows ___how many books were collected___

The most books collected was ___22___.

That number was collected during the month of ___April___.

• During which month were the most books collected?

___April___

Step 4 Look Back	Is the solution reasonable?
	Does your answer make sense? (Yes) No

Use with Grade 2, Chapter 8, Lesson 5, pages 287–288. (240)

Daily Homework

 8·5 **Problem Solving: Strategy**
Make a Table

Fill in the table. Then answer the questions.

Tim's class sold 12 boxes of mint cookies and 10 boxes of chip cookies. They also sold 14 boxes of nut cookies and 9 boxes of oatmeal cookies.

Boxes of Cookies Sold				
Kind	Mint	Chip	Nut	Oatmeal
How Many?	12	10	14	9

1. What kind of cookie sold the fewest? ___oatmeal___

2. How many more boxes of nut cookies were sold than oatmeal cookies? ___5___ boxes

3. How many boxes of mint cookies and nut cookies were sold in all? ___26___ boxes

4. How could you find out how many boxes of cookies were sold in all?

___I could add the number of boxes for each kind of cookie.___

Spiral Review

Add or subtract.

5.
64 − 36 28	22 + 65 87	34 + 47 81	72 − 49 23	55 − 31 24	43 + 48 91

Grade 2, Chapter 8, Lesson 5, Cluster B **73**

Chapter 8 ~ Lesson 6

Practice

Represent Data in Different Ways

Use data from the tally chart to make the bar graph.
Answer each question.

Favorite Foods

Spaghetti	HHH IIII
Hamburger	IIII
Pizza	HHH IIII
Yogurt	HHH I

Favorite Foods

Food (Spaghetti, Hamburger, Pizza, Yogurt) vs Number of Votes 0 1 2 3 4 5 6 7 8 9 10

1. Which food got 6 votes? _____ yogurt _____

2. From which data display did you get your answer for question 1?
Explain. ___ Possible answer: The graph because ___
___ I can see by looking which food got the most votes. ___

3. Which food got the most votes? _____ pizza _____

4. Which food got the least votes? _____ hamburger _____

5. From which data display did you get your answer for question 4?
Explain. ___ Possible answer: The graph because ___
___ I can see by looking which food got the least votes. ___

Use with Grade 2, Chapter 8, Lesson 6, pages 289–290. (241)

Reteach

Represent Data in Different Ways

You can show the same data different ways.
You can use charts, pictographs, or bar graphs.

Favorite Playground Toys

Seesaw	HHH
Monkey Bars	HHH III
Swings	III

1. Use the data from the tally chart to make the pictograph.

Favorite Playground Toys

Each ☺ stands for 1 vote.

2. Use the data from the pictograph to color the bar graph.

Favorite Playground Toys

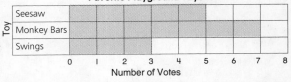

Toy (Seesaw, Monkey Bars, Swings) vs Number of Votes 0 1 2 3 4 5 6 7 8

Use with Grade 2, Chapter 8, Lesson 6, pages 289–290. (242)

Enrich

Represent Data in Different Ways

Let's Go, Team!

Find out how many players are on each kind of team.

Record the data in the tally chart.

Show the data in a pictograph and a bar graph.

Students' pictographs and bar graphs may vary. Possible graphs are given.

Sports	Baseball	Basketball	Football	Soccer
Tally	HHH IIII	HHH	HHH HHH I	HHH HHH I
Total	9	5	11	11

Favorite Sports

Sports	Number of Players
Baseball	🏃🏃🏃🏃🏃
Basketball	🏃🏃🏃
Football	🏃🏃🏃🏃🏃🏃
Soccer	🏃🏃🏃🏃🏃🏃

Each 🏃 stands for 2 players.

Favorite Sports

Baseball, Basketball, Football, Soccer vs 0 1 2 3 4 5 6 7 8 9 10 11 12

Use with Grade 2, Chapter 8, Lesson 6, pages 289–290. (243)

Daily Homework

8-6 Represent Data in Different Ways

Use the data from the tally table to make the bar graph. Answer each question.

Favorite Sport

Soccer	HHH II
Swimming	HHH I
Softball	IIII

1. Which sport got 4 votes?
_____ softball _____

2. From which data display did you get your answer for question 1? Explain.
___ Answers will vary. ___

Favorite Sport

Soccer, Swimming, Softball vs 0 1 2 3 4 5 6 7 8

3. Which sport got the most votes? _____ soccer _____

4. From which data display did you get your answer for question 3? Explain.
___ Possible answer: The graph; I can see by looking ___
___ which sport got the most votes. ___

Spiral Review

5. Matt has 1 quarter, 2 dimes, and 2 pennies.
His brother gives him 2 more pennies.
How much money does Matt have now? _____ 49¢ _____

Chapter 8 ~ Lesson 7

Practice

Range and Mode

P 8-7 PRACTICE

Use the data. Answer each question.

Tim's team scored this many points in the last 5 games.

2   5   9   4   4

1. What is the range of the numbers? _____7_____

2. What is the mode of the numbers? _____4_____

Annie's team scored this many points in 6 games.

1   6   3   3   9   5

3. What is the range of the numbers? _____8_____

4. What is the mode of the numbers? _____3_____

This is the number of children on each team.

22   25   25   21   25

5. What is the range of the numbers? _____4_____

6. What is the mode of the numbers? _____25_____

This many bags of popcorn were sold at the last 6 games.

37   21   44   44   32   27

7. What is the range of the numbers? _____23_____

8. What is the mode of the numbers? _____44_____

Reteach

Range and Mode

R 8-7 RETEACH

Here are some numbers in a set of data.   5   5   7   9   11

Find the **range**.	Find the **mode**.
Subtract the least number from the greatest number.	The mode is the number that appears most often.
The greatest number is 11. The least number is 5.	5 appears more than the other numbers.
$11 - 5 = 6$ 6 The range is _____6_____.	The mode is _____5_____.

Look at each set of data. Find the range. Find the mode.

1. Data: 3   4   4   6   8
greatest number − least number = range

_8_ − _3_ = _5_

The range is _5_ .

The mode is the number that appears most often. The mode is _4_.

2. Data: 5   9   9   11   12   13
greatest number − least number = range

_13_ − _5_ = _8_

The range is _8_ .

The mode is the number that appears most often. The mode is _9_.

3. Data: 10   11   11   13   11   14

_14_ − _10_ = _4_

The range is _4_ .

The mode is _11_ .

4. Data: 9   12   13   20   20

_20_ − _9_ = _11_

The range is _11_ .

The mode is _20_ .

Enrich

Range and Mode
At the Zoo

E 8-7 ENRICH

The zoo has special movies about Jungle Animals.
The pictograph shows how many tickets were sold for each show.

Movie Ticket Sales

Big Cats	🎟🎟🎟🎟🎟
Leaping Lizards	🎟🎟🎟🎟🎟🎟
Jungle Birds	🎟🎟🎟🎟🎟🎟🎟🎟
Monkey Business	🎟🎟🎟🎟🎟🎟🎟🎟🎟
Baby Elephants	🎟🎟🎟🎟🎟

Each 🎟 stands for 2 tickets.

Read the graph. How many tickets were sold for each show?

Big Cats	Leaping Lizards	Jungle Birds	Monkey Business	Baby Elephants
10	12	16	18	10

1. What is the range for the data? _8_ tickets

2. What is the mode for the data? _10_ tickets

3. What was the total number of tickets sold? _66_ tickets

Daily Homework

 8-7 Range and Mode

Use the data. Answer each question.
The following numbers show how many baseball caps the school store sold in the past five weeks.

5   3   10   24   5

1. What is the range of the numbers? _____21_____

2. What is the mode of the numbers? _____5_____

The following numbers show how many pencils the school store sold in the last five weeks.

25   36   18   25   16

3. What is the range of the numbers? _____20_____

4. What is the mode of the numbers? _____25_____

Spiral Review

5. John began watching a movie at 1:00. The movie ended at 3:00. How long did he spend watching the movie?

_____2_____ hours

6. Carla started playing soccer at 2:00. She played for 1 hour and 30 minutes. At what time did she finish playing soccer?

_3_ : _30_

Chapter 8 ~ Lesson 8

Part A Worksheet

Problem Solving: Application

Make a Picture

Part A | 8-8 WORKSHEET | Decision Making

Plan a mural showing favorite school activities.

Select some activities.

Record them in the table.

Survey your classmates.

Tables may vary.

Favorite School Activities	

Use with Grade 2, Chapter 8, Lesson 8, pages 293–294. (247)

Part A Worksheet

Problem Solving: Application

Make a Picture

Part A | 8-8 WORKSHEET | Decision Making

1. Which activities will you show on your mural?

Answers may vary.

2. Tell how you made your decision.

Answers may vary.

3. Use the information you collected to make a graph.

Check students' graphs.

Work Space

Use with Grade 2, Chapter 8, Lesson 8, pages 293–294. (248)

Part B Worksheet

Problem Solving: Application

What Is Your Favorite Season?

Part B | 8-8 WORKSHEET | Math & Science

1. Draw the symbols you chose for each season.
Record your data. Check students' work.

Our Favorite Season

🍁	
❄	
🍄	
🌼	

2. List the seasons in order, from your class's favorite to least favorite.

3. What if you asked other students in your school to name their favorite season?
What do you think they would name? Explain your thinking.

Use with Grade 2, Chapter 8, Lesson 8, pages 295–296. (249)

Chapter 9 ~ Lesson 1

Practice

Inch and Foot

Find these objects.
Estimate. Then measure and record.
Write how many inches or feet. Estimates and measures may vary.

	Estimate	Measure
1.	about _____	about _____
2.	about _____	about _____
3.	about _____	about _____
4.	about _____	about _____
5.	about _____	about _____
6.	about _____	about _____

Use with Grade 2, Chapter 9, Lesson 1, pages 309–310. (250)

Reteach

Inch and Foot

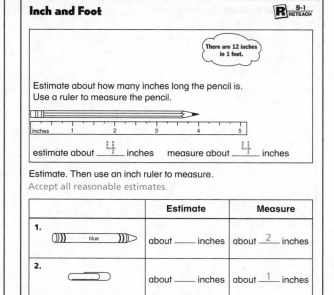

There are 12 inches in 1 foot.

Estimate about how many inches long the pencil is.
Use a ruler to measure the pencil.

estimate about _____ inches   measure about _____ inches

Estimate. Then use an inch ruler to measure.
Accept all reasonable estimates.

	Estimate	Measure
1. blue	about _____ inches	about _2_ inches
2.	about _____ inches	about _1_ inches
3.	about _____ inches	about _1_ inches
4. chalk	about _____ inches	about _2_ inches

Use with Grade 2, Chapter 9, Lesson 1, pages 309–310. (251)

Enrich

Inch and Foot
Dinosaur Data

Find how many inches.
Then use the chart to answer each question.

Feet	1	2	3	4	5	6
Inches	12	24	36	48	60	72

1. A dinosaur bone measures 4 feet long. How many inches is the bone?

___48___ inches

A scientist digs a hole 5 feet deep to find a dinosaur. How many inches deep is the hole?

___60___ inches

2. *Compsagnathus* was one of the smallest dinosaurs. It measured about 2 feet long. How many inches is that?

___24___ inches

A dinosaur named *Protoceratops* measured 72 inches long. How many feet long is that?

___6___ feet

3. An early kind of crocodile was the *Terrestrisuchus*. It was only 1 foot 8 inches long. How many inches is that?

___20___ inches

The *Psittarosaurus* was a dinosaur with a head like a parrot. This dinosaur was 6 feet 6 inches long. How many inches is that?

___78___ inches

Would you use feet or inches to measure?
Circle the best answer.

4. the length of a dinosaur

(feet)   inches

the length of a dinosaur egg

feet   (inches)

Use with Grade 2, Chapter 9, Lesson 1, pages 309–310. (252)

Daily Homework

9-1   ### Inch and Foot

Find these objects.   Estimates and measures may vary.
Estimate. Then measure and record.
Write how many inches or feet.

	Estimate	Measure
1.	possible answer: 5 feet about _____	
2.	possible answer: 15 inches about _____	
3.	possible answer: 5 inches about _____	

Solve.

4. A piece of notebook paper is about 9 inches wide. How wide are two pieces of paper taped side by side? ___18___ inches

Spiral Review

Add or subtract. Complete the fact family.

5. $6 + 7 = $ ___13___ $13 - 6 = $ ___7___

$7 + $ ___6___ $ = 13$ ___13___ $ - 7 = 6$

Chapter 9 ~ Lesson 2

Practice

Inches, Feet, and Yards

P 9-2 PRACTICE

Estimate.
Find an object for each length. Objects and measures may vary.

	Write your object.	Measure.
1. about 2 inches	_____	about _____
2. about 6 inches	_____	about _____
3. about 11 inches	_____	about _____
4. about 18 inches	_____	about _____
5. about 2 feet	_____	about _____
6. about 2 yards	_____	about _____
7. about 3 yards	_____	about _____

Use with Grade 2, Chapter 9, Lesson 2, pages 311–312. (253)

Reteach

Inches, Feet, and Yards

R 9-2 RETEACH

There are 3 feet in 1 yard.

estimate about _____ yard   measure about _____ yard

Find these objects. Estimate. Then measure and record. Write how many inches or how many inches and feet. Estimates and measures may vary.

		Estimate	Measure
1.		about _____	about _____
2.		about _____	about _____
3.		about _____	about _____
4.		about _____	about _____

Use with Grade 2, Chapter 9, Lesson 2, pages 311–312. (254)

Enrich

Inches, Feet, and Yards
More Dinosaur Data

E 9-2 ENRICH

Find how many feet.
Then use the chart to answer each question.

Yards	1	2	3	4	5	6
Feet	3	6	9	12	15	18

1. The head of an *Allosaurus* was about 3 feet long. How many yards is that?

_____1_____ yard

A scientist found a dinosaur nest that was about 9 feet long. How many yards is that?

_____3_____ yards

2. A *Tyrannosaurus* stood about 6 yards high. How many feet high is that?

_____18_____ feet

An *Iguanodon* was about 10 yards long. How many feet long was the *Iguanodon*?

_____30_____ feet

3. The *Emeus crassus* was a bird that didn't fly. It is like the kiwi bird today. The *Emeus crassus* was 1 yard 2 feet tall. How many feet is that?

_____5_____ feet

The skeleton of a *Deinonychus* was found in Montana. This fast dinosaur was 3 yards 1 foot long. How many feet is that?

_____10_____ feet

Would you use yards, feet, or inches to measure? Circle the best answer.

4. The length of a dinosaur footprint?

inch   (foot)   yard

The height of a very tall dinosaur?

inch   foot   (yard)

Use with Grade 2, Chapter 9, Lesson 2, pages 311–312. (255)

Daily Homework

9-2 Inches, Feet, and Yards

Find these objects.
Estimate. Then measure and record. Write how many inches, feet, or yards. Estimates and measures may vary.

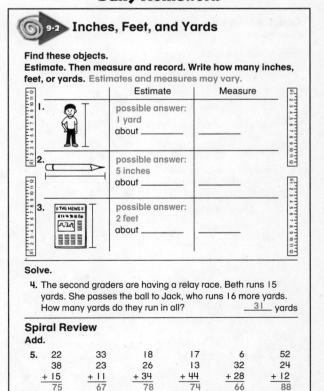

		Estimate	Measure
1.		possible answer: 1 yard about _____	_____
2.		possible answer: 5 inches about _____	_____
3.		possible answer: 2 feet about _____	_____

Solve.

4. The second graders are having a relay race. Beth runs 15 yards. She passes the ball to Jack, who runs 16 more yards. How many yards do they run in all?   _____31_____ yards

Spiral Review
Add.

5.	22	33	18	17	6	52
	38	23	26	13	32	24
	+ 15	+ 11	+ 34	+ 44	+ 28	+ 12
	75	67	78	74	66	88

Grade 2, Chapter 9, Lesson 2, Cluster A **77**

Chapter 9 ~ Lesson 3

Practice

Cup, Pint, Quart

Circle the better estimate.

1.

(more than 1 cup)
less than 1 cup

more than 1 cup
(less than 1 cup)

2.

(more than 1 cup)
less than 1 cup

more than 1 pint
(less than 1 pint)

3.

(more than 1 pint)
less than 1 pint

more than 1 pint
less than 1 pint

4.

(more than 1 quart)
less than 1 quart

more than 1 quart
(less than 1 quart)

Use with Grade 2, Chapter 9, Lesson 3, pages 313–314. (256)

Reteach

Cup, Pint, Quart

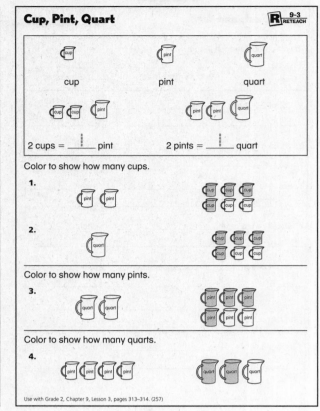

2 cups = _____ pint   2 pints = _____ quart

Color to show how many cups.

1.

2.

Color to show how many pints.

3.

Color to show how many quarts.

4.

Use with Grade 2, Chapter 9, Lesson 3, pages 313–314. (257)

Enrich

Cup, Pint, Quart
Fruit Punch

Amanda is making fruit punch.

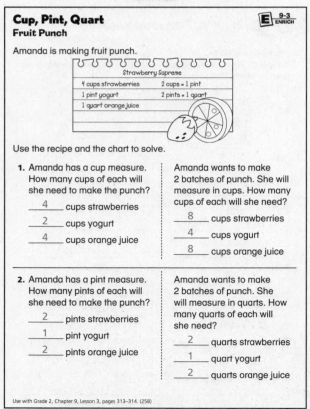

Strawberry Supreme

4 cups strawberries	2 cups = 1 pint
1 pint yogurt	2 pints = 1 quart
1 quart orange juice	

Use the recipe and the chart to solve.

1. Amanda has a cup measure. How many cups of each will she need to make the punch?

____4____ cups strawberries

____2____ cups yogurt

____4____ cups orange juice

Amanda wants to make 2 batches of punch. She will measure in cups. How many cups of each will she need?

____8____ cups strawberries

____4____ cups yogurt

____8____ cups orange juice

2. Amanda has a pint measure. How many pints of each will she need to make the punch?

____2____ pints strawberries

____1____ pint yogurt

____2____ pints orange juice

Amanda wants to make 2 batches of punch. She will measure in quarts. How many quarts of each will she need?

____2____ quarts strawberries

____1____ quart yogurt

____2____ quarts orange juice

Use with Grade 2, Chapter 9, Lesson 3, pages 313–314. (258)

Daily Homework

9-3 Cup, Pint, Quart

Circle the better estimate.

1.

more than 1 quart
(less than 1 quart)

2.

(more than 1 quart)
less than 1 quart

3.

more than 1 pint
(less than 1 pint)

4.

(more than 1 cup)
less than 1 cup

Write the answer.

5. Jamie drinks a cup of water at lunch. He drinks a pint of water at dinner. Does he drink more water at lunch or at dinner?   _____dinner_____

6. Rich uses 4 quarts of water to fill the fish bowl. He uses 3 quarts to water the plants. How many quarts of water does he use in all?   ____7____ quarts

Spiral Review

Add.

7.

67	43	21	39	46	19
+ 25	+ 14	+ 27	+ 42	+ 29	+ 35
92	57	48	81	75	54

78 Grade 2, Chapter 9, Lesson 3, Cluster A

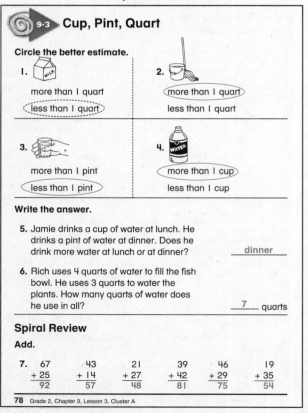

Chapter 9 ~ Lesson 4

Practice

Ounce and Pound

Circle the better estimate.

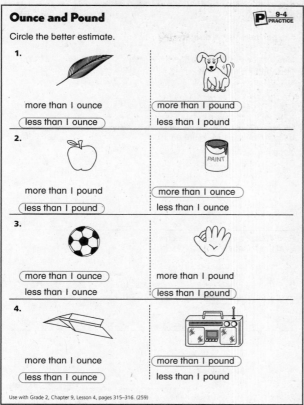

1.
more than I ounce
(less than I ounce)

(more than I pound)
less than I pound

2.
more than I pound
(less than I pound)

(more than I ounce)
less than I ounce

3.
(more than I ounce)
less than I ounce

more than I pound
(less than I pound)

4.
(more than I ounce)
(less than I ounce)

(more than I pound)
less than I pound

Use with Grade 2, Chapter 9, Lesson 4, pages 315–316. (259)

Reteach

Ounce and Pound

You can estimate if something is more or less than a pound.

There are 16 ounces in 1 pound.

(more than I pound)
(less than I pound)

(more than I ounce)
less than I ounce

Circle the better estimate.

1.
(more than I pound)
less than I pound

more than I ounce
(less than I ounce)

2.
more than I pound
(less than I pound)

more than I ounce
(less than I ounce)

3.
(more than I pound)
less than I pound

(more than I ounce)
less than I ounce

Use with Grade 2, Chapter 9, Lesson 4, pages 315–316. (260)

Enrich

Ounce and Pound
Fruit Balance

Balance the scale.
Tell how many of each fruit you need.

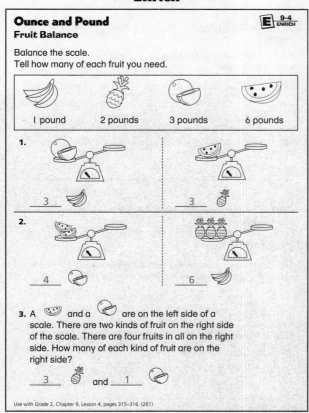

I pound	2 pounds	3 pounds	6 pounds

1.
_3_
_3_

2.
_4_
_6_

3. A 🍉 and a 🍊 are on the left side of a scale. There are two kinds of fruit on the right side of the scale. There are four fruits in all on the right side. How many of each kind of fruit are on the right side?

_3_ 🍍 and _1_ 🍊

Use with Grade 2, Chapter 9, Lesson 4, pages 315–316. (261)

Daily Homework

9-4 Ounce and Pound

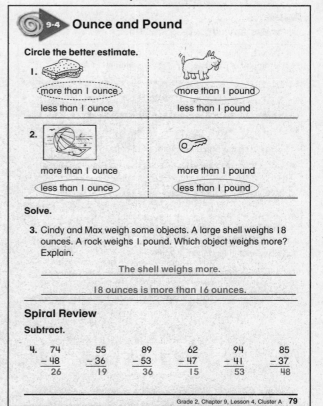

Circle the better estimate.

1.
(more than I ounce)
less than I ounce

(more than I pound)
less than I pound

2.
more than I ounce
(less than I ounce)

more than I pound
(less than I pound)

Solve.

3. Cindy and Max weigh some objects. A large shell weighs 18 ounces. A rock weighs 1 pound. Which object weighs more? Explain.

___The shell weighs more.___

___18 ounces is more than 16 ounces.___

Spiral Review
Subtract.

4.	74	55	89	62	94	85
	− 48	− 36	− 53	− 47	− 41	− 37
	26	19	36	15	53	48

Grade 2, Chapter 9, Lesson 4, Cluster A **79**

Chapter 9 ~ Lesson 5

Practice

Perimeter

Find the perimeter of each figure. Use an inch ruler.

1.

$\underline{2} + \underline{2} + \underline{2} = \underline{6}$ inches

2.

$\underline{1} + \underline{1} + \underline{1} + \underline{1} = \underline{4}$ inches

3.

$\underline{1} + \underline{2} + \underline{1} + \underline{2} = \underline{6}$ inches

4.

$\underline{1} + \underline{1} + \underline{1} + \underline{1} + \underline{1} = \underline{5}$ inches

Use with Grade 2, Chapter 9, Lesson 5, pages 317–318. (262)

Reteach

Perimeter

The perimeter is the distance around a figure.
Measure each side of the figure.
Then add the measures.

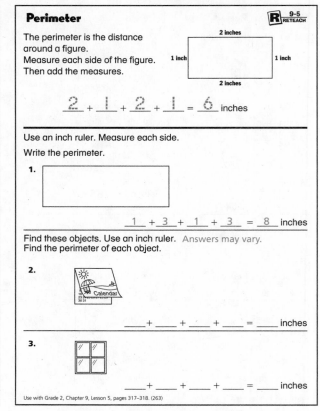

$\underline{2} + \underline{1} + \underline{2} + \underline{1} = \underline{6}$ inches

Use an inch ruler. Measure each side.
Write the perimeter.

1.

$\underline{1} + \underline{3} + \underline{1} + \underline{3} = \underline{8}$ inches

Find these objects. Use an inch ruler. Answers may vary.
Find the perimeter of each object.

2.

____ + ____ + ____ + ____ = ____ inches

3.

____ + ____ + ____ + ____ = ____ inches

Use with Grade 2, Chapter 9, Lesson 5, pages 317–318. (263)

Enrich

Perimeter

All the Way Around   Check students' drawings.

1. Draw a shape with a perimeter of 6 units.	Draw a shape with a perimeter of 10 units.

2. Draw a shape with a perimeter of 15 units.

3. Use an inch ruler. Find the perimeter.

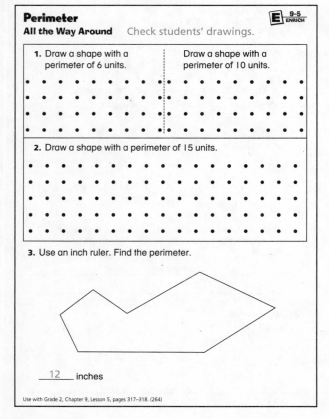

$\underline{12}$ inches

Use with Grade 2, Chapter 9, Lesson 5, pages 317–318. (264)

Daily Homework

9-5 Perimeter

Find the perimeter of each figure.
Use an inch ruler.

1.

$\underline{1} + \underline{1} + \underline{1} + \underline{1} = \underline{4}$ inches

2.

$\underline{1} + \underline{1} + \underline{1} + \underline{2} = \underline{5}$ inches

3.

$\underline{1} + \underline{1} + \underline{1} = \underline{3}$ inches

Problem Solving

4. 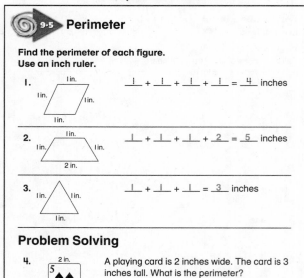 A playing card is 2 inches wide. The card is 3 inches tall. What is the perimeter?

$\underline{2} + \underline{3} + \underline{2} + \underline{3} = \underline{10}$ inches

Spiral Review

Circle the better estimate.

5. 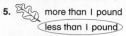 more than 1 pound
(less than 1 pound)

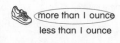 (more than 1 ounce)
less than 1 ounce

Chapter 9 ~ Lesson 6

Practice

Area

Color to show the number of square units. Sample answers are given.

1.

5 square units | 4 square units

2.

6 square units | 8 square units

3.

12 square units | 15 square units

Use with Grade 2, Chapter 9, Lesson 6, pages 319–320. (265)

Reteach

Area

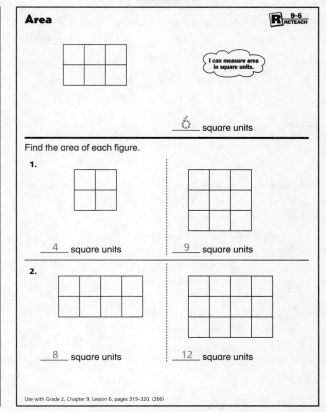

I can measure area in square units.

_6_ square units

Find the area of each figure.

1.

_4_ square units | _9_ square units

2.

_8_ square units | _12_ square units

Use with Grade 2, Chapter 9, Lesson 6, pages 319–320. (266)

Enrich

Area
Picture This

Count the number of square units in the shaded figure.

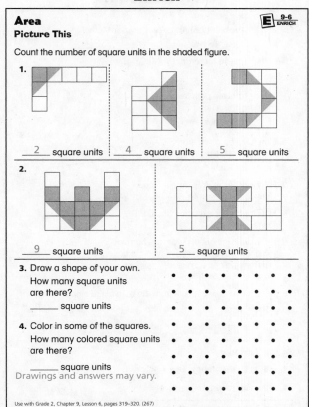

1.

_2_ square units | _4_ square units | _5_ square units

2.

_9_ square units | _5_ square units

3. Draw a shape of your own. How many square units are there?

_____ square units

4. Color in some of the squares. How many colored square units are there?

_____ square units

Drawings and answers may vary.

Use with Grade 2, Chapter 9, Lesson 6, pages 319–320. (267)

Daily Homework

9-6 Area

Sample answers are given.

Color to show the number of square units.

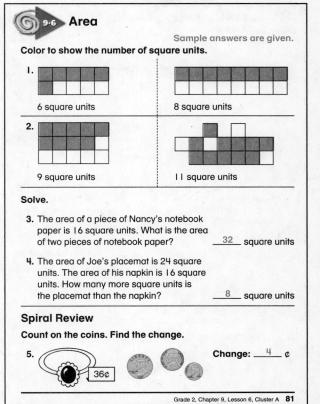

1.

6 square units | 8 square units

2.

9 square units | 11 square units

Solve.

3. The area of a piece of Nancy's notebook paper is 16 square units. What is the area of two pieces of notebook paper? _32_ square units

4. The area of Joe's placemat is 24 square units. The area of his napkin is 16 square units. How many more square units is the placemat than the napkin? _8_ square units

Spiral Review

Count on the coins. Find the change.

5. 36¢   Change: _4_ ¢

Chapter 9 ~ Lesson 7

Practice

Problem Solving: Reading for Math
Use Maps

P 9-7 PRACTICE Reading Skill

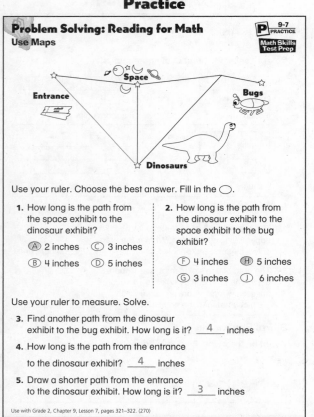

Use your ruler to measure. Solve.

1. How long is the path from the bird house
   to the monkey house? __3__ inches

2. How long is the path from the monkey
   house to the penguin area? __2__ inches

3. How long is the path from the bird house
   to the monkey house to the penguin area?
   __5__ inches

4. How long is the other path from
   the bird house to the penguin area? __6__ inches

5. Draw a shorter path from the bird house
   to the penguin area. How long is it? __4__ inches

Practice

Problem Solving: Reading for Math
Use Maps

P 9-7 PRACTICE Math Skills Test Prep

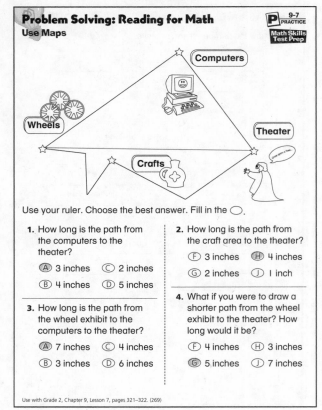

Use your ruler. Choose the best answer. Fill in the ◯.

1. How long is the path from
   the computers to the
   theater?
   Ⓐ 3 inches   Ⓒ 2 inches
   Ⓑ 4 inches   Ⓓ 5 inches

2. How long is the path from
   the craft area to the theater?
   Ⓕ 3 inches   Ⓗ 4 inches
   Ⓖ 2 inches   Ⓙ 1 inch

3. How long is the path from
   the wheel exhibit to the
   computers to the theater?
   Ⓐ 7 inches   Ⓒ 4 inches
   Ⓑ 3 inches   Ⓓ 6 inches

4. What if you were to draw a
   shorter path from the wheel
   exhibit to the theater? How
   long would it be?
   Ⓕ 4 inches   Ⓗ 3 inches
   Ⓖ 5 inches   Ⓙ 7 inches

Practice

Problem Solving: Reading for Math
Use Maps

P 9-7 PRACTICE Math Skills Test Prep

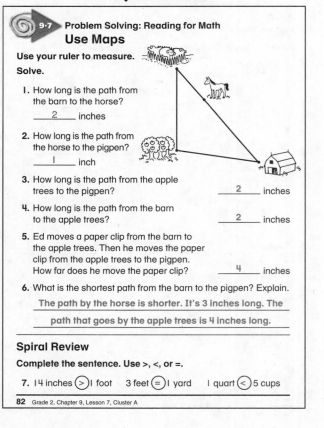

Use your ruler. Choose the best answer. Fill in the ◯.

1. How long is the path from
   the space exhibit to the
   dinosaur exhibit?
   Ⓐ 2 inches   Ⓒ 3 inches
   Ⓑ 4 inches   Ⓓ 5 inches

2. How long is the path from
   the dinosaur exhibit to the
   space exhibit to the bug
   exhibit?
   Ⓕ 4 inches   Ⓗ 5 inches
   Ⓖ 3 inches   Ⓙ 6 inches

Use your ruler to measure. Solve.

3. Find another path from the dinosaur
   exhibit to the bug exhibit. How long is it? __4__ inches

4. How long is the path from the entrance
   to the dinosaur exhibit? __4__ inches

5. Draw a shorter path from the entrance
   to the dinosaur exhibit. How long is it? __3__ inches

Daily Homework

9-7 Problem Solving: Reading for Math
Use Maps

Use your ruler to measure.
Solve.

1. How long is the path from
   the barn to the horse?
   __2__ inches

2. How long is the path from
   the horse to the pigpen?
   __1__ inch

3. How long is the path from the apple
   trees to the pigpen? __2__ inches

4. How long is the path from the barn
   to the apple trees? __2__ inches

5. Ed moves a paper clip from the barn to
   the apple trees. Then he moves the paper
   clip from the apple trees to the pigpen.
   How far does he move the paper clip? __4__ inches

6. What is the shortest path from the barn to the pigpen? Explain.
   The path by the horse is shorter. It's 3 inches long. The
   path that goes by the apple trees is 4 inches long.

Spiral Review

Complete the sentence. Use >, <, or =.

7. 14 inches ⊛>⊛ 1 foot   3 feet ⊛=⊛ 1 yard   1 quart ⊛<⊛ 5 cups

Chapter 9 ~ Lesson 8

Practice

Problem Solving: Strategy
Guess and Check

P 9-8 PRACTICE

How long is each path?
Estimate the length. Then use a ruler to check.

Accept any reasonable estimates.

1.

Estimate _____ inches   Check __5__ inches

2.

Estimate _____ inches   Check __6__ inches

3.

Estimate _____ inches   Check __7__ inches

Mixed Strategy Review

Solve.

4. Celia made 16 chocolate
   brownies. She made 13
   butterscotch brownies. How
   many brownies did she
   make?
   __29__ brownies

5. **Create a problem** for which
   you would guess and check
   to solve. Share it with others.

   _____

   _____

Use with Grade 2, Chapter 9, Lesson 8, pages 325–326. (271)

Reteach

Problem Solving: Strategy
Guess and Check

R 9-8 RETEACH

Page 326, Problem 3

How long is the path on the next page?
Estimate the length. Then use a ruler to check.

Estimate _____ inches   Check _____ inches

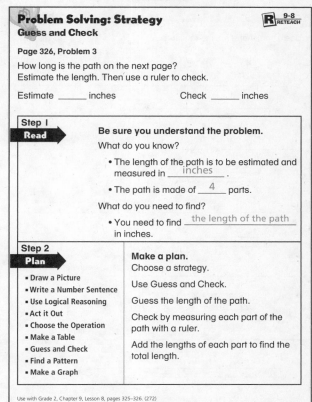

Step 1 Read	Be sure you understand the problem.

Be sure you understand the problem.

What do you know?

- The length of the path is to be estimated and measured in __inches__.
- The path is made of __4__ parts.

What do you need to find?

- You need to find __the length of the path__ in inches.

Step 2 Plan

Make a plan.
Choose a strategy.

- Draw a Picture
- Write a Number Sentence
- Use Logical Reasoning
- Act it Out
- Choose the Operation
- Make a Table
- Guess and Check
- Find a Pattern
- Make a Graph

Use Guess and Check.

Guess the length of the path.

Check by measuring each part of the path with a ruler.

Add the lengths of each part to find the total length.

Use with Grade 2, Chapter 9, Lesson 8, pages 325–326. (272)

Reteach

Problem Solving: Strategy
Guess and Check

R 9-8 RETEACH

Step 3 Solve

Carry out your plan.

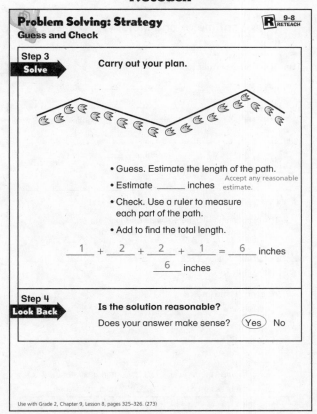

- Guess. Estimate the length of the path.
- Estimate _____ inches   Accept any reasonable estimate.
- Check. Use a ruler to measure each part of the path.
- Add to find the total length.

__1__ + __2__ + __2__ + __1__ = __6__ inches

__6__ inches

Step 4 Look Back

Is the solution reasonable?

Does your answer make sense?   (Yes)   No

Use with Grade 2, Chapter 9, Lesson 8, pages 325–326. (273)

© McGraw-Hill School Division

Daily Homework

9-8 **Problem Solving: Strategy**
Guess and Check

How long is each path? Estimate the length. Then use a ruler to check.

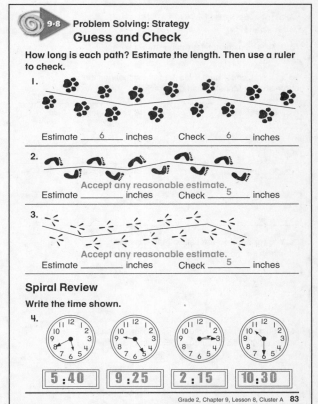

1.

Estimate __6__ inches   Check __6__ inches

2.

Accept any reasonable estimate.
Estimate _____ inches   Check __5__ inches

3.

Accept any reasonable estimate.
Estimate _____ inches   Check __5__ inches

Spiral Review

Write the time shown.

4.

| 5:40 | 9:25 | 2:15 | 10:30 |

Grade 2, Chapter 9, Lesson 8, Cluster A 83

Chapter 9 ~ Lesson 9

Practice

Centimeter and Meter

P 9-9 PRACTICE

Use a centimeter ruler to measure.

1.

about __4__ centimeters

2.

about __9__ centimeters

3.

about __6__ centimeters

4.

about __5__ centimeters

5.

about __3__ centimeters

6. about __12__ centimeters

Reteach

Centimeter and Meter

R 9-9 RETEACH

You can use a centimeter ruler to measure.

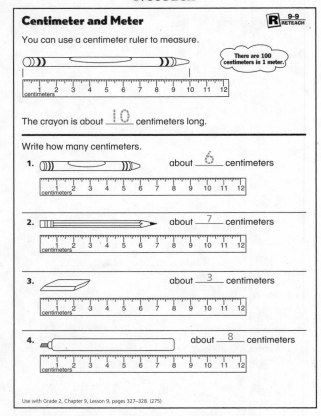

There are 100 centimeters in 1 meter.

1 2 3 4 5 6 7 8 9 10 11 12 centimeters

The crayon is about __10__ centimeters long.

Write how many centimeters.

1. about __6__ centimeters

1 2 3 4 5 6 7 8 9 10 11 12 centimeters

2. about __7__ centimeters

1 2 3 4 5 6 7 8 9 10 11 12 centimeters

3. about __3__ centimeters

1 2 3 4 5 6 7 8 9 10 11 12 centimeters

4. about __8__ centimeters

1 2 3 4 5 6 7 8 9 10 11 12 centimeters

Enrich

Centimeter and Meter
Scavenger Hunt

E 9-9 ENRICH

You will need a centimeter ruler. Play with a team of 4.

Go on a scavenger hunt. Find something that has the length shown. Measure and draw pictures. Answers may vary.

1. 5 centimeters	10 centimeters
2. 20 centimeters	50 centimeters

3. You will need a meter stick. Find something that is about 1 meter long. Draw a picture of it.

4. Would you use centimeters or meters to measure the length of a playground? Explain your answer.

____Meters; there would be too many centimeters, so____
____meters would be easier to count.____

Daily Homework

9-9 Centimeter and Meter

Find these objects.
Use a centimeter ruler to measure. Measures may vary.

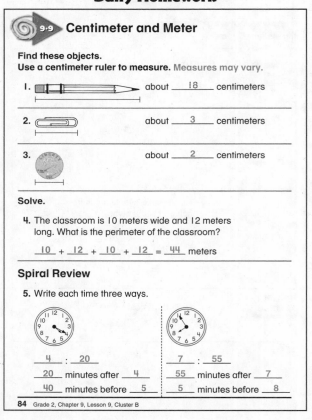

1. about __18__ centimeters

2. about __3__ centimeters

3. about __2__ centimeters

Solve.

4. The classroom is 10 meters wide and 12 meters long. What is the perimeter of the classroom?

__10__ + __12__ + __10__ + __12__ = __44__ meters

Spiral Review

5. Write each time three ways.

__4__ : __20__

__20__ minutes after __4__

__40__ minutes before __5__

__7__ : __55__

__55__ minutes after __7__

__5__ minutes before __8__

Chapter 9 ~ Lesson 10

Practice

Gram and Kilogram

P 9-10 PRACTICE

Circle the better estimate.

1.

lighter than 1 kilogram *(circled)*
heavier than 1 kilogram
about the same as 1 kilogram

lighter than 1 kilogram
heavier than 1 kilogram
about the same as 1 kilogram *(circled)*

2.

lighter than 1 kilogram
heavier than 1 kilogram *(circled)*
about the same as 1 kilogram

lighter than 1 kilogram *(circled)*
heavier than 1 kilogram
about the same as 1 kilogram

3.

lighter than 1 kilogram
heavier than 1 kilogram
about the same as 1 kilogram *(circled)*

lighter than 1 kilogram
heavier than 1 kilogram *(circled)*
about the same as 1 kilogram

Use with Grade 2, Chapter 9, Lesson 10, pages 329–330. (277)

Reteach

Gram and Kilogram

R 9-10 RETEACH

There are 1,000 grams in 1 kilogram.
Your math book is about 1 kilogram.

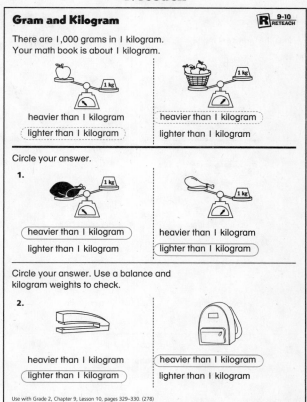

heavier than 1 kilogram
lighter than 1 kilogram *(circled)*

heavier than 1 kilogram *(circled)*
lighter than 1 kilogram

Circle your answer.

1.

heavier than 1 kilogram *(circled)*
lighter than 1 kilogram

heavier than 1 kilogram
lighter than 1 kilogram *(circled)*

Circle your answer. Use a balance and kilogram weights to check.

2.

heavier than 1 kilogram
lighter than 1 kilogram *(circled)*

heavier than 1 kilogram *(circled)*
lighter than 1 kilogram

Use with Grade 2, Chapter 9, Lesson 10, pages 329–330. (278)

Enrich

Gram and Kilogram
The Farmers Market

E 9-10 ENRICH

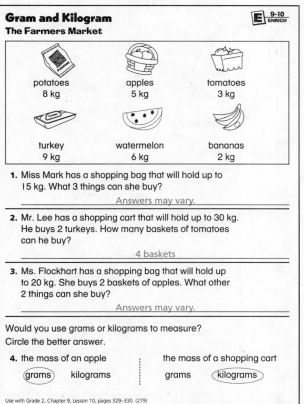

potatoes 8 kg
apples 5 kg
tomatoes 3 kg
turkey 9 kg
watermelon 6 kg
bananas 2 kg

1. Miss Mark has a shopping bag that will hold up to 15 kg. What 3 things can she buy?

_____ Answers may vary.

2. Mr. Lee has a shopping cart that will hold up to 30 kg. He buys 2 turkeys. How many baskets of tomatoes can he buy?

_____ 4 baskets

3. Ms. Flockhart has a shopping bag that will hold up to 20 kg. She buys 2 baskets of apples. What other 2 things can she buy?

_____ Answers may vary.

Would you use grams or kilograms to measure?
Circle the better answer.

4. the mass of an apple

(grams) kilograms

the mass of a shopping cart

grams (kilograms)

Use with Grade 2, Chapter 9, Lesson 10, pages 329–330. (279)

Daily Homework

9·10 Gram and Kilogram

Choose the better estimate.

1.

lighter than 1 kilogram
heavier than 1 kilogram *(circled)*
about the same as 1 kilogram

lighter than 1 kilogram *(circled)*
heavier than 1 kilogram
about the same as 1 kilogram

2.

lighter than 1 kilogram *(circled)*
heavier than 1 kilogram
about the same as 1 kilogram

lighter than 1 kilogram
heavier than 1 kilogram
about the same as 1 kilogram *(circled)*

Problem Solving

3. Martin buys 12 kilograms of birdseed. The birds eat 3 kilograms of birdseed. How much birdseed is left? _____ 9 _____ kilograms

Spiral Review

Draw the clock hands to show the end time.

4. 2 hours later:

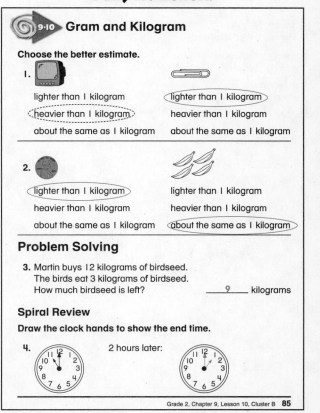

Grade 2, Chapter 9, Lesson 10, Cluster B **85**

Chapter 9 ~ Lesson 11

Practice

Liter

9-11 PRACTICE

Circle the better estimate.

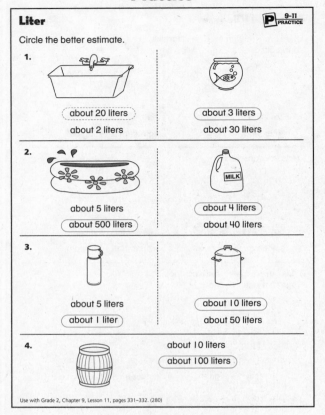

1.
- about 20 liters
- about 2 liters

- about 3 liters
- about 30 liters

2.
- about 5 liters
- about 500 liters

- about 4 liters
- about 40 liters

3.
- about 5 liters
- about 1 liter

- about 10 liters
- about 50 liters

4.
- about 10 liters
- about 100 liters

Use with Grade 2, Chapter 9, Lesson 11, pages 331–332. (280)

Reteach

Liter

9-11 RETEACH

A liter is used to measure liquids.

A bottle holds about ____ liter.

1. Ring the things that hold about 1 liter.

2. Ring the things that hold more than 1 liter.

3. Ring the things that hold less than 1 liter.

Use with Grade 2, Chapter 9, Lesson 11, pages 331–332. (281)

Enrich

Liter

9-11 ENRICH

Franny's Fish Store

Franny's Fish Store has these fish tanks. Franny needs to fill each tank.

How many of each container does she need to fill each tank?

Possible answers are shown.

Write the number below each container.

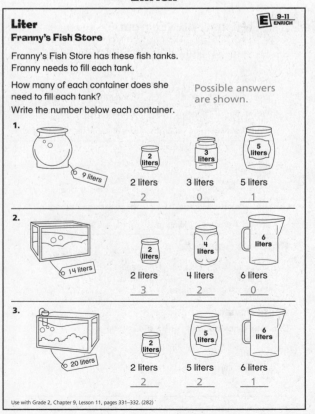

1. 9 liters

2 liters	3 liters	5 liters
2	0	1

2. 14 liters

2 liters	4 liters	6 liters
3	2	0

3. 20 liters

2 liters	5 liters	6 liters
2	2	1

Use with Grade 2, Chapter 9, Lesson 11, pages 331–332. (282)

Daily Homework

9-11 Liter

Choose the better estimate.

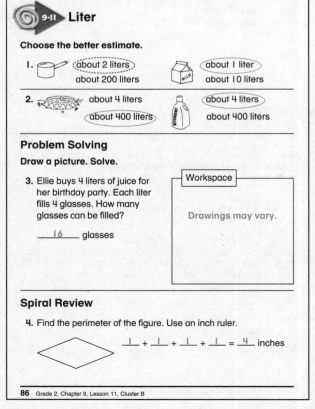

1.
- about 2 liters
- about 200 liters

- about 1 liter
- about 10 liters

2.
- about 4 liters
- about 400 liters

- about 4 liters
- about 400 liters

Problem Solving

Draw a picture. Solve.

3. Ellie buys 4 liters of juice for her birthday party. Each liter fills 4 glasses. How many glasses can be filled?

____16____ glasses

Workspace

Drawings may vary.

Spiral Review

4. Find the perimeter of the figure. Use an inch ruler.

$\underline{1} + \underline{1} + \underline{1} + \underline{1} = \underline{4}$ inches

Chapter 9 ~ Lesson 12

Practice

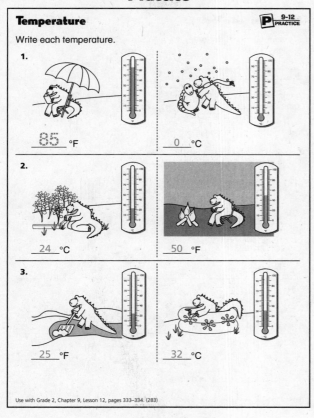

Temperature

Write each temperature.

1.

_85_ °F   _0_ °C

2.

_24_ °C   _50_ °F

3.

_25_ °F   _32_ °C

Use with Grade 2, Chapter 9, Lesson 12, pages 333–334. (283)

Reteach

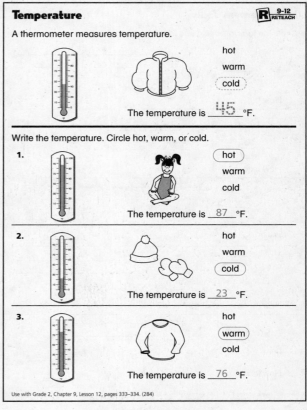

Temperature

A thermometer measures temperature.

hot
warm
(cold)

The temperature is _45_ °F.

Write the temperature. Circle hot, warm, or cold.

1. (hot) warm cold

The temperature is _87_ °F.

2. hot warm (cold)

The temperature is _23_ °F.

3. hot (warm) cold

The temperature is _76_ °F.

Use with Grade 2, Chapter 9, Lesson 12, pages 333–334. (284)

Enrich

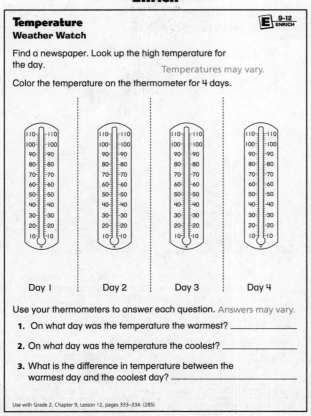

Temperature
Weather Watch

Find a newspaper. Look up the high temperature for the day. Temperatures may vary.

Color the temperature on the thermometer for 4 days.

Day 1   Day 2   Day 3   Day 4

Use your thermometers to answer each question. Answers may vary.

1. On what day was the temperature the warmest? _____

2. On what day was the temperature the coolest? _____

3. What is the difference in temperature between the warmest day and the coolest day? _____

Use with Grade 2, Chapter 9, Lesson 12, pages 333–334. (285)

Daily Homework

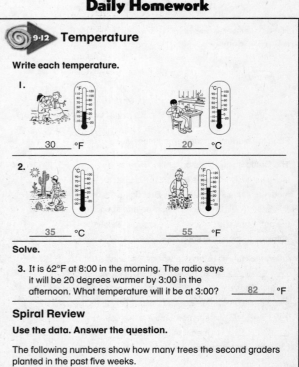

9·12 Temperature

Write each temperature.

1.

_30_ °F   _20_ °C

2.

_35_ °C   _55_ °F

Solve.

3. It is 62°F at 8:00 in the morning. The radio says it will be 20 degrees warmer by 3:00 in the afternoon. What temperature will it be at 3:00? _82_ °F

Spiral Review

Use the data. Answer the question.

The following numbers show how many trees the second graders planted in the past five weeks.

4, 7, 6, 12, 7

4. What is the range of the numbers? _8_

Grade 2, Chapter 9, Lesson 12, Cluster B **87**

Chapter 9 ~ Lesson 13

Practice

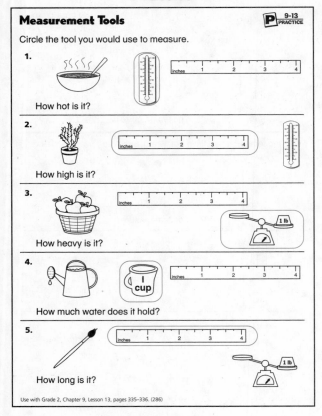

Measurement Tools

Circle the tool you would use to measure.

1. How hot is it?

2. How high is it?

3. How heavy is it?

4. How much water does it hold?

5. How long is it?

Reteach

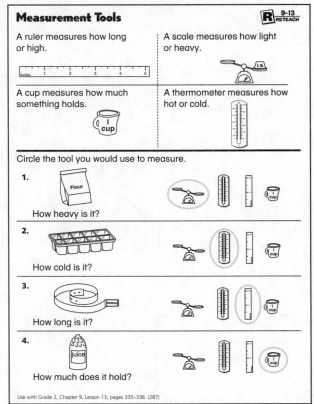

Measurement Tools

A ruler measures how long or high.

A scale measures how light or heavy.

A cup measures how much something holds.

A thermometer measures how hot or cold.

Circle the tool you would use to measure.

1. How heavy is it?

2. How cold is it?

3. How long is it?

4. How much does it hold?

Enrich

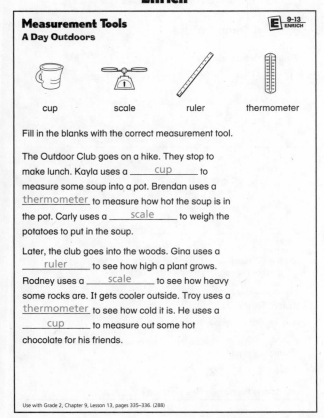

Measurement Tools
A Day Outdoors

cup   scale   ruler   thermometer

Fill in the blanks with the correct measurement tool.

The Outdoor Club goes on a hike. They stop to make lunch. Kayla uses a ____cup____ to measure some soup into a pot. Brendan uses a _thermometer_ to measure how hot the soup is in the pot. Carly uses a ____scale____ to weigh the potatoes to put in the soup.

Later, the club goes into the woods. Gina uses a ____ruler____ to see how high a plant grows. Rodney uses a ____scale____ to see how heavy some rocks are. It gets cooler outside. Troy uses a _thermometer_ to see how cold it is. He uses a ____cup____ to measure out some hot chocolate for his friends.

Daily Homework

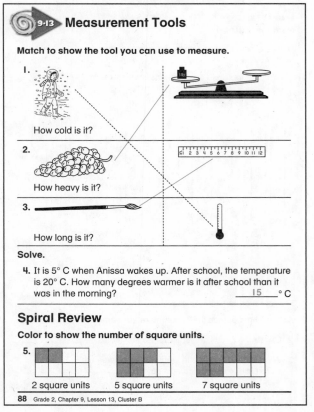

9-13 Measurement Tools

Match to show the tool you can use to measure.

1. How cold is it?

2. How heavy is it?

3. How long is it?

Solve.

4. It is 5° C when Anissa wakes up. After school, the temperature is 20° C. How many degrees warmer is it after school than it was in the morning? ____15____ ° C

Spiral Review

Color to show the number of square units.

5.
2 square units   5 square units   7 square units

Chapter 9 ~ Lesson 14

Part A Worksheet

Problem Solving: Application
Build a Dinosaur Diorama

Part A 9-14 WORKSHEET Decision Making

Plan a dinosaur diorama.

Decide what you will show.

You may use these dinosaurs.

Part A Worksheet

Problem Solving: Application
Build a Dinosaur Diorama

Part A 9-14 WORKSHEET Decision Making

List the items you used in your dinosaur diorama.

Measure and record the length, width, or height of each.

Check students' work.

Item	Length, Width, or Height

Part B Worksheet

Problem Solving: Application
What Can a Footprint Tell Us?

Part B 9-14 WORKSHEET Math & Science

1. Tell the length of each.

   Dinosaur footprint ___53___ inches

   Your footprint _____ inches

2. How much longer is the dinosaur footprint than your footprint?

   _____

3. How many times longer is the dinosaur footprint than your footprint?

   _____

4. Name another animal that you think has a larger footprint than yours. Explain your thinking.

   Answers may vary. Possible answer: An elephant would

   have a larger footprint because it is much larger than I am.

5. Name another animal that you think has a smaller footprint than yours. Explain your thinking.

   Answers may vary. Possible answer: A cat would have a

   smaller footprint because it is much smaller than I am.

Chapter 10 ~ Lesson 1

Practice

Solid Figures

Circle each named solid figure. Write how many faces, vertices, and edges.

Name	Solid Figure	Faces	Vertices	Edges
1. rectangular prism		6	8	12
2. pyramid		5	5	8
3. cube		6	8	12
4. pyramid		5	5	8
5. rectangular prism		6	8	12

Reteach

Solid Figures

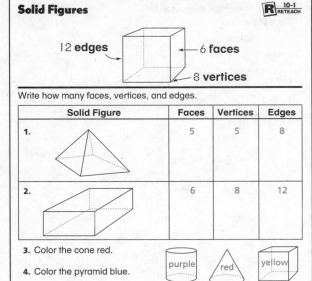

12 edges — 6 faces — 8 vertices

Write how many faces, vertices, and edges.

Solid Figure	Faces	Vertices	Edges
1.	5	5	8
2.	6	8	12

3. Color the cone red.

4. Color the pyramid blue.

5. Color the sphere green.

6. Color the cube yellow.

7. Color the cylinder purple.

8. Color the rectangular prism orange.

purple   red   yellow   orange   green   blue

Enrich

Solid Figures
What Solid Am I?

Trace each shape on a piece of paper.

Cut out the shapes. Fold along the dotted lines to make a solid figure.

Write the name of the solid figure. Choose from the list.

> cone
> cube
> cylinder
> pyramid
> rectangular prism

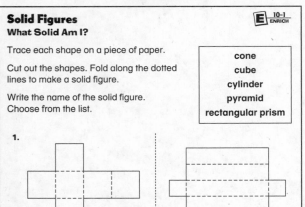

1.

cube   rectangular prism

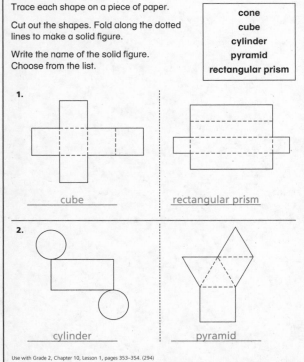

2.

cylinder   pyramid

Daily Homework

10-1 Solid Figures

Circle the solid figure that answers each question.

1. Which has 6 faces?

2. Which has 8 vertices?

3. Which has 8 edges?

4. Which has 5 faces?

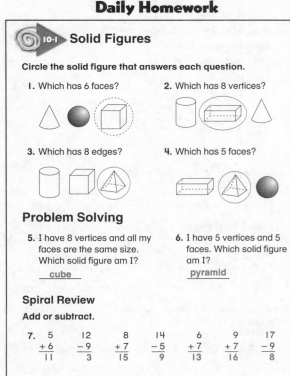

Problem Solving

5. I have 8 vertices and all my faces are the same size. Which solid figure am I?

cube

6. I have 5 vertices and 5 faces. Which solid figure am I?

pyramid

Spiral Review
Add or subtract.

7.						
5	12	8	14	6	9	17
+6	−9	+7	−5	+7	+7	−9
11	3	15	9	13	16	8

Chapter 10 ~ Lesson 2

Practice

Solid and Plane Figures

Circle each solid figure you can trace to make shapes.

1.

2.

3.

Reteach

Solid and Plane Figures

4 angles ← → 4 sides

Write how many sides and angles.

	Plane Figure	Sides	Angles
1.		4	4
2.		0	0
3.		3	3

4. Color the circle red.

5. Color the square blue.

6. Color the triangle green.

7. Color the rectangle yellow.

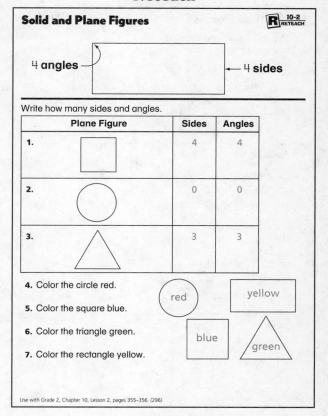

Enrich

Solid and Plane Figures
Fish for Solid Shapes

Cut out the cards below. Mix up the cards.

Give each player two cards. Put the rest in a pile face down. Take turns with a partner.

- See if you can make a solid shape with the cards in your hand. If so, put them down and take another card.

- If not, ask your partner for a shape you need.

- If your partner does not have that shape, take a card from the pile.

cube

rectangular prism

cylinder

cone

pyramid

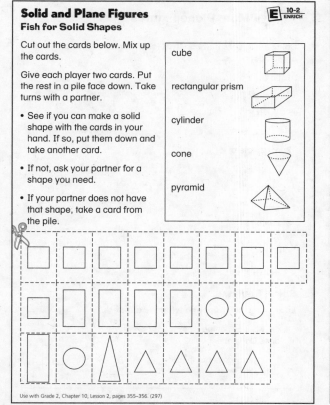

Daily Homework

10-2 Solid and Plane Figures

Circle each solid figure you can trace to make the shapes.

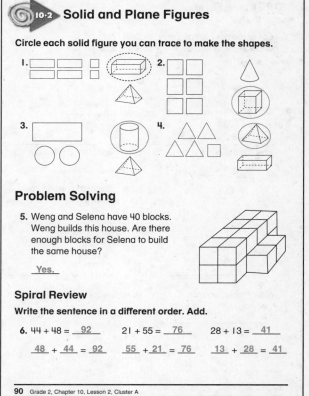

Problem Solving

5. Weng and Selena have 40 blocks. Weng builds this house. Are there enough blocks for Selena to build the same house?

___Yes.___

Spiral Review

Write the sentence in a different order. Add.

6. 44 + 48 = __92__   21 + 55 = __76__   28 + 13 = __41__

__48__ + __44__ = 92   __55__ + __21__ = 76   __13__ + __28__ = 41

Chapter 10 ~ Lesson 3

Practice

P 10-3 PRACTICE

MORE Plane Figures

Tell how many sides and angles.
Then color each named figure.

1. quadrilateral

_____ sides

_____ angles

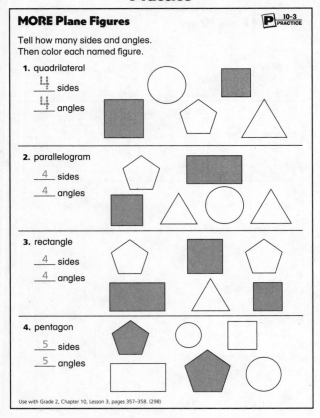

2. parallelogram

__4__ sides

__4__ angles

3. rectangle

__4__ sides

__4__ angles

4. pentagon

__5__ sides

__5__ angles

Use with Grade 2, Chapter 10, Lesson 3, pages 357–358. (298)

Reteach

R 10-3 RETEACH

MORE Plane Figures

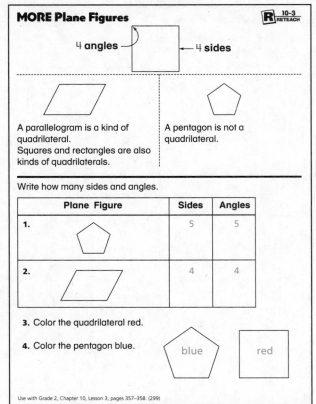

4 angles ← 4 sides

A parallelogram is a kind of quadrilateral.
Squares and rectangles are also kinds of quadrilaterals.

A pentagon is not a quadrilateral.

Write how many sides and angles.

Plane Figure	Sides	Angles
1.	5	5
2.	4	4

3. Color the quadrilateral red.

4. Color the pentagon blue.

blue   red

Use with Grade 2, Chapter 10, Lesson 3, pages 357–358. (299)

Enrich

E 10-3 ENRICH

MORE Plane Figures
Shape Shifts

1. Look at the dot pattern. Draw the next quadrilateral. Write how many dots in each.

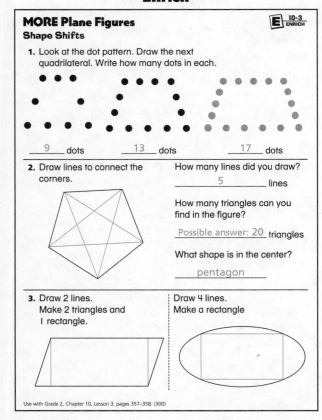

__9__ dots   __13__ dots   __17__ dots

2. Draw lines to connect the corners.

How many lines did you draw?

__5__ lines

How many triangles can you find in the figure?

Possible answer: 20 triangles

What shape is in the center?

__pentagon__

3. Draw 2 lines.
Make 2 triangles and
1 rectangle.

Draw 4 lines.
Make a rectangle

Use with Grade 2, Chapter 10, Lesson 3, pages 357–358. (300)

Daily Homework

10-3 More Plane Figures

Color the figures named. Then tell how many sides and angles each has.

1. parallelogram

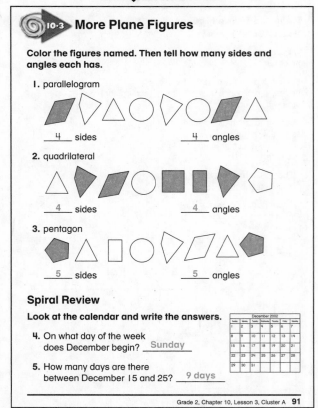

__4__ sides   __4__ angles

2. quadrilateral

__4__ sides   __4__ angles

3. pentagon

__5__ sides   __5__ angles

Spiral Review

Look at the calendar and write the answers.

4. On what day of the week does December begin? __Sunday__

5. How many days are there between December 15 and 25? __9 days__

December 2002

Grade 2, Chapter 10, Lesson 3, Cluster A **91**

Chapter 10 ~ Lesson 4

Practice

Make Figures

The pattern blocks were used to make new figures.
Complete the chart. Answers may vary. Sample new figures are given.

Pattern blocks I used	New figure	How many sides?	How many corners?	Name of new figure
1.		6	6	hexagon
2.		4	4	square
3.		4	4	square
4.		4	4	rectangle

Use with Grade 2, Chapter 10, Lesson 4, pages 359–360. (301)

Reteach

Make Figures

Use △ and ☐ to make figures.

__2__ triangles   __2__ rectangles

__4__ sides __4__ corners   __4__ sides __4__ corners

Use triangles to make new figures.

	How many sides?	How many corners?
1. Make a hexagon.	6	6
2. Make a trapezoid.	4	4

Use squares to make a new figure.

	How many sides?	How many corners?
3. Make a quadrilateral.	4	4

Use with Grade 2, Chapter 10, Lesson 4, pages 359–360. (302)

Enrich

Make Figures
Which Blocks Do You Use?

Use pattern blocks to make each figure.
Write how many of each kind of block you use.

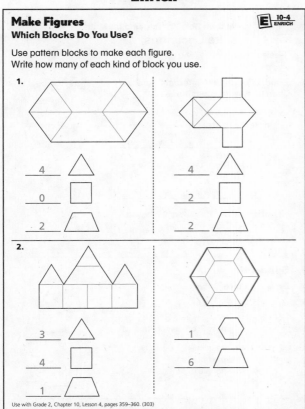

1.

__4__   __4__

__0__   __2__

__2__   __2__

2.

__3__   __1__

__4__   __6__

__1__

Use with Grade 2, Chapter 10, Lesson 4, pages 359–360. (303)

Daily Homework

10-4 Make Figures

Use pattern blocks to make new figures. Complete the chart.

Use these blocks.	Make a new figure.	How many sides?	How many corners?	Name of new figure
1.		4	4	parallelogram
2.		6	6	hexagon
3.		4	4	rectangle

Problem Solving

4. Kira made this figure using 2 pattern blocks.
What were the figures that Kira used?

_____ square and trapezoid _____

Draw a line to show how Kira put the figures together.

Spiral Review

Subtract.

5.

65	59	73	66	84	75
− 9	− 27	− 47	− 38	− 31	− 57
56	32	26	28	53	18

Chapter 10~ Lesson 5

Practice

Problem Solving: Reading for Math
Make Decisions

Andre is building a house.
He uses different figures.

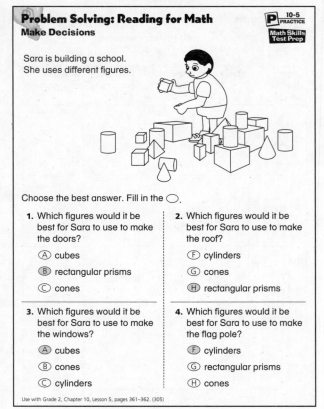

Build a house. Use different figures.
Then answer the questions.

1. Which figure did you use to make the door? Why?

_____

_____

Answers may vary. Possible answer: Drawing may show rectangular prism. A door is taller than it is wide.

2. Which figures did you use to make the windows? Why?

_____

_____

Answers may vary. Possible answer: Drawing may show cubes and rectangular prisms. Windows have square corners.

3. Which figure did you use to make the roof? Why?

_____

_____

Answers may vary. Possible answer: Drawing may show triangular prism. Roofs are slanted.

4. What does the front of the house look like? Draw the house.

_____

_____

Drawings may vary.

Use with Grade 2, Chapter 10, Lesson 5, pages 361–362. (304)

Practice

Problem Solving: Reading for Math
Make Decisions

Sara is building a school.
She uses different figures.

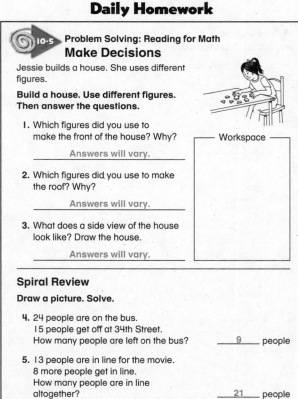

Choose the best answer. Fill in the ◯.

1. Which figures would it be best for Sara to use to make the doors?
   - Ⓐ cubes
   - Ⓑ rectangular prisms
   - Ⓒ cones

2. Which figures would it be best for Sara to use to make the roof?
   - Ⓕ cylinders
   - Ⓖ cones
   - Ⓗ rectangular prisms

3. Which figures would it be best for Sara to use to make the windows?
   - Ⓐ cubes
   - Ⓑ cones
   - Ⓒ cylinders

4. Which figures would it be best for Sara to use to make the flag pole?
   - Ⓕ cylinders
   - Ⓖ rectangular prisms
   - Ⓗ cones

Use with Grade 2, Chapter 10, Lesson 5, pages 361–362. (305)

Practice

Problem Solving: Reading for Math
Make Decisions

Clayton is building a barn.
He uses different figures.

Choose the best answer. Fill in the ◯.

1. Which figures would it be best for Clayton to use to make the doors?
   - Ⓐ cones
   - Ⓑ rectangular prisms
   - Ⓒ cylinders

2. Which figures would it be best for Clayton to use to make the silo?
   - Ⓕ cylinders
   - Ⓖ cubes
   - Ⓗ rectangular prisms

Build a barn. Use different figures.
Then answer the questions.

3. Which figures did you use to make the main part? Why?

Answers may vary. Possible answer: rectangular prisms; the

walls of a barn are straight sides that make square corners.

4. What does the front of the barn look like? Draw the barn.
Drawings may vary.

Use with Grade 2, Chapter 10, Lesson 5, pages 361–362. (306)

Daily Homework

10-5

Problem Solving: Reading for Math
Make Decisions

Jessie builds a house. She uses different figures.

**Build a house. Use different figures.
Then answer the questions.**

1. Which figures did you use to make the front of the house? Why?

Answers will vary.

2. Which figures did you use to make the roof? Why?

Answers will vary.

3. What does a side view of the house look like? Draw the house.

Answers will vary.

Workspace

Spiral Review

Draw a picture. Solve.

4. 24 people are on the bus.
15 people get off at 34th Street.
How many people are left on the bus? _____9_____ people

5. 13 people are in line for the movie.
8 more people get in line.
How many people are in line altogether? _____21_____ people

Grade 2, Chapter 10, Lesson 5, Cluster A **93**

Chapter 10 ~ Lesson 6

Practice

Problem Solving: Strategy
Act It Out

10-6 PRACTICE

Use triangles and squares to make each figure.

1.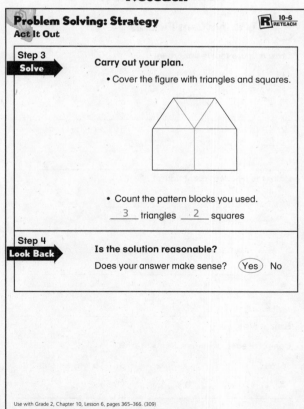
__2__ triangles

2.
__6__ triangles

3.
__1__ squares __2__ triangles

4.
__2__ triangles __2__ squares

5.
__1__ triangles __2__ squares

6.
__6__ triangles __2__ squares

Mixed Strategy Review
Solve.

7. Jenny had 35 strawberries in a bowl. She ate 11 of them. How many strawberries does she have left?
__24__ strawberries

8. **Create a problem** you would act out to solve. Share it with others.
_____
_____

Use with Grade 2, Chapter 10, Lesson 6, pages 365–366. (307)

Reteach

Problem Solving: Strategy
Act It Out

10-6 RETEACH

Page 366, Problem 4
Use triangles and squares to make the figure.

_____ triangles _____ squares

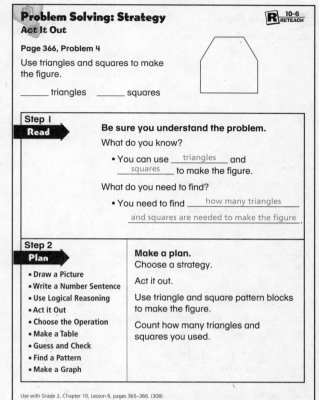

Step 1 Read	Be sure you understand the problem. What do you know? • You can use __triangles__ and __squares__ to make the figure. What do you need to find? • You need to find __how many triangles and squares are needed to make the figure__
Step 2 Plan	**Make a plan.** Choose a strategy. Act it out. Use triangle and square pattern blocks to make the figure. Count how many triangles and squares you used.

- Draw a Picture
- Write a Number Sentence
- Use Logical Reasoning
- Act it Out
- Choose the Operation
- Make a Table
- Guess and Check
- Find a Pattern
- Make a Graph

Use with Grade 2, Chapter 10, Lesson 6, pages 365–366. (308)

Reteach

Problem Solving: Strategy
Act It Out

10-6 RETEACH

Step 3 Solve	Carry out your plan. • Cover the figure with triangles and squares.

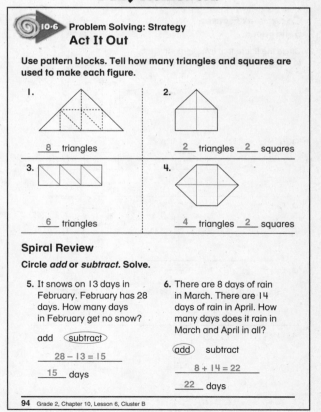

• Count the pattern blocks you used.
__3__ triangles __2__ squares

Step 4 Look Back	**Is the solution reasonable?** Does your answer make sense? (Yes) No

Use with Grade 2, Chapter 10, Lesson 6, pages 365–366. (309)

© McGraw-Hill School Division

Daily Homework

10-6 **Problem Solving: Strategy**
Act It Out

Use pattern blocks. Tell how many triangles and squares are used to make each figure.

1.
__8__ triangles

2.
__2__ triangles __2__ squares

3.
__6__ triangles

4.
__4__ triangles __2__ squares

Spiral Review

Circle *add* or *subtract*. Solve.

5. It snows on 13 days in February. February has 28 days. How many days in February get no snow?
add (subtract)
$28 - 13 = 15$
__15__ days

6. There are 8 days of rain in March. There are 14 days of rain in April. How many days does it rain in March and April in all?
(add) subtract
$8 + 14 = 22$
__22__ days

94 Grade 2, Chapter 10, Lesson 6, Cluster B

Chapter 10 ~ Lesson 7

Practice

Congruent Figures

P 10-7 PRACTICE

Draw a figure that is congruent.

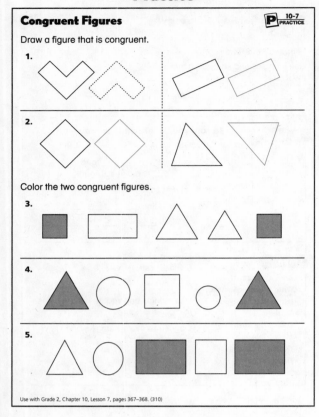

1.

2.

Color the two congruent figures.

3.

4.

5.

Use with Grade 2, Chapter 10, Lesson 7, pages 367–368. (310)

Reteach

Congruent Figures

R 10-7 RETEACH

Congruent figures have the same size and shape.

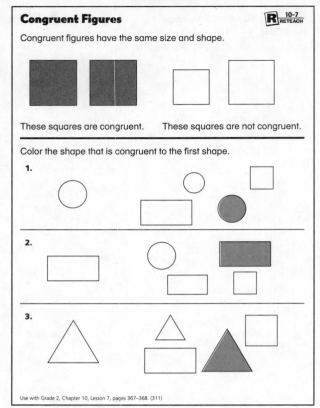

These squares are congruent.   These squares are not congruent.

Color the shape that is congruent to the first shape.

1.

2.

3.

Use with Grade 2, Chapter 10, Lesson 7, pages 367–368. (311)

Enrich

Congruent Figures
Solid Faces

E 10-7 ENRICH

Circle the figure that is congruent to the given face of this solid.

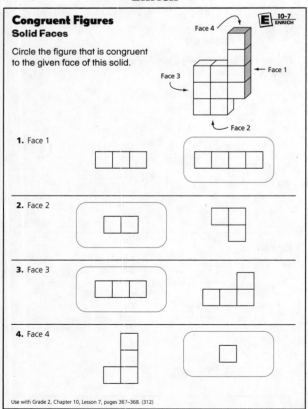

Face 4
Face 1
Face 3
Face 2

1. Face 1

2. Face 2

3. Face 3

4. Face 4

Use with Grade 2, Chapter 10, Lesson 7, pages 367–368. (312)

Daily Homework

10-7 Congruent Figures

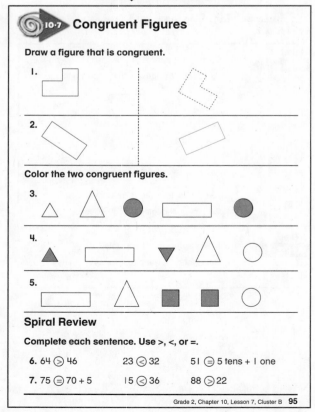

Draw a figure that is congruent.

1.

2.

Color the two congruent figures.

3.

4.

5.

Spiral Review

Complete each sentence. Use >, <, or =.

6. $64 > 46$ $23 < 32$ $51 = 5$ tens + 1 one

7. $75 = 70 + 5$ $15 < 36$ $88 > 22$

Chapter 10 ~ Lesson 8

Practice

Symmetry

Draw a matching part for the figure.

1.

2.

3.

Reteach

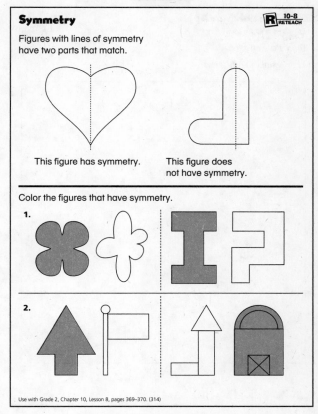

Symmetry

Figures with lines of symmetry have two parts that match.

This figure has symmetry.   This figure does not have symmetry.

Color the figures that have symmetry.

1.

2.

Enrich

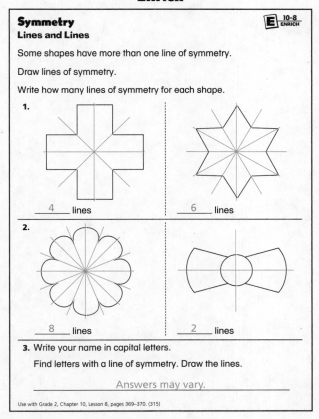

Symmetry
Lines and Lines

Some shapes have more than one line of symmetry.

Draw lines of symmetry.

Write how many lines of symmetry for each shape.

1.

 4 lines   6 lines

2.

 8 lines   2 lines

3. Write your name in capital letters.

Find letters with a line of symmetry. Draw the lines.

Answers may vary.

Daily Homework

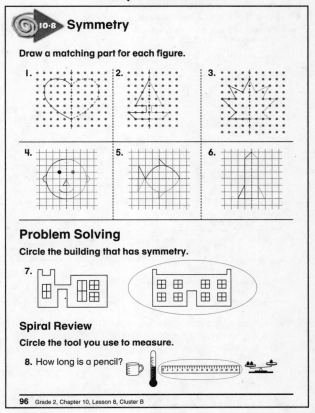

10-8 Symmetry

Draw a matching part for each figure.

1.   2.   3.

4.   5.   6.

Problem Solving

Circle the building that has symmetry.

7.

Spiral Review

Circle the tool you use to measure.

8. How long is a pencil?

Chapter 10 ~ Lesson 9

Part A Worksheet

Problem Solving: Application
Design a City Building

Part A | 10-9 WORKSHEET | Decision Making

Plan a city building.

Draw what it will look like.

Check students' drawings.

Part A Worksheet

Problem Solving: Application
Design a City Building

Part A | 10-9 WORKSHEET | Decision Making

Tell what shapes you used in your building.

Tell why you used each shape.

Kind of Shape	Why Used

Check students' work.

Part B Worksheet

Problem Solving: Application
What Kinds of Shapes Can You Find at Playgrounds? Answers may vary.

Part B | 10-9 WORKSHEET | Math & Science

1. What playground structure did you build?

_____

2. Tell about the shapes you used to build your structure.

Kind of Shape	How Many	Why Shape Used

3. What shape did you use most often?

_____

4. What shape did you use least often?

_____

5. What if you designed another playground structure.
What shape would you use most often?
Tell why you think this.

_____

Chapter 11 ~ Lesson 1

Practice

Halves, Fourths, and Eighths

P 11-1 PRACTICE

Color one part of each figure.
Then write the fraction for the part.

1. $\frac{1}{2}$ $\frac{1}{8}$ $\frac{1}{4}$

2. $\frac{1}{2}$ $\frac{1}{2}$ $\frac{1}{4}$

3. $\frac{1}{4}$ $\frac{1}{8}$ $\frac{1}{2}$

4. $\frac{1}{8}$ $\frac{1}{2}$ $\frac{1}{4}$

Use with Grade 2, Chapter 11, Lesson 1, pages 387–388. (319)

Reteach

Halves, Fourths, and Eighths

R 11-1 RETEACH

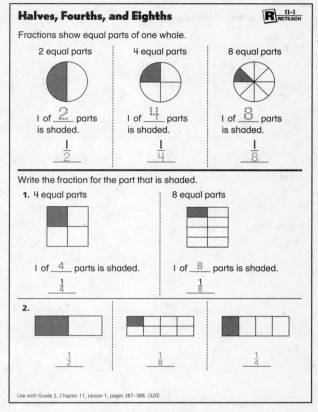

Fractions show equal parts of one whole.

2 equal parts   4 equal parts   8 equal parts

1 of _2_ parts is shaded.   1 of _4_ parts is shaded.   1 of _8_ parts is shaded.

$\frac{1}{2}$ $\frac{1}{4}$ $\frac{1}{8}$

Write the fraction for the part that is shaded.

1. 4 equal parts   8 equal parts

1 of _4_ parts is shaded.   1 of _8_ parts is shaded.

$\frac{1}{4}$ $\frac{1}{8}$

2. $\frac{1}{2}$ $\frac{1}{8}$ $\frac{1}{4}$

Use with Grade 2, Chapter 11, Lesson 1, pages 387–388. (320)

Enrich

Halves, Fourths, and Eighths
Pattern Block Shapes

E 11-1 ENRICH

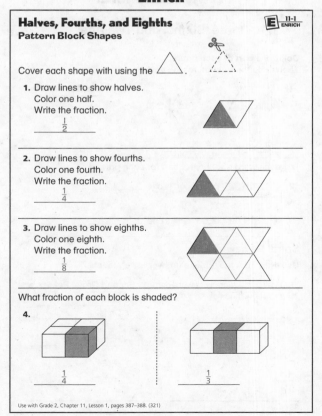

Cover each shape with using the △.

1. Draw lines to show halves.
   Color one half.
   Write the fraction.

   $\frac{1}{2}$

2. Draw lines to show fourths.
   Color one fourth.
   Write the fraction.

   $\frac{1}{4}$

3. Draw lines to show eighths.
   Color one eighth.
   Write the fraction.

   $\frac{1}{8}$

What fraction of each block is shaded?

4. $\frac{1}{4}$ $\frac{1}{3}$

Use with Grade 2, Chapter 11, Lesson 1, pages 387–388. (321)

Daily Homework

11-1 Halves, Fourths, and Eighths

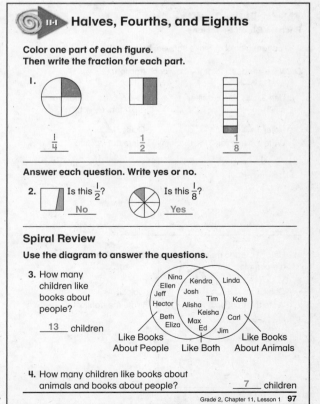

Color one part of each figure.
Then write the fraction for each part.

1. $\frac{1}{4}$ $\frac{1}{2}$ $\frac{1}{8}$

Answer each question. Write yes or no.

2. Is this $\frac{1}{2}$?   __No__   Is this $\frac{1}{8}$?   __Yes__

Spiral Review

Use the diagram to answer the questions.

3. How many children like books about people?

   __13__ children

   Nina, Ellen, Jeff, Hector, Beth, Eliza — Kendra, Josh, Alisha, Keisha, Max, Ed, Tim — Linda, Kate, Carl, Jim

   Like Books About People   Like Both   Like Books About Animals

4. How many children like books about animals and books about people?   __7__ children

Chapter 11 ~ Lesson 2

Practice

Thirds, Sixths, Twelfths

11-2 PRACTICE

Color one part of each figure.
Then write the fraction for the part.

1.

$\frac{1}{6}$　　$\frac{1}{12}$　　$\frac{1}{6}$

2.

$\frac{1}{3}$　　$\frac{1}{12}$　　$\frac{1}{3}$

Write the word and the fraction for each word.

3. Each part is one __sixth__, or $\frac{1}{6}$.

4. Each part is one __third__, or $\frac{1}{3}$.

5. Each part is one __twelfth__, or $\frac{1}{12}$.

Use with Grade 2, Chapter 11, Lesson 2, pages 389–390. (322)

Reteach

Thirds, Sixths, Twelfths

11-2 RETEACH

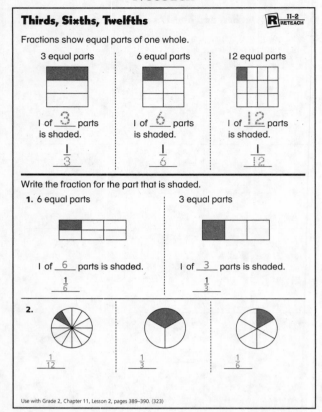

Fractions show equal parts of one whole.

| 3 equal parts | 6 equal parts | 12 equal parts |

I of __3__ parts is shaded.　　I of __6__ parts is shaded.　　I of __12__ parts is shaded.

$\frac{1}{3}$　　$\frac{1}{6}$　　$\frac{1}{12}$

Write the fraction for the part that is shaded.

1. 6 equal parts　　　3 equal parts

I of __6__ parts is shaded.　　I of __3__ parts is shaded.

$\frac{1}{6}$　　$\frac{1}{3}$

2.

$\frac{1}{12}$　　$\frac{1}{3}$　　$\frac{1}{6}$

Use with Grade 2, Chapter 11, Lesson 2, pages 389–390. (323)

Enrich

Thirds, Sixths, Twelfths
Pattern Block Fractions

11-2 ENRICH

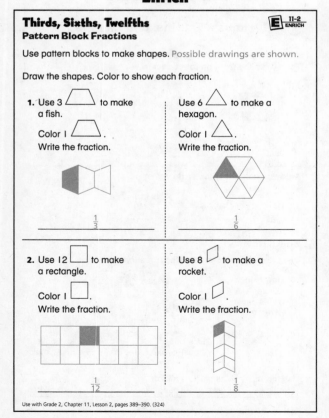

Use pattern blocks to make shapes. Possible drawings are shown.

Draw the shapes. Color to show each fraction.

1. Use 3 ⬡ to make a fish.

Color I ⬡.
Write the fraction.

$\frac{1}{3}$

Use 6 △ to make a hexagon.

Color I △.
Write the fraction.

$\frac{1}{6}$

2. Use 12 ☐ to make a rectangle.

Color I ☐.
Write the fraction.

$\frac{1}{12}$

Use 8 ◇ to make a rocket.

Color I ◇.
Write the fraction.

$\frac{1}{8}$

Use with Grade 2, Chapter 11, Lesson 2, pages 389–390. (324)

Daily Homework

11-2 Thirds, Sixths, and Twelfths

Color one part of each figure.
Then write the fraction for the part.

1.

$\frac{1}{3}$　　$\frac{1}{12}$　　$\frac{1}{6}$

Write the word and the fraction for each part.

2. Each part is one __third__, or $\frac{1}{3}$.

3. Each part is one __twelfth__, or $\frac{1}{12}$.

Spiral Review

Use data from the table to answer the question.

4. How many more cats were at the pet show than fish?

___7___ cats

Second Grade Pet Show

Cats	ⵏⵏⵏ ⵏⵏⵏ II
Dogs	ⵏⵏⵏ III
Fish	ⵏⵏⵏ
Hamsters	III

Chapter 11 ~ Lesson 3

Practice

P 11-3 PRACTICE

MORE Fractions

Write the fraction for the part that is shaded.

1.

$\frac{3}{8}$ $\frac{2}{4}$ $\frac{2}{6}$

2.

$\frac{4}{12}$ $\frac{5}{6}$ $\frac{2}{3}$

Color to show the fraction.

3.

$\frac{5}{8}$ $\frac{3}{4}$ $\frac{3}{6}$

4.

$\frac{9}{12}$ $\frac{2}{3}$ $\frac{2}{8}$

Use with Grade 2, Chapter 11, Lesson 3, pages 391–392. (325)

Reteach

R 11-3 RETEACH

MORE Fractions

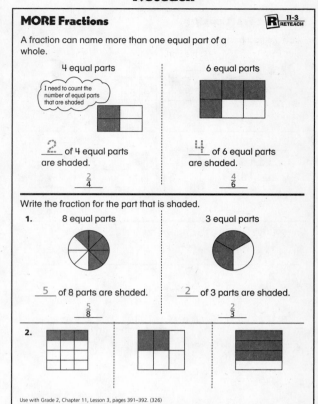

A fraction can name more than one equal part of a whole.

4 equal parts

I need to count the number of equal parts that are shaded

$\underline{2}$ of 4 equal parts are shaded.

$\frac{2}{4}$

6 equal parts

$\underline{4}$ of 6 equal parts are shaded.

$\frac{4}{6}$

Write the fraction for the part that is shaded.

1. 8 equal parts   3 equal parts

$\underline{5}$ of 8 parts are shaded. $\underline{2}$ of 3 parts are shaded.

$\frac{5}{8}$ $\frac{2}{3}$

2.

Use with Grade 2, Chapter 11, Lesson 3, pages 391–392. (326)

Enrich

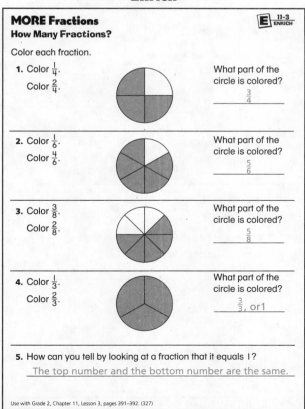

E 11-3 ENRICH

MORE Fractions

How Many Fractions?

Color each fraction.

1. Color $\frac{1}{4}$.
Color $\frac{2}{4}$.

What part of the circle is colored?
$\frac{3}{4}$

2. Color $\frac{1}{6}$.
Color $\frac{4}{6}$.

What part of the circle is colored?
$\frac{5}{6}$

3. Color $\frac{3}{8}$.
Color $\frac{2}{8}$.

What part of the circle is colored?
$\frac{5}{8}$

4. Color $\frac{1}{3}$.
Color $\frac{2}{3}$.

What part of the circle is colored?
$\frac{3}{3}$, or 1

5. How can you tell by looking at a fraction that it equals 1?
The top number and the bottom number are the same.

Use with Grade 2, Chapter 11, Lesson 3, pages 391–392. (327)

Daily Homework

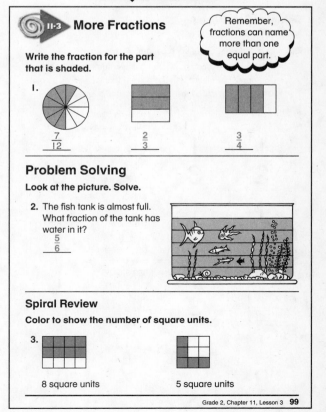

11-3 **More Fractions**

Remember, fractions can name more than one equal part.

Write the fraction for the part that is shaded.

1.

$\frac{7}{12}$ $\frac{2}{3}$ $\frac{3}{4}$

Problem Solving

Look at the picture. Solve.

2. The fish tank is almost full. What fraction of the tank has water in it?
$\frac{5}{6}$

Spiral Review

Color to show the number of square units.

3.

8 square units   5 square units

Grade 2, Chapter 11, Lesson 3 **99**

Chapter 11 ~ Lesson 4

Practice

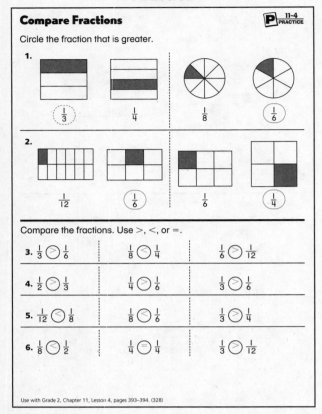

Compare Fractions — P 11-4 PRACTICE

Circle the fraction that is greater.

1. $\frac{1}{3}$ (circled) $\frac{1}{4}$ $\frac{1}{8}$ $\frac{1}{6}$ (circled)

2. $\frac{1}{12}$ $\frac{1}{6}$ (circled) $\frac{1}{6}$ $\frac{1}{4}$ (circled)

Compare the fractions. Use >, <, or =.

3. $\frac{1}{3}$ > $\frac{1}{6}$ 　 $\frac{1}{8}$ < $\frac{1}{4}$ 　 $\frac{1}{6}$ > $\frac{1}{12}$

4. $\frac{1}{2}$ > $\frac{1}{3}$ 　 $\frac{1}{4}$ > $\frac{1}{6}$ 　 $\frac{1}{3}$ > $\frac{1}{6}$

5. $\frac{1}{12}$ < $\frac{1}{8}$ 　 $\frac{1}{8}$ < $\frac{1}{6}$ 　 $\frac{1}{3}$ > $\frac{1}{4}$

6. $\frac{1}{8}$ < $\frac{1}{2}$ 　 $\frac{1}{4}$ = $\frac{1}{4}$ 　 $\frac{1}{3}$ > $\frac{1}{12}$

Use with Grade 2, Chapter 11, Lesson 4, pages 393–394. (328)

Reteach

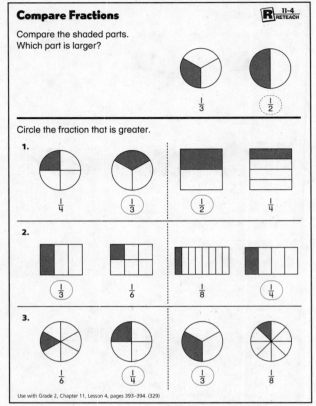

Compare Fractions — R 11-4 RETEACH

Compare the shaded parts.
Which part is larger?

$\frac{1}{3}$ $\frac{1}{2}$ (circled)

Circle the fraction that is greater.

1. $\frac{1}{4}$ $\frac{1}{3}$ (circled) $\frac{1}{2}$ (circled) $\frac{1}{4}$

2. $\frac{1}{3}$ (circled) $\frac{1}{6}$ $\frac{1}{8}$ $\frac{1}{4}$ (circled)

3. $\frac{1}{6}$ $\frac{1}{4}$ (circled) $\frac{1}{3}$ (circled) $\frac{1}{8}$

Use with Grade 2, Chapter 11, Lesson 4, pages 393–394. (329)

Enrich

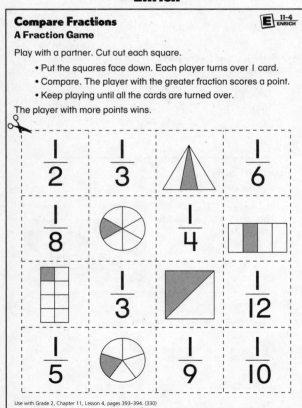

Compare Fractions — E 11-4 ENRICH
A Fraction Game

Play with a partner. Cut out each square.

• Put the squares face down. Each player turns over 1 card.
• Compare. The player with the greater fraction scores a point.
• Keep playing until all the cards are turned over.

The player with more points wins.

$\frac{1}{2}$ 　 $\frac{1}{3}$ 　 △ 　 $\frac{1}{6}$

$\frac{1}{8}$ 　 ○ 　 $\frac{1}{4}$ 　 ▭

▦ 　 $\frac{1}{3}$ 　 ◨ 　 $\frac{1}{12}$

$\frac{1}{5}$ 　 ○ 　 $\frac{1}{9}$ 　 $\frac{1}{10}$

Use with Grade 2, Chapter 11, Lesson 4, pages 393–394. (330)

Daily Homework

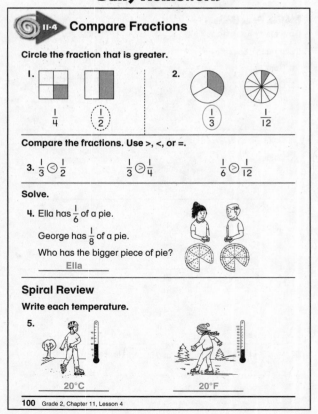

11-4 **Compare Fractions**

Circle the fraction that is greater.

1. $\frac{1}{4}$ $\frac{1}{2}$ (circled)   　2. $\frac{1}{3}$ (circled) $\frac{1}{12}$

Compare the fractions. Use >, <, or =.

3. $\frac{1}{3}$ < $\frac{1}{2}$ 　 $\frac{1}{3}$ > $\frac{1}{4}$ 　 $\frac{1}{6}$ > $\frac{1}{12}$

Solve.

4. Ella has $\frac{1}{6}$ of a pie.

George has $\frac{1}{8}$ of a pie.

Who has the bigger piece of pie?

___Ella___

Spiral Review

Write each temperature.

5. ___20°C___ 　 ___20°F___

Chapter 11 ~ Lesson 5

Practice

Problem Solving: Reading for Math
Making Predictions

P 11-5 PRACTICE Reading Skill

Callie and Ben worked at the bake sale.

Callie sold $\frac{1}{2}$ of a cake.

Ben sold $\frac{1}{8}$ of a cake.

Predict part of which cake Ben sold.

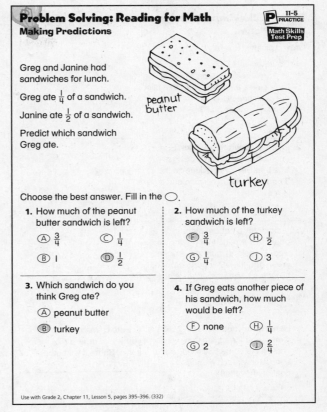
carrot cake
chocolate

Solve.

1. How much of the carrot cake is left? $\frac{1}{2}$

2. How much of the chocolate cake is left? $\frac{7}{8}$

3. Part of which cake do you think Ben sold? __chocolate__

4. Is it possible that Ben sold more cake than Callie?

   Explain.
   It is possible because his cake was larger.

5. If Callie sold another piece of her cake, how much would be left? __none__

6. If Ben sold another piece of his cake, how much would be left? $\frac{6}{8}$

Practice

Problem Solving: Reading for Math
Making Predictions

P 11-5 PRACTICE Math Skills Test Prep

Greg and Janine had sandwiches for lunch.

Greg ate $\frac{1}{4}$ of a sandwich.

Janine ate $\frac{1}{2}$ of a sandwich.

Predict which sandwich Greg ate.

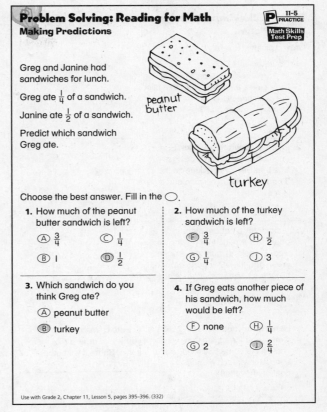
peanut butter
turkey

Choose the best answer. Fill in the ◯.

1. How much of the peanut butter sandwich is left?
   - Ⓐ $\frac{3}{4}$
   - Ⓒ $\frac{1}{4}$
   - Ⓑ 1
   - Ⓓ $\frac{1}{2}$

2. How much of the turkey sandwich is left?
   - Ⓕ $\frac{3}{4}$
   - Ⓗ $\frac{1}{2}$
   - Ⓖ $\frac{1}{4}$
   - Ⓙ 3

3. Which sandwich do you think Greg ate?
   - Ⓐ peanut butter
   - Ⓑ turkey

4. If Greg eats another piece of his sandwich, how much would be left?
   - Ⓕ none
   - Ⓗ $\frac{1}{4}$
   - Ⓖ 2
   - Ⓙ $\frac{2}{4}$

Practice

Problem Solving: Reading for Math
Making Predictions

P 11-5 PRACTICE Math Skills Test Prep

Terry and Mitch were eating cookies at a class party.

Terry had eaten $\frac{1}{6}$ of her cookie.

Mitch had eaten $\frac{1}{3}$ of his cookie.

Predict which cookie Mitch is eating.

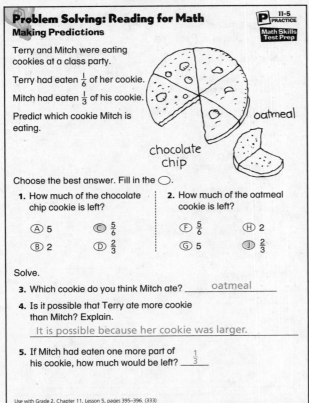
oatmeal
chocolate chip

Choose the best answer. Fill in the ◯.

1. How much of the chocolate chip cookie is left?
   - Ⓐ 5
   - Ⓒ $\frac{5}{6}$
   - Ⓑ 2
   - Ⓓ $\frac{2}{3}$

2. How much of the oatmeal cookie is left?
   - Ⓕ $\frac{5}{6}$
   - Ⓗ 2
   - Ⓖ 5
   - Ⓙ $\frac{2}{3}$

Solve.

3. Which cookie do you think Mitch ate? __oatmeal__

4. Is it possible that Terry ate more cookie than Mitch? Explain.
   It is possible because her cookie was larger.

5. If Mitch had eaten one more part of his cookie, how much would be left? $\frac{1}{3}$

Daily Homework

11-5 Problem Solving: Reading for Math
Making Predictions

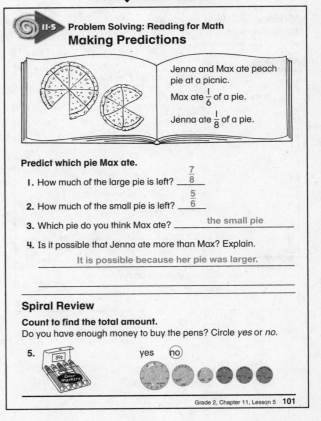

Jenna and Max ate peach pie at a picnic.

Max ate $\frac{1}{6}$ of a pie.

Jenna ate $\frac{1}{8}$ of a pie.

Predict which pie Max ate.

1. How much of the large pie is left? $\frac{7}{8}$

2. How much of the small pie is left? $\frac{5}{6}$

3. Which pie do you think Max ate? __the small pie__

4. Is it possible that Jenna ate more than Max? Explain.
   It is possible because her pie was larger.

Spiral Review

Count to find the total amount.
Do you have enough money to buy the pens? Circle *yes* or *no*.

5. yes ⓝo

Chapter 11 ~ Lesson 6

Practice

Problem Solving: Strategy
Draw a Picture

Draw a picture. Solve.

1. Courtney cuts a pizza into 8 slices that are the same size. Three slices have olives on them. The other slices are plain cheese. What fraction of the pizza has olives on it?

   $\frac{3}{8}$

2. Laura is decorating a cake. She puts red sprinkles on 2 parts of it. She puts yellow sprinkles on the other 3 parts of it. What fraction of the cake is red?

   $\frac{2}{5}$

3. Victor folds a square piece of paper into 4 parts that are the same size. He colors 1 part of the paper green and the other parts orange. What fraction of the paper is orange?

Mixed Strategy Review

Solve.

4. Henry had 1 quarter, 3 dimes, and 9 pennies in his pocket. He spent 35¢ for a snack. How much money does he have left?

   29 ¢

5. **Create a problem** for which you would draw a picture to solve. Share it with others.

   _____

   _____

Reteach

Problem Solving: Strategy
Draw a Picture

Page 400, Problem 2
Jackie makes a big banner for the school party. She paints 4 parts of it blue. It has 5 equal parts. She paints 1 part yellow. What fraction of the banner is yellow?

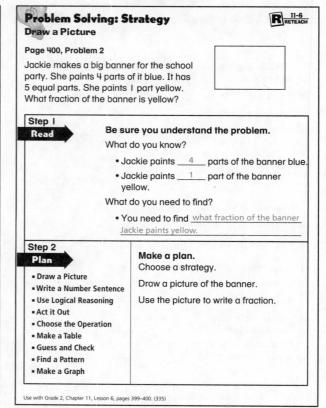

Step 1 Read	Be sure you understand the problem.
	What do you know?
	• Jackie paints ___4___ parts of the banner blue.
	• Jackie paints ___1___ part of the banner yellow.
	What do you need to find?
	• You need to find _what fraction of the banner Jackie paints yellow._

Step 2 Plan	Make a plan.
• Draw a Picture	Choose a strategy.
• Write a Number Sentence	Draw a picture of the banner.
• Use Logical Reasoning	Use the picture to write a fraction.
• Act it Out	
• Choose the Operation	
• Make a Table	
• Guess and Check	
• Find a Pattern	
• Make a Graph	

Reteach

Problem Solving: Strategy
Draw a Picture

Step 3 Solve	Carry out your plan.
	• Draw a picture of the banner.
	• There are ___4___ blue parts and ___1___ yellow part.
	There are ___5___ parts in all.

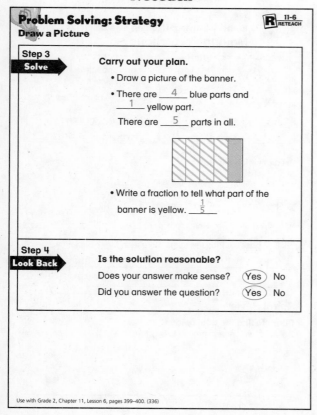

| | • Write a fraction to tell what part of the banner is yellow. $\frac{1}{5}$ |

Step 4 Look Back	Is the solution reasonable?
	Does your answer make sense? (Yes) No
	Did you answer the question? (Yes) No

Daily Homework

11-6

Problem Solving: Strategy
Draw a Picture

Draw a picture. Solve.

	Workspace
1. Jen and Seth paint a big square on the playground. They divide the square into 4 equal parts. They paint 2 of the 4 parts blue. What fraction of the square is blue?	$\frac{2}{4}$
2. A pizza is cut into 12 pieces. 5 of the pieces have peppers on them. What fraction of the pizza has peppers on it?	$\frac{5}{12}$
3. Nick bakes a pan of brownies. He divides the pan into 12 parts. He puts frosting on 8 parts. What fraction of the brownie pan has frosting on it?	$\frac{8}{12}$

Spiral Review

Write the time for each clock.

4.

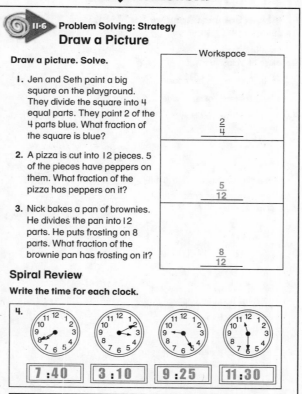

| 7:40 | 3:10 | 9:25 | 11:30 |

Chapter 11 ~ Lesson 7

Practice

Fractions of a Group

Color to show each fraction.

1. $\frac{5}{6}$ ▦▦▦▦▦☐

2. $\frac{7}{12}$ ▦▦▦▦▦▦▦☐☐☐☐☐

3. $\frac{5}{8}$ ▦▦▦▦▦☐☐☐

Look at the picture. Write the fraction.

4. What fraction of the animals are starfish?

$\frac{2}{4}$ → total number of starfish
→ total number of animals

5. What fraction of the animals are goldfish?

$\frac{5}{8}$ → total number of goldfish
→ total number of animals

6. What fraction of the animals are dolphins?

$\frac{3}{6}$ → total number of dolphins
→ total number of animals

Use with Grade 2, Chapter 11, Lesson 7, pages 401–402. (337)

Reteach

Fractions of a Group

You can show a fraction of a group. ☐ ☐ ▦

How many counters are white? _2_ $\frac{2}{}$ → white counters

How many counters are there in all? _3_ $\frac{}{3}$ → in all

$\frac{2}{3}$ are white.

Write the fraction.

1. ☐ ☐ ☐ ▦

How many counters are white? _3_ $\frac{3}{}$ → white counters
How many counters are there in all? _4_ $\frac{}{4}$ → in all

$\frac{3}{4}$ are white.

2. ☐ ☐ ☐ ☐ ▦ ▦

How many counters are white? _4_ $\frac{4}{}$ → white counters
How many counters are there in all? _6_ $\frac{}{6}$ → in all

$\frac{4}{6}$ are white.

3. ☐ ☐ ☐ ☐ ☐ ☐ ☐ ▦

How many counters are white? _7_ $\frac{7}{}$ → white counters
How many counters are there in all? _8_ $\frac{}{8}$ → in all

$\frac{7}{8}$ are white.

Use with Grade 2, Chapter 11, Lesson 7, pages 401–402. (338)

Enrich

Fractions of a Group
Pet Farm

1. How many horses are not grey?

_____4_____

What fraction of the horses are not grey?

$\frac{4}{6}$

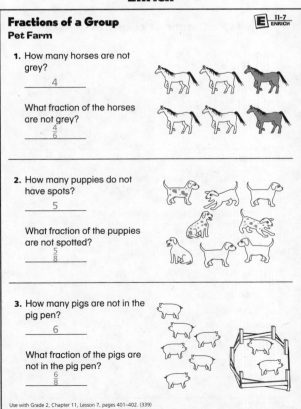

2. How many puppies do not have spots?

_____5_____

What fraction of the puppies are not spotted?

$\frac{5}{8}$

3. How many pigs are not in the pig pen?

_____6_____

What fraction of the pigs are not in the pig pen?

$\frac{6}{8}$

Use with Grade 2, Chapter 11, Lesson 7, pages 401–402. (339)

Daily Homework

11-7 Fractions of a Group

Color to show each fraction.

1. $\frac{1}{3}$ ● ○ ○   2. $\frac{3}{4}$ ● ● ● ○

Look at the picture. Find the fraction.

3. What fraction of the apples are shaded?

$\frac{1}{4}$ → number of shaded apples
→ total number of apples

4. What fraction of the cherries are shaded?

$\frac{7}{12}$ → number of shaded cherries
→ total number of cherries

Look at the picture. Answer the question.

5. Kyra has 6 cookies. 2 are oatmeal cookies. 4 are chocolate cookies. What fraction of the cookies are oatmeal?

$\frac{2}{6}$

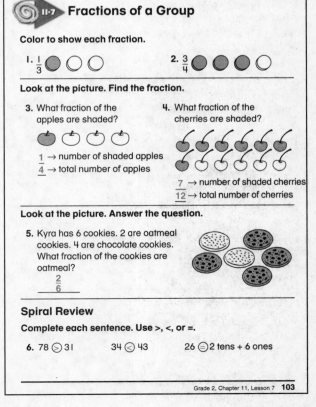

Spiral Review

Complete each sentence. Use >, <, or =.

6. 78 ⊙ 31   34 ⊙ 43   26 ⊙ 2 tens + 6 ones

Chapter 11 ~ Lesson 8

Practice

MORE Fractions of a Group

P 11-8 PRACTICE

Color to show the fraction.

1. $\frac{5}{6}$ of the fish are green.

$\frac{3}{4}$ of the fish are pink.

$\frac{3}{3}$ of the fish are blue.

2. $\frac{3}{8}$ of the fish are red.

$\frac{1}{2}$ of the fish are yellow.

$\frac{1}{6}$ of the fish are orange.

Use the picture. Write the fraction.

3. $\frac{2}{6}$ of the fish are striped.

$\frac{3}{6}$ of the fish are spotted.

$\frac{1}{6}$ of the fish are white.

Reteach

MORE Fractions of a Group

R 11-8 RETEACH

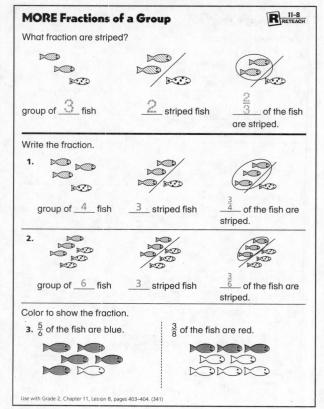

What fraction are striped?

group of __3__ fish   __2__ striped fish $\frac{2}{3}$ of the fish are striped.

Write the fraction.

1. group of __4__ fish   __3__ striped fish $\frac{3}{4}$ of the fish are striped.

2. group of __6__ fish   __3__ striped fish $\frac{3}{6}$ of the fish are striped.

Color to show the fraction.

3. $\frac{5}{6}$ of the fish are blue. $\frac{3}{8}$ of the fish are red.

Enrich

MORE Fractions of a Group

E 11-8 ENRICH

Betsy's Party

The graph shows the party supplies that Betsy bought.

Betsy's Party Supplies	
party hats	🎉🎉🎉🎉🎉🎉
noisemakers	📯📯📯📯📯📯📯📯
balloons	🎈🎈🎈🎈🎈

Color the pictures to help you solve each problem.

1. There are 8 yellow noisemakers. What fraction of the noisemakers are yellow?
$\frac{8}{12}$, or $\frac{2}{3}$

There are 3 red balloons. What fraction of the balloons are red?
$\frac{3}{6}$, or $\frac{1}{2}$

2. There are 6 green party hats. What fraction of the party hats are green?
$\frac{6}{8}$, or $\frac{3}{4}$

Betsy buys 4 more green hats. What fraction of the hats are green now?
$\frac{10}{12}$, or $\frac{5}{6}$

3. There are 15 balloons. Color 10 balloons red. What fraction of the balloons are red?
$\frac{10}{15}$, or $\frac{2}{3}$

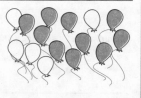

Daily Homework

11-8 More Fractions of a Group

Color to show the fraction.

1. $\frac{1}{2}$ of the circles are red.

$\frac{3}{4}$ of the circles are orange.

$\frac{1}{3}$ of the circles are yellow.

Answer the question.

2. Zoe has 2 red apples and 6 yellow apples. How many apples does she have altogether?   __8__ apples

What fraction of the apples are yellow? $\frac{6}{8}$ or $\frac{3}{4}$

Spiral Review

Match the faces with the solid figures.

3. 4 triangles and 1 square

4. 2 circles

5. 6 squares

Chapter 11 ~ Lesson 9

Practice

Most Likely and Least Likely Outcomes

P PRACTICE 11-9

Look at the shells. Which kind are you most likely to
pick? Which kind are you least likely to pick?

	most likely	least likely
1. 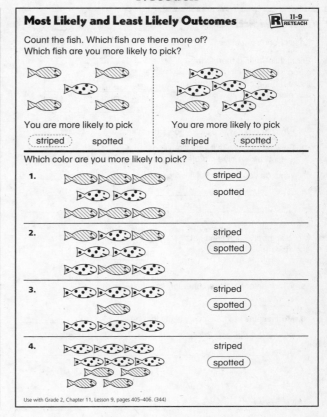		
2.		
3.		

Use with Grade 2, Chapter 11, Lesson 9, pages 405–406. (343)

Reteach

Most Likely and Least Likely Outcomes

R RETEACH 11-9

Count the fish. Which fish are there more of?
Which fish are you more likely to pick?

You are more likely to pick — (striped) spotted

You are more likely to pick — striped (spotted)

Which color are you more likely to pick?

1.	(striped) spotted
2.	striped (spotted)
3.	striped (spotted)
4.	striped (spotted)

Use with Grade 2, Chapter 11, Lesson 9, pages 405–406. (344)

Enrich

Most Likely and Least Likely Outcomes
Spinner Fun

You will need (red) (blue) (green) (yellow)

E ENRICH 11-9

1. Color some parts of the spinner red.
Color some parts of the spinner blue.
Are you more likely to spin red or blue?
___Answers may vary.___

2. Color some parts of the spinner red.
Color some parts of the spinner
yellow.
Are you more likely to spin red
or yellow?
___Answers may vary.___

3. Color some parts of the spinner blue.
Color some parts of the spinner yellow.
Color some parts of the spinner green.
Are you most likely to spin blue, green,
or yellow?
___Answers may vary.___

4. Look back at exercise 3. Do you think that
everyone in your class got the same answer you
did? Tell why or why not. No, everyone did not color the
same number of spaces each color, so the most likely
color to spin would be different.

Use with Grade 2, Chapter 11, Lesson 9, pages 405–406. (345)

Daily Homework

11-9 Most Likely and Least Likely
Outcomes

**Look at the items. Circle the one you are most likely to pick.
Circle the one you are least likely to pick.**

	most likely	least likely
1.		
2.		

Answer the questions.

3. Edna has 8 candies in a bag. 5 candies are
silver, 2 are green, and 1 is blue. Edna
chooses a candy without looking. Which
color is Edna most likely to pick? ___silver___

Which color is Edna least likely to pick? ___blue___

Spiral Review

Write the next three even numbers.

4. 24 __26__ __28__ __30__   48 __50__ __52__ __54__

Chapter 11 ~ Lesson 10

Practice

Make Predictions

Answer each question.

Each child picks a marble from a bag without looking. So far, these are the marbles each child has picked.

Marbles	
Blue marbles	////
Green marbles	+HT /
Yellow marbles	+HT +HT ////
Red marbles	+HT

1. Which marble was picked most often? _____ yellow

2. Sally picks next. Is it very likely that she will pick a blue marble? _____ no

3. What do you predict Sally will pick next? _____ a yellow marble

4. Why? _Possible answer: there are more yellow marbles than marbles of other colors._

Next, the children play a game with a spinner. Each child gets one spin.

Spins	
Red spins	+HT
Blue spins	+HT +HT /
Yellow spins	////

5. Which color did the spinner land on the least often? _____ yellow

6. Martin spins next. Is it very likely that he will spin blue? _____ yes

7. Why? _Possible answer: blue is the color that appears the most._

Reteach

Make Predictions

This spinner is more likely to land on

- stripes
- spots
- white

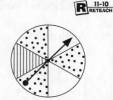

1. Make a prediction. What color do you predict you will land on the most? _____ Answers may vary.

2. Use a paper clip and pencil to spin. Spin the spinner 10 times. Record each spin. Answers may vary.

Spots	Stripes	White

Answer each question. Answers may vary.

3. What color did you land on the most? _____

4. How many times did the spinner land on spots? _____

5. Was your prediction right? _____

6. If you spin again, will you change your prediction? _Answers may vary, but should reflect what their prediction and results were for the first spin._

Enrich

Make Predictions
Picking Cubes

Put 5 red cubes and 5 blue cubes in a bag.
Pick one cube without looking.
Mark the tally chart for the color you picked.
Put the cube back in the bag.
Keep picking cubes and marking the tally chart.
Do it 10 times in all.

red	blue

Write the number of red cubes and blue cubes you picked.

1. I picked _____ red cubes.

2. I picked _____ blue cubes.

What if you try this again.

How many of each color will you pick this time?

3. I will pick _____ red cubes.

4. I will pick _____ blue cubes.

Now try it again.

Pick cubes and mark the tally chart.

Do it 10 more times.

See if you are right.

red	blue

Check students' work.
Answers may vary.

Daily Homework

11-10 Make Predictions

Answer each question.

Each second grader picked a button from a bag without looking. So far, these are the buttons each child picked.

Buttons	
pink button	+HT /
blue button	+HT +HT //
green button	+HT
silver button	////

1. Which button was picked most often? _____ blue button

2. Andy picks next. Is it very likely that he will pick a silver button? _____ No.

3. What do you predict Andy will pick? _____ a blue button

4. Why? _____ Possible answer: because there are more blue buttons than other colors.

Spiral Review

Write the number that comes between.

5. 59   14   37   20

   60   15   38   21

   61   16   39   22

Chapter 11 ~ Lesson 11

Part A Worksheet

Problem Solving: Application
Sea Animal Game

Part A 11-11 WORKSHEET Decision Making

Plan a board game.

Use a game board and yellow and orange crayons.

Use fractions in your rules.

Use these game boards to try some sample games.

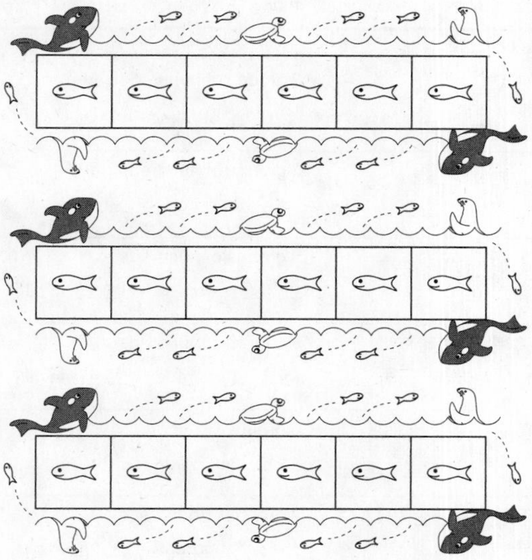

Use with Grade 2, Chapter 11, Lesson 11, pages 409–410. (349)

Part A Worksheet

Problem Solving: Application
Sea Animal Game

Part A 11-11 WORKSHEET Decision Making

1. Record the rules of your game. Check students' work.

Sea Animal Game

____

____

____

____

____

____

2. What if you wanted to change the rules to make them harder?
Record the new rules of your game.

Sea Animal Game

____

____

____

____

____

____

____

Use with Grade 2, Chapter 11, Lesson 11, pages 409–410. (350)

Part B Worksheet

Problem Solving: Application
Why is Water Important?

Part B 11-11 WORKSHEET Math & Science

1. Record what happened when you put oil in the jar.

____

____

What happened when you added soap to the jar?

____

____

2. When was it easier to remove oil from the water?

before adding soap

3. What if you were trying to clean oil off a bird after an oil spill.
Would you use soap?
Explain your thinking.

Answers may vary. Possible answer: Yes, because the soap would help the oil dissolve.

____

____

____

Use with Grade 2, Chapter 11, Lesson 11, pages 411–412. (351)

Chapter 12 ~ Lesson 1

Practice

Hundreds

3 groups of hundreds

_____3_____ hundreds = __300__ in all

Write how many.

1. 6 groups of hundreds
   __6__ hundreds
   _600_ in all

   9 groups of hundreds
   __9__ hundreds
   _900_ in all

2. 4 groups of hundreds
   __4__ hundreds
   _400_ in all

   2 groups of hundreds
   __2__ hundreds
   _200_ in all

3. 7 groups of hundreds
   __7__ hundreds
   _700_ in all

   I group of hundreds
   __1__ hundred
   _100_ in all

4. 5 groups of hundreds
   __5__ hundreds
   _500_ in all

   8 groups of hundreds
   __8__ hundreds
   _800_ in all

5. 2 groups of hundreds
   __2__ hundreds
   _200_ in all

   6 groups of hundreds
   __6__ hundreds
   _600_ in all

Reteach

Hundreds

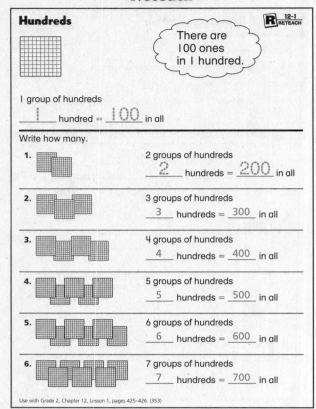

There are
100 ones
in 1 hundred.

I group of hundreds

_____I_____ hundred = __100__ in all

Write how many.

1. 2 groups of hundreds
   __2__ hundreds = _200_ in all

2. 3 groups of hundreds
   __3__ hundreds = _300_ in all

3. 4 groups of hundreds
   __4__ hundreds = _400_ in all

4. 5 groups of hundreds
   __5__ hundreds = _500_ in all

5. 6 groups of hundreds
   __6__ hundreds = _600_ in all

6. 7 groups of hundreds
   __7__ hundreds = _700_ in all

Enrich

Hundreds
100s of Beads

The crafts club is making necklaces.

The bar graph shows how many beads are in each box.

Colors of Beads

	0	100	200	300	400	500	600	700	800	900
red										
blue										
green										
yellow										

1. How many blue beads are there? _500_

2. How many yellow beads are there? _200_

3. How many red beads are there? _900_

4. How many more green beads are there than blue beads? _100_

5. How many more red beads are there than yellow beads? _700_

6. Write a problem about the graph. Solve it. Give it to a classmate to solve.

_____ Answers may vary. _____

Daily Homework

12-1 Hundreds

Write how many.

1. 6 groups of hundreds
   __6__ hundreds =
   _600_ in all

   4 groups of hundreds
   __4__ hundreds =
   _400_ in all

2. 8 groups of hundreds
   __8__ hundreds =
   _800_ in all

   5 groups of hundreds
   __5__ hundreds =
   _500_ in all

Problem Solving

4. Which group has more?

   _____ Group B has more. _____

   How do you know?

   __ I counted how many hundreds __
   __ were in each group __
   __ and then compared. __

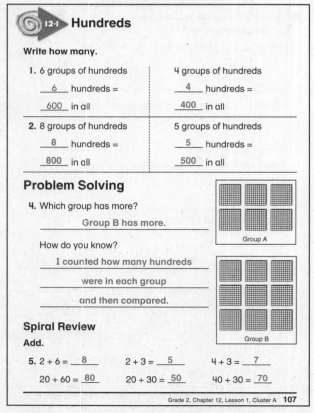

Group A

Group B

Spiral Review

Add.

5. $2 + 6 =$ _8_ $2 + 3 =$ _5_ $4 + 3 =$ _7_

   $20 + 60 =$ _80_ $20 + 30 =$ _50_ $40 + 30 =$ _70_

Chapter 12 ~ Lesson 2

Practice

Hundreds, Tens, and Ones

You can use hundreds, tens and ones to show 409.

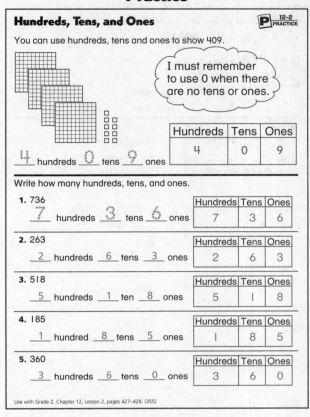

I must remember to use 0 when there are no tens or ones.

__4__ hundreds __0__ tens __9__ ones

Hundreds	Tens	Ones
4	0	9

Write how many hundreds, tens, and ones.

1. 736

__7__ hundreds __3__ tens __6__ ones

Hundreds	Tens	Ones
7	3	6

2. 263

__2__ hundreds __6__ tens __3__ ones

Hundreds	Tens	Ones
2	6	3

3. 518

__5__ hundreds __1__ ten __8__ ones

Hundreds	Tens	Ones
5	1	8

4. 185

__1__ hundred __8__ tens __5__ ones

Hundreds	Tens	Ones
1	8	5

5. 360

__3__ hundreds __6__ tens __0__ ones

Hundreds	Tens	Ones
3	6	0

Use with Grade 2, Chapter 12, Lesson 2, pages 427–428. (355)

Reteach

Hundreds, Tens, and Ones

You can use hundreds, tens, and ones to show 243.

Count the hundreds. Count the tens. Count the ones.

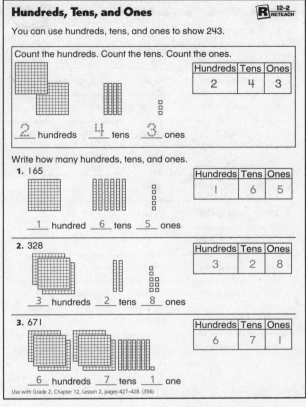

Hundreds	Tens	Ones
2	4	3

__2__ hundreds __4__ tens __3__ ones

Write how many hundreds, tens, and ones.

1. 165

__1__ hundred __6__ tens __5__ ones

Hundreds	Tens	Ones
1	6	5

2. 328

__3__ hundreds __2__ tens __8__ ones

Hundreds	Tens	Ones
3	2	8

3. 671

__6__ hundreds __7__ tens __1__ one

Hundreds	Tens	Ones
6	7	1

Use with Grade 2, Chapter 12, Lesson 2, pages 427–428. (356)

Enrich

Hundreds, Tens, and Ones
Bull's-Eye!

Max likes to play Bull's-Eye. Each ball shows a hit.

Write the points for each game.

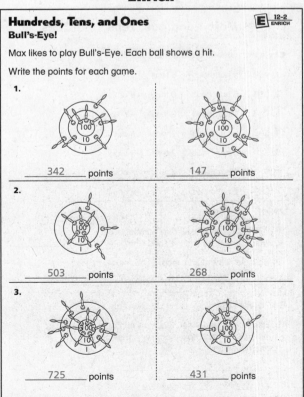

1. 342 points   147 points

2. 503 points   268 points

3. 725 points   431 points

Use with Grade 2, Chapter 12, Lesson 2, pages 427–428. (357)

Daily Homework

12-2 Hundreds, Tens, and Ones

Write how many hundreds, tens, and ones.

1. 357 __3__ hundreds

__5__ tens __7__ ones

hundreds	tens	ones
3	5	7

2. 424 __4__ hundreds

__2__ tens __4__ ones

hundreds	tens	ones
4	2	4

3. 740 __7__ hundreds

__4__ tens __0__ ones

hundreds	tens	ones
7	4	0

Write the number.

4. 8 hundreds 0 tens 3 ones __803__

5. 5 hundreds 7 tens 2 ones __572__

Solve.

6. Sophie has 5 hundreds. Cassandra has 3 hundreds. How many do they have in all?

__800__

7. Nate has 9 hundreds. Joe has 4 hundreds. How many more hundreds does Nate have?

__500__

Spiral Review

8. Color to show the fraction one fourth. Write the fraction.

$\frac{1}{4}$

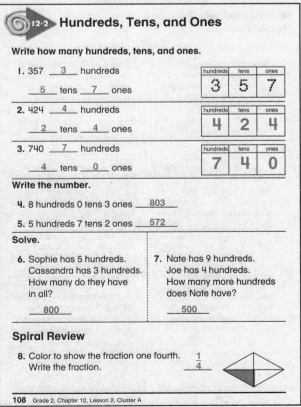

108 Grade 2, Chapter 12, Lesson 2, Cluster A

Chapter 12 ~ Lesson 3

Practice

MORE Hundreds, Tens, and Ones

P 12-3 PRACTICE

Circle the value of each dark digit.

1. 6**2**4	(6 hundreds)	6 tens	6 ones
2. 41**5**	5 hundreds	5 tens	(5 ones)
3. 3**9**1	9 hundreds	(9 tens)	9 ones
4. 18**2**	2 hundreds	2 tens	(2 ones)
5. 7**0**3	0 hundreds	(0 tens)	0 ones
6. **8**73	(8 hundreds)	8 tens	8 ones
7. 32**4**	4 hundreds	4 tens	(4 ones)
8. **1**97	(1 hundred)	1 ten	1 one
9. 4**6**9	6 hundreds	(6 tens)	6 ones
10. 7**2**1	2 hundreds	(2 tens)	2 ones
11. 42**7**	7 hundreds	7 tens	(7 ones)
12. **2**93	(2 hundreds)	2 tens	2 ones

Use with Grade 2, Chapter 12, Lesson 3, pages 429–430. (358)

Reteach

MORE Hundreds, Tens, and Ones

R 12-3 RETEACH

Place value can help you tell the value of a digit.

Hundreds	Tens	Ones
4	7	1

The value of the 4 is
(4 hundreds)
4 tens
4 ones

Write the number. Circle the value of the digit.

1.
Hundreds	Tens	Ones
5	3	6

536

The value of the 6 is
6 hundreds
6 tens
(6 ones)

2.
Hundreds	Tens	Ones
9	2	4

924

The value of the 2 is
2 hundreds
(2 tens)
2 ones

3.
Hundreds	Tens	Ones
8	1	7

817

The value of the 8 is
(8 hundreds)
8 tens
8 ones

4.
Hundreds	Tens	Ones
3	2	9

329

The value of the 3 is
(3 hundreds)
3 tens
3 ones

Use with Grade 2, Chapter 12, Lesson 3, pages 429–430. (359)

Enrich

MORE Hundreds, Tens, and Ones
Number Riddles

E 12-3 ENRICH

Solve each riddle.

1. I have a 3 in my tens place. My hundreds digit is 4 greater than my ones digit. My ones digit is 2. What number am I? __632__

H	T	O
6	3	2

I have a 6 in my tens place. My ones digit is 4 less than my tens digit. My hundreds digit is 1. What number am I? __162__

H	T	O
1	6	2

2. I have a 3 in my tens place. My ones digit is 2 greater than the tens digit. My hundreds digit is 2 less than the tens digit. What number am I? __135__

H	T	O
1	3	5

My tens digit is a 5. My ones digit is 2 less than 5 and the same as my hundreds digit. What number am I? __353__

H	T	O
3	5	3

3. I have a 7 as my ones digit. My tens digit is 3 less than my ones digit. My hundreds digit is 1 greater than my tens digit. What number am I? __547__

H	T	O
5	4	7

My ones digit is an even number less than 4. My tens digit is 3 greater than the ones digit. My hundreds digit is the same as the tens digit. What number am I? __552__

H	T	O
5	5	2

Use with Grade 2, Chapter 12, Lesson 3, pages 429–430. (360)

Daily Homework

12-3 More Hundreds, Tens, and Ones

Circle the value of each underlined digit.

1. **4**59	(4 hundreds)	5 tens	9 ones
2. 5**0**8	5 hundreds	(0 tens)	8 ones
3. 7**2**4	7 hundreds	(2 tens)	4 ones
4. **5**96	(5 hundreds)	9 tens	6 ones
5. 32**4**	3 hundreds	2 tens	(4 ones)
6. 5**7**0	5 hundreds	(7 tens)	0 ones
7. 28**9**	2 hundreds	8 tens	(9 ones)

Solve.

8. What is the greatest 3-digit number you can write using the digits 2, 8, and 6? ___862___

9. How many hundreds, tens, and ones are in 461?

___4___ hundreds ___6___ tens ___1___ one

Spiral Review

10. Use a centimeter ruler. Measure each side. Write about how many centimeters around the shape is.

___2___ + ___2___ + ___3___ + ___3___

+ ___3___ = ___13___ centimeters

Chapter 12 ~ Lesson 4

Practice

Counting On or Back by Hundreds

Count on or back by hundreds. Write each number.

1. One hundred more than 715 is __815__.

2. One hundred less than 327 is __227__.

3. One hundred more than 382 is __482__.

4. One hundred less than 425 is __325__.

5. One hundred more than 367 is __467__.

6. One hundred less than 672 is __572__.

7. Two hundred more than 649 is __849__.

8. Three hundred less than 432 is __132__.

9. Four hundred more than 146 is __546__.

10. Three hundred more than 162 is __462__.

11. Two hundred less than 748 is __548__.

12. Four hundred more than 406 is __806__.

Use with Grade 2, Chapter 12, Lesson 4, pages 431–432. (361)

Reteach

Counting On or Back by Hundreds

You can count on or back by hundreds.

I can count on by one hundred.

I can count back by one hundred.

214
One hundred more is __314__.

235
One hundred less is __135__.

Count on by hundreds.
Use place-value models to show each number.
Write each number.

1. 782
   One hundred more is __882__.

   439
   One hundred more is __539__.

2. 152
   One hundred more is __252__.

   391
   One hundred more is __491__.

3. 608
   Two hundred more is __808__.

   214
   Four hundred more is __614__.

Count back by hundreds.
Use place-value models to show each number.
Write each number.

4. 893
   One hundred less is __793__.

   540
   One hundred less is __440__.

5. 674
   One hundred less is __574__.

   908
   One hundred less is __808__.

6. 750
   Four hundred less is __350__.

   418
   Three hundred less is __118__.

Use with Grade 2, Chapter 12, Lesson 4, pages 431–432. (362)

Enrich

Counting On or Back by Hundreds
Keep Counting

Count on or back. Write each number in the box.

Then count on or back from that number.

1. Start with	Count back 100.	Count on 10.	Count back 1.
417	317	327	326

2. Start with	Count on 200.	Count back 20.	Count on 2.
573	773	753	755

3. Start with	Count back 300.	Count on 30.	Count back 3.
945	645	675	672

4. Start with	Count on 200.	Count back 30.	Count on 1.
294	494	464	465

5. Start with	Count back 100.	Count on 20.	Count back 3.
658	558	578	575

6. Start with	Count on 300.	Count back 30.	Count on 2.
360	660	630	632

Use with Grade 2, Chapter 12, Lesson 4, pages 431–432. (363)

Daily Homework

12-4 **Counting On or Back by Hundreds**

Count on or back by hundreds. Write each number.

1. One hundred more than 841 is __941__.

2. One hundred less than 602 is __502__.

3. One hundred more than 263 is __363__.

4. One hundred less than 316 is __216__.

5. Two hundred more than 555 is __755__.

6. Three hundred more than 128 is __428__.

7. Three hundred less than 754 is __454__.

8. Four hundred more than 250 is __650__.

Problem Solving

9. Holly has 139 buttons in a jar. She adds 200 more buttons to the jar. How many buttons does Holly have in all?

   __339__ buttons

10. Keith has 567 beads. He puts 300 beads on a string. How many beads does Keith have left?

    __267__ beads

Spiral Review
Add.

11.

8	7	4¢	6	8	7
+8	+4	+9¢	+9	+5	+8
16	11	13¢	15	13	15

110 Grade 2, Chapter 12, Lesson 4, Cluster A

Chapter 12 ~ Lesson 5

Practice

Numbers to 1,000

P 12-5 PRACTICE

Write each number. Write each word.

1.

Hundreds	Tens	Ones
6	3	9

639

six hundred thirty-nine

2.

Hundreds	Tens	Ones
4	1	7

417

four hundred seventeen

3.

Hundreds	Tens	Ones
9	2	5

925

nine hundred twenty-five

4.

Hundreds	Tens	Ones
8	0	3

803

eight hundred three

5.

Hundreds	Tens	Ones
7	8	2

782

seven hundred eighty-two

6.

Hundreds	Tens	Ones
2	4	0

240

two hundred forty

Use with Grade 2, Chapter 12, Lesson 5, pages 433–434. (364)

Reteach

Numbers to 1,000

R 12-5 RETEACH

Hundreds	Tens	Ones
5	4	3

Write the number: 543

You can write the word name for this number.

five hundred forty-three

Write each number. Write each word name.

1.

Hundreds	Tens	Ones
3	0	0

300

three hundred

2.

Hundreds	Tens	Ones
4	6	0

460

four hundred sixty

3.

Hundreds	Tens	Ones
6	2	0

620

six hundred twenty

4.

Hundreds	Tens	Ones
7	3	9

739

seven hundred thirty-nine

5.

Hundreds	Tens	Ones
1	8	2

182

one hundred eighty-two

Use with Grade 2, Chapter 12, Lesson 5, pages 433–434. (365)

Enrich

Numbers to 1,000
Number Play

E 12-5 ENRICH

Cut off the bottom part of the page. Put it aside.
Write two different numbers. Possible answers are shown.
Now finish the bottom of the page.

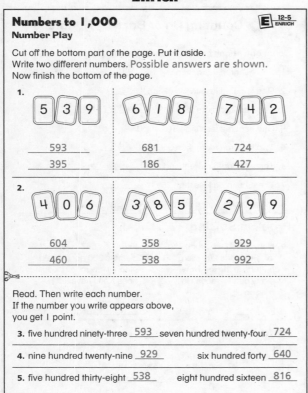

1.

5 3 9 — 593 / 395

6 1 8 — 681 / 186

7 4 2 — 724 / 427

2.

4 0 6 — 604 / 460

3 8 5 — 358 / 538

2 9 9 — 929 / 992

Read. Then write each number.
If the number you write appears above,
you get 1 point.

3. five hundred ninety-three __593__   seven hundred twenty-four __724__

4. nine hundred twenty-nine __929__   six hundred forty __640__

5. five hundred thirty-eight __538__   eight hundred sixteen __816__

Use with Grade 2, Chapter 12, Lesson 5, pages 433–434. (366)

Daily Homework

12-5 Numbers to 1,000

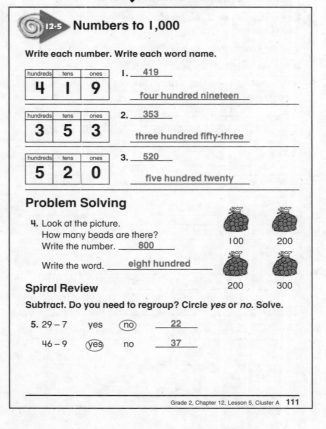

Write each number. Write each word name.

1.

hundreds	tens	ones
4	1	9

419

four hundred nineteen

2.

hundreds	tens	ones
3	5	3

353

three hundred fifty-three

3.

hundreds	tens	ones
5	2	0

520

five hundred twenty

Problem Solving

4. Look at the picture.
How many beads are there?
Write the number. __800__

Write the word. __eight hundred__

100   200

200   300

Spiral Review

Subtract. Do you need to regroup? Circle *yes* or *no*. Solve.

5. 29 − 7   yes   (no)   __22__

46 − 9   (yes)   no   __37__

Chapter 12 ~ Lesson 6

Practice

Expanded Form

Write each number in expanded form.

1. 378   300 + 70 + 8
2. 725   700 + 20 + 5
3. 148   100 + 40 + 8
4. 581   500 + 80 + 1
5. 904   900 + 0 + 4
6. 284   200 + 80 + 4
7. 373   300 + 70 + 3
8. 550   500 + 50 + 0
9. 847   800 + 40 + 7
10. 458   400 + 50 + 8
11. 921   900 + 20 + 1
12. 780   700 + 80 + 0

Use with Grade 2, Chapter 12, Lesson 6, pages 435–436. (367)

Reteach

Expanded Form

You can show a number by writing it in hundreds, tens, and ones. This is called expanded form.

427 = four hundreds 2 tens 7 ones

or

400 + 20 + 7

Write each number in expanded form.

1. 185   100 + 80 + 5   341   300 + 40 + 1
2. 774   700 + 70 + 4   916   900 + 10 + 6
3. 638   600 + 30 + 8   240   200 + 40 + 0

Use with Grade 2, Chapter 12, Lesson 6, pages 435–436. (368)

Enrich

Expanded Form
A Crafts Fair

Read the story. Then answer each question.

The Pearl Street School held a crafts fair. There were 200 + 40 + 7 students at the fair. Each booth sold different things. The first grade class used 100 + 90 + 3 strings to make pot holders. The second grade used 600 + 50 + 1 beads to make necklaces. The third grade used 400 + 20 + 8 pieces of yarn to make puppets. There were 500 + 20 + 6 parents at the fair. There were 700 + 80 + 3 cups of juice sold at the fair. Everyone had a good time.

1. How many pieces of yarn did the third grade use? __428__ pieces
2. How many students were at the fair? __247__ students
3. How many pieces of string did the first grade use? __193__ pieces
4. How many parents were at the fair? __526__ parents
5. How many cups of juice were sold? __783__ cups
6. How many beads did the second grade use? __651__ beads

Use with Grade 2, Chapter 12, Lesson 6, pages 435–436. (369)

Daily Homework

 Expanded Form

Write each number in expanded form.

1. 566   500 + 60 + 6
2. 830   800 + 30 + 0
3. 271   200 + 70 + 1
4. 304   300 + 0 + 4
5. 989   900 + 80 + 9
6. 742   700 + 40 + 2

Solve.

7. Charlie glues 246 buttons to his puppet. Write this number in expanded form.

   __200 + 40 + 6__

8. Julie has 7 beads. Mona has 20 beads. Zack has 100 beads. How many beads do they have in all?

   __127__

Spiral Review

9. Circle the clock that shows the same time.

112   Grade 2, Chapter 12, Lesson 6, Cluster A

Chapter 12 ~ Lesson 7

Practice

Problem Solving: Reading for Math
Problem and Solutions

Charlie is making a mosaic with different shaped tiles. He uses 4 square tiles, 4 rectangle tiles, and 4 triangle tiles. What pattern does Charlie make?

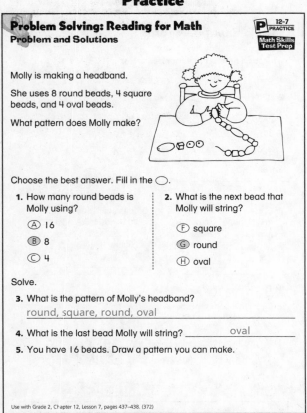

Solve.

1. How many rectangle tiles are in Charlie's mosaic?

____4____ rectangle tiles

2. What is the pattern of Charlie's mosaic?

square, rectangle, triangle

3. What is the last tile Charlie will add to his mosaic?

triangle

4. You have 12 tiles.
Draw a pattern you can make.

Use with Grade 2, Chapter 12, Lesson 7, pages 437–438. (370)

Practice

Problem Solving: Reading for Math
Problem and Solutions

Suzanne is planting flowers along a fence. She has 10 tulips, 5 daffodils, and 5 daisies. What pattern does Suzanne make?

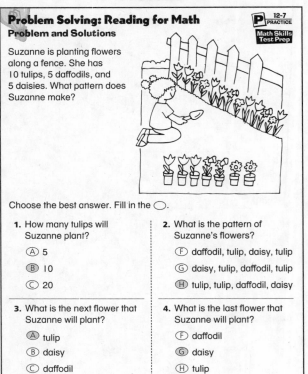

Choose the best answer. Fill in the ○.

1. How many tulips will Suzanne plant?
- Ⓐ 5
- Ⓑ 10
- Ⓒ 20

2. What is the pattern of Suzanne's flowers?
- Ⓕ daffodil, tulip, daisy, tulip
- Ⓖ daisy, tulip, daffodil, tulip
- Ⓗ tulip, tulip, daffodil, daisy

3. What is the next flower that Suzanne will plant?
- Ⓐ tulip
- Ⓑ daisy
- Ⓒ daffodil

4. What is the last flower that Suzanne will plant?
- Ⓕ daffodil
- Ⓖ daisy
- Ⓗ tulip

Use with Grade 2, Chapter 12, Lesson 7, pages 437–438. (371)

Practice

Problem Solving: Reading for Math
Problem and Solutions

Molly is making a headband.

She uses 8 round beads, 4 square beads, and 4 oval beads.

What pattern does Molly make?

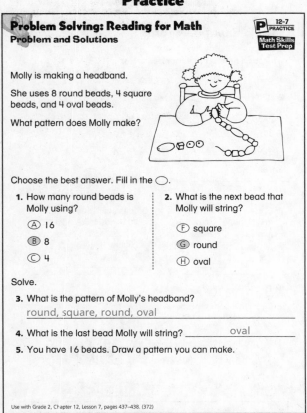

Choose the best answer. Fill in the ○.

1. How many round beads is Molly using?
- Ⓐ 16
- Ⓑ 8
- Ⓒ 4

2. What is the next bead that Molly will string?
- Ⓕ square
- Ⓖ round
- Ⓗ oval

Solve.

3. What is the pattern of Molly's headband?
round, square, round, oval

4. What is the last bead Molly will string? ____oval____

5. You have 16 beads. Draw a pattern you can make.

Use with Grade 2, Chapter 12, Lesson 7, pages 437–438. (372)

Daily Homework

12-7 Problem Solving: Reading for Math
Problems and Solutions

Solve.

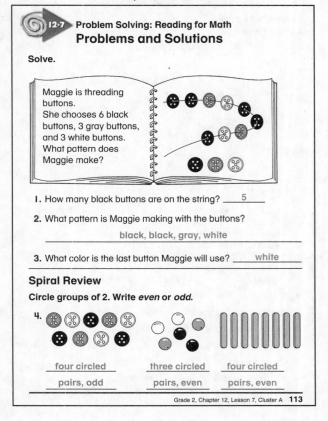

Maggie is threading buttons. She chooses 6 black buttons, 3 gray buttons, and 3 white buttons. What pattern does Maggie make?

1. How many black buttons are on the string? ____5____

2. What pattern is Maggie making with the buttons?

black, black, gray, white

3. What color is the last button Maggie will use? ____white____

Spiral Review

Circle groups of 2. Write *even* or *odd*.

4.

four circled	three circled	four circled
pairs, odd	pairs, even	pairs, even

Grade 2, Chapter 12, Lesson 7, Cluster A **113**

Chapter 12 ~ Lesson 8

Practice

Problem Solving: Strategy
Find a Pattern

Continue each pattern. Write what will most likely come next.

1. _____ black

2. _____ white

3. _____ circle

4. _____ moon

Mixed Strategy Review

Solve.

5. Haley had a pizza cut into 8 equal pieces. She ate 3 pieces. What fraction of the pizza is left?

$\frac{5}{8}$

6. **Create a problem** for which you would find a pattern to solve. Share it with others.

_____

Reteach

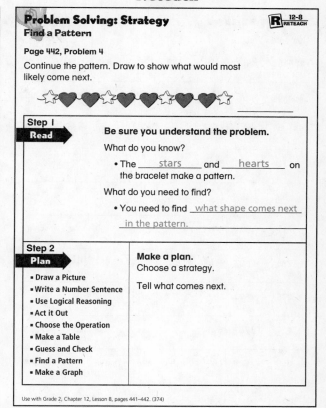

Problem Solving: Strategy
Find a Pattern

Page 442, Problem 4

Continue the pattern. Draw to show what would most likely come next.

_____

Step 1 Read	Be sure you understand the problem.
	What do you know?
	• The ___stars___ and ___hearts___ on the bracelet make a pattern.
	What do you need to find?
	• You need to find __what shape comes next__ __in the pattern.__

Step 2 Plan	Make a plan. Choose a strategy.
▪ Draw a Picture	Tell what comes next.
▪ Write a Number Sentence	
▪ Use Logical Reasoning	
▪ Act it Out	
▪ Choose the Operation	
▪ Make a Table	
▪ Guess and Check	
▪ Find a Pattern	
▪ Make a Graph	

Reteach

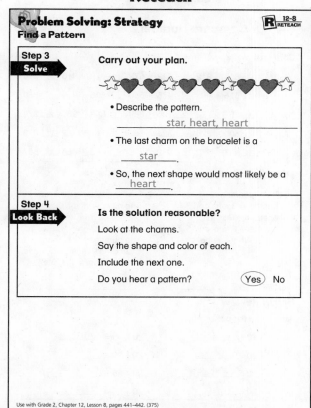

Problem Solving: Strategy
Find a Pattern

Step 3 Solve	Carry out your plan.
	• Describe the pattern.
	__star, heart, heart__
	• The last charm on the bracelet is a __star__.
	• So, the next shape would most likely be a __heart__.

Step 4 Look Back	Is the solution reasonable?
	Look at the charms.
	Say the shape and color of each.
	Include the next one.
	Do you hear a pattern? (Yes) No

Daily Homework

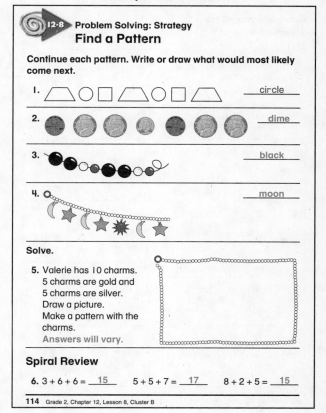

12·8 **Problem Solving: Strategy**
Find a Pattern

Continue each pattern. Write or draw what would most likely come next.

1. _____ circle

2. _____ dime

3. _____ black

4. _____ moon

Solve.

5. Valerie has 10 charms. 5 charms are gold and 5 charms are silver. Draw a picture. Make a pattern with the charms. *Answers will vary.*

Spiral Review

6. $3 + 6 + 6 = $ __15__ $5 + 5 + 7 = $ __17__ $8 + 2 + 5 = $ __15__

Chapter 12 ~ Lesson 9

Practice

Compare Numbers
P 12-9 PRACTICE

Compare. Write >, <, or =.

1. 415 $<$ 451 | 623 $<$ 678 | 730 $<$ 830 | 178 $>$ 168
2. 375 $=$ 375 | 549 $<$ 560 | 248 $>$ 239 | 773 $<$ 785
3. 109 $<$ 111 | 382 $>$ 379 | 445 $<$ 545 | 990 $>$ 909
4. 272 $<$ 275 | 818 $>$ 816 | 357 $=$ 357 | 734 $>$ 699
5. 643 $>$ 637 | 256 $<$ 261 | 429 $>$ 421 | 153 $>$ 152
6. 317 $<$ 371 | 588 $<$ 598 | 761 $<$ 769 | 848 $=$ 848
7. 285 $<$ 287 | 638 $>$ 632 | 954 $<$ 957 | 465 $>$ 456
8. 275 $<$ 375 | 717 $=$ 717 | 539 $<$ 542 | 311 $<$ 313
9. 827 $>$ 789 | 690 $<$ 711 | 431 $<$ 438 | 321 $<$ 323
10. 555 $>$ 525 | 684 $>$ 648 | 698 $=$ 698 | 547 $>$ 544

Use with Grade 2, Chapter 12, Lesson 9, pages 443–444. (376)

Reteach

Compare Numbers
R 12-9 RETEACH

You can compare numbers using >, <, or =.

> First compare the hundreds. If the hundreds are the same, compare the tens. If the tens are the same, compare the ones.

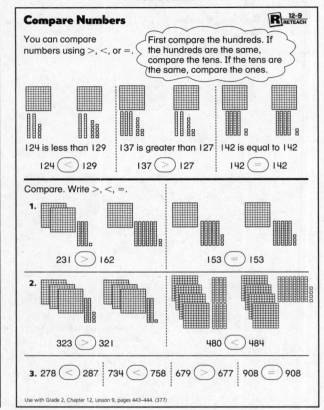

124 is less than 129 | 137 is greater than 127 | 142 is equal to 142

124 $<$ 129 | 137 $>$ 127 | 142 $=$ 142

Compare. Write >, <, =.

1. 231 $>$ 162 | 153 $=$ 153

2. 323 $>$ 321 | 480 $<$ 484

3. 278 $<$ 287 | 734 $<$ 758 | 679 $>$ 677 | 908 $=$ 908

Use with Grade 2, Chapter 12, Lesson 9, pages 443–444. (377)

Enrich

Compare Numbers
E 12-9 ENRICH
A Number Game

Play with a partner.

Scoring Chart	
Name	Points

- Each player drops a counter on the game board.
- Compare numbers.
- The player with the greater number gets 1 point.

The first player to reach 10 points wins.

3 tens 4 ones 2 hundreds	500 + 60 + 7	(blocks)	H T O 4 3 1
600 + 30 + 0	(blocks)	5 ones 6 tens 3 hundreds	H T O 9 5 2
(blocks)	H T O 6 7 4	100 + 70 + 9	5 tens 9 ones 9 hundreds
800 + 60 + 3	7 ones 8 hundreds 4 ones	H T O 7 8 9	(blocks)

Use with Grade 2, Chapter 12, Lesson 9, pages 443–444. (378)

Daily Homework

12-9 **Compare Numbers**

Compare. Write >, <, or =.

1. 864 $<$ 865 | 812 $<$ 822 | 678 $=$ 678 | 410 $>$ 310
2. 578 $>$ 516 | 483 $<$ 485 | 560 $>$ 555 | 960 $>$ 860
3. 502 $=$ 502 | 122 $>$ 120 | 844 $=$ 844 | 280 $>$ 279
4. 599 $<$ 600 | 325 $>$ 323 | 167 $<$ 761 | 862 $<$ 873
5. 467 $>$ 458 | 912 $<$ 932 | 343 $=$ 343 | 760 $>$ 587

Problem Solving

6. I am greater than 4 hundreds 3 tens and 3 ones. I am less than 4 hundreds 3 tens and 5 ones. What number am I?

   434

7. Nancy is waiting for a bus. The number of the bus is greater than 1 hundred 9 tens and 2 ones. The number is less than 1 hundred 9 tens and 4 ones. What number is the bus?

   193

Spiral Review

Add. Look for patterns.

8. 30 + 10 = 40 | 20 + 15 = 35
   30 + 20 = 50 | 20 + 20 = 40
   30 + 30 = 60 | 20 + 25 = 45
   30 + 40 = 70 | 20 + 30 = 50

Practice

Order Numbers

P 12-10 PRACTICE

Write the number that comes just before.

1. 775 776 | 397 398 | 449 450

2. 118 119 | 510 511 | 981 982

3. 543 544 | 878 879 | 199 200

Write the number that comes just after.

4. 471 472 | 399 400 | 761 762

5. 122 123 | 840 841 | 599 600

6. 940 941 | 284 285 | 676 677

Write the number that comes between.

7. 615 616 617 | 799 800 801 | 443 444 445

8. 313 314 315 | 898 899 900 | 627 628 629

9. 100 101 102 | 255 256 257 | 533 534 535

Use with Grade 2, Chapter 12, Lesson 10, pages 445–446. (379)

Reteach

Order Numbers

R 12-10 RETEACH

A number that comes **just before** is one less than a number.

346 347

A number that comes **between** is one more than the first number and one less than the other number.

416 417 418

A number that comes **just after** is one more than a number.

570 571

Circle the number that comes just before.

1. 554 | 989
   558 (557) | 990 987
   560 | 991

Circle the number that comes just after.

2. 816 | 299
   819 818 | 298 294
   (820) | 297

Circle the number that comes between.

3. (478) | 145
   477 475 479 | 142 (143) 144
   480 | 141

Write the number

just before	just after	between
4. 737 738	595 596	337 338 339
5. 499 500	329 330	179 180 181

Use with Grade 2, Chapter 12, Lesson 10, pages 445–446. (380)

Enrich

Order Numbers
Let's Come to Order

E 12-10 ENRICH

Play with a partner.

• Write your name on 2 cards each.

• Use a paper clip and a pencil to spin.

• Spin a number.

• Write the number on your card if you can.

The player who fills both cards first wins.

Spinner: 287 415 970 842 613 156 340 581 776 498 369 491

Card 1	Card 2
Name _____	Name _____
Write the number that is	Write the number that is
just before 415 416	just before 156 157
just after 612 613	just after 580 581
between 286 287 288	between 969 970 971

Card 3	Card 4
Name _____	Name _____
Write the number that is	Write the number that is
just before 776 777	just before 369 370
just after 339 340	just after 490 491
between 841 842 843	between 497 498 499

Use with Grade 2, Chapter 12, Lesson 10, pages 445–446. (381)

Daily Homework

12-10 Order Numbers

Write the number that comes just after.

1. 764 765 | 207 208 | 652 653 | 284 285

2. 835 836 | 914 915 | 101 102 | 342 343

Write the number that comes just before.

3. 196 197 | 284 285 | 986 987 | 658 659

4. 570 571 | 454 455 | 620 621 | 376 377

Write the number that comes between.

5. 288 289 290 | 405 406 407 | 961 962 963

6. 755 756 757 | 682 683 684 | 510 511 512

Problem Solving
Circle your answer.

7. Which number is closest to 500?   498   510   (501)

8. Which number is closest to 800?   750   (825)   850

Spiral Review
Write the number in three different ways.

9. 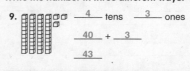 4 tens 3 ones
   40 + 3
   43

116 Grade 2, Chapter 12, Lesson 10, Cluster B

Chapter 12 ~ Lesson 11

Practice

Number Patterns

The numbers go up by ones, tens, or hundreds.
Write the missing numbers in each pattern.
Then write the pattern.

                                    Count By

1. 715, 725, __735__, 745, __755__   ones (tens) hundreds

2. 673, __674__, 675, __676__, 677   (ones) tens hundreds

3. 491, __591__, 691, __791__, 891   ones tens (hundreds)

4. __838__, 839, __840__, 841, 842   (ones) tens hundreds

5. __129__, 229, __329__, 429, 529   ones tens (hundreds)

6. 548, 648, __748__, __848__, 948   ones tens (hundreds)

7. __295__, 395, 495, 595, __695__   ones tens (hundreds)

8. 579, 589, 599, __609__, __619__   ones (tens) hundreds

Use with Grade 2, Chapter 12, Lesson 11, pages 447–448. (382)

Reteach

Number Patterns

You can use number patterns to help you count.
Count by tens.

340, 350, __360__, 370, __380__, 390

Count by hundreds.

400, 500, 600, __700__, 800, __900__

Count by tens. Write the numbers.

1. 220, 230, __240__, 250, __260__, 270, 280

2. 510, 520, 530, __540__, 550, __560__, 570

3. 135, 145, 155, __165__, 175, __185__, 195

4. 747, 757, __767__, __777__, 787, 797, 807

5. 313, __323__, 333, 343, __353__, 363, 373

Count by hundreds. Write the numbers.

6. 200, 300, 400, __500__, 600 __700__, 800

7. 350, 450, 550, __650__, __750__, 850, 950

8. 182, __282__, 382, 482, __582__, 682, 782

Use with Grade 2, Chapter 12, Lesson 11, pages 447–448. (383)

Enrich

Number Patterns
What's the Pattern?

Complete the patterns.
Write the numbers.

1. Start with: 433	
Count by: tens	433, 443, 453, 463, 473, 483, 493

2. Start with: 668	
Count by: twos	668, 670, 672, 674, 676, 678, 680

3. Start with: 523	
Count by: fives	523, 528, 533, 538, 543, 548, 553

4. Start with: 129	
Count by: threes	129, 132, 135, 138, 141, 144, 147

5. Start with: 840	
Count by: tens	840, 850, 860, 870, 880, 890, 900

Use with Grade 2, Chapter 12, Lesson 11, pages 447–448. (384)

Daily Homework

 12-11 **Number Patterns**

The numbers go up by ones, tens, or hundreds. Write the
missing numbers in each pattern. Then circle the pattern.

	Numbers	Pattern: Count By
1.	810, 820, 830, __840__, 850, __860__	ones (tens) hundreds
2.	400, 500, 600, __700__, 800, __900__	ones tens (hundreds)
3.	345, 346, __347__, 348, 349, __350__	(ones) tens hundreds
4.	425, 525, 625, __725__, __825__, 925	ones tens (hundreds)
5.	523, 524, __525__, 526, 527, __528__	(ones) tens hundreds

Problem Solving

6. Pedro counts pennies in groups of ten.
   How many pennies does Pedro have if he has 6 groups?

Number of groups	1	2	3	4	5	6
Number of pennies	10	20	30	40	50	60

Spiral Review

Complete the number sentence.

7. __3__ + 9 = 12   11 = __7__ + 4   5 + __5__ = 10

Grade 2, Chapter 12, Lesson 11, Cluster B **117**

Chapter 12 ~ Lesson 12

Part A Worksheet

Problem Solving: Application
Make a Bracelet

Plan to make a bracelet.

Color each shape bead a different color.

Cut out the beads.

Choose the ones you want to use.

Make a pattern.

Part A Worksheet

Problem Solving: Application
Make a Bracelet

1. Draw a picture of your bracelet.

Check students' work.

2. Describe the pattern you used.

_____

_____

_____

Part B Worksheet

Problem Solving: Application
How Well Does Sound Move Through String?

1. Record how well you can hear
on your string phones.
Write **1** for great, **2** for O.K., or **3** for poor. Answers may vary.

Length	Rating
30-foot phone	
20-foot phone	
10-foot phone	

2. Write your phones in order from best to worst.

_____

_____

_____

_____

3. What if you want to make a phone
that works even better?
How long would you make the string?
Explain your thinking.

_____

_____

Chapter 13 ~ Lesson 1

Practice

Add Hundreds

P 13-1 PRACTICE

Count on by hundreds to add.

1.
300	200	700	200	100
+ 100	+ 400	+ 100	+ 300	+ 400
400	600	800	500	500

2.
600	300	600	800	400
+ 100	+ 200	+ 200	+ 100	+ 500
700	500	800	900	900

3.
500	400	500	200	100
+ 200	+ 200	+ 300	+ 200	+ 700
700	600	800	400	800

4.
300	400	100	200	100
+ 300	+ 300	+ 100	+ 200	+ 800
600	700	200	400	900

Problem Solving

5. There are 400 students in the second grade. There are 300 students in the third grade. How many students are there in all?

   __700__ students

6. There are 200 children that take the bus to school. There are 200 children that walk to school. How many children are there in all?

   __400__ children

Use with Grade 2, Chapter 13, Lesson 1, pages 465–466. (388)

Reteach

Add Hundreds

R 13-1 RETEACH

Count on by hundreds.

Add: 200 + 300

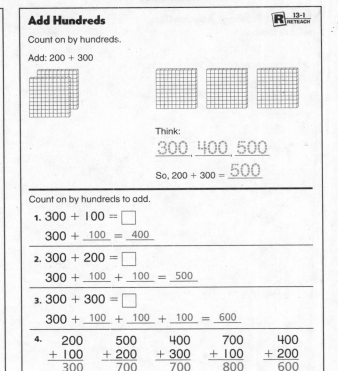

Think:

300, 400, 500

So, 200 + 300 = __500__

Count on by hundreds to add.

1. 300 + 100 = ☐

   300 + __100__ = __400__

2. 300 + 200 = ☐

   300 + __100__ + __100__ = __500__

3. 300 + 300 = ☐

   300 + __100__ + __100__ + __100__ = __600__

4.
200	500	400	700	400
+ 100	+ 200	+ 300	+ 100	+ 200
300	700	700	800	600

Use with Grade 2, Chapter 13, Lesson 1, pages 465–466. (389)

Enrich

Add Hundreds
Add Up to 1,000

E 13-1 ENRICH

Cut out the spinner.
Use a pencil and a paperclip to spin.
Play with a partner. Take turns.

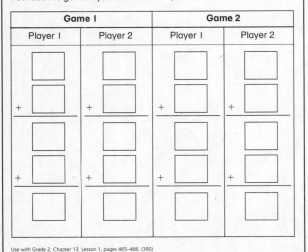

- Spin a number.
- Write the number in the game card.
- Add after each spin.

The first player to reach 1,000 wins.
You lose the game if your sum is over 1,000.

Game 1		Game 2	
Player 1	Player 2	Player 1	Player 2
☐	☐	☐	☐
+ ☐	+ ☐	+ ☐	+ ☐
☐	☐	☐	☐
+ ☐	+ ☐	+ ☐	+ ☐

Use with Grade 2, Chapter 13, Lesson 1, pages 465–466. (390)

Daily Homework

13-1 Add Hundreds

Count on by hundreds to add.

1. 200 + 600 = __800__   100 + 300 = __400__   300 + 400 = __700__

2. 500 + 100 = __600__   600 + 300 = __900__   200 + 700 = __900__

3.
200	500	300	400	700	600
+ 200	+ 400	+ 300	+ 500	+ 200	+ 100
400	900	600	900	900	700

4.
400	100	400	300	500	600
+ 200	+ 400	+ 300	+ 600	+ 200	+ 200
600	500	700	900	700	800

Problem Solving

5. The school kitchen collects food scraps to compost. In one month, the kitchen collected 300 pounds of scraps. The next month they collected 400 pounds of scraps. How many pounds of scraps were collected in all?

   __700__ pounds

6. The school sponsors a car wash. The first graders wash 100 cars. The third graders wash 400 cars. How many cars are washed in all?

   __500__ cars

Spiral Review

Write how many hundreds, tens, and ones.

7. 452 __4__ hundreds __5__ tens __2__ ones

© McGraw-Hill School Division

Chapter 13 ~ Lesson 2

Practice

3-Digit Addition Without Regrouping

Find each sum.

1.

Hundreds	Tens	Ones
5	1	2
+2	3	1
7	4	3

Hundreds	Tens	Ones
3	7	5
+1	0	1
4	7	6

2.
327	411	524	158	341
+ 401	+ 273	+ 215	+ 120	+ 235
728	684	739	278	576

3.
196	313	136	261	473
+ 203	+ 145	+ 163	+ 122	+ 102
399	458	299	383	575

4.
463	211	438	522	217
+ 133	+ 211	+ 250	+ 147	+ 232
596	422	688	669	449

Problem Solving

5. On Monday, 127 children helped clean up the park. On Tuesday, 231 children helped clean up. How many children helped clean up the park?

___358___ children

6. The children collected 219 bottles the first week. They collected 330 bottles the second week. How many bottles did they collect in all?

___549___ bottles

Use with Grade 2, Chapter 13, Lesson 2, pages 469–471. (391)

Reteach

3-Digit Addition Without Regrouping

Add: 241 + 125

Add the ones. | Add the tens. | Add the hundreds.

Hundreds	Tens	Ones
2	4	1
+1	2	5
		6

Hundreds	Tens	Ones
2	4	1
+1	2	5
	6	6

Hundreds	Tens	Ones
2	4	1
+1	2	5
3	6	6

Find each sum.

1.
Hundreds	Tens	Ones
1	1	3
+1	4	5
2	5	8

Hundreds	Tens	Ones
2	3	7
+2	1	2
4	4	9

2.
Hundreds	Tens	Ones
2	5	4
+1	3	4
3	8	8

Hundreds	Tens	Ones
4	2	1
+2	4	6
6	6	7

3.
Hundreds	Tens	Ones
2	4	0
+3	5	2
5	9	2

Hundreds	Tens	Ones
5	2	6
+3	3	1
8	5	7

Use with Grade 2, Chapter 13, Lesson 2, pages 469–470. (392)

Enrich

3-Digit Addition Without Regrouping
3-Digit Number Play

Look at the numbers on the mailboxes. Read the clues. Find the numbers.

1. The sum of these two numbers is 838. Their ones digits are the same.

___524___ , ___314___

2. The sum of these two numbers is 993. The sum of their digits is 21.

___461___ , ___532___

3. The sum of these two numbers is 386. One addend counts up 100 from the other.

___243___ , ___143___

4. The sum of these two numbers is 729. The hundreds digit in one addend is an odd number.

___415___ , ___314___

5. The sum of these two numbers is 644. The sum of their digits is 14.

___304___ , ___314___

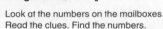
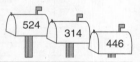
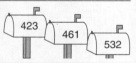

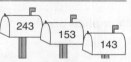
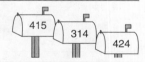
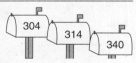

Use with Grade 2, Chapter 13, Lesson 2, pages 469–470. (393)

Daily Homework

13-2 **3-Digit Addition Without Regrouping**

Find each sum.

1.
hundreds	tens	ones
5	1	4
+ 4	5	4
9	6	8

hundreds	tens	ones
1	7	3
+ 2	2	6
1	9	9

hundreds	tens	ones
2	8	3
+ 1	0	6
3	8	9

2.
538	614	936	318	211
+ 241	+ 173	+ 21	+ 600	+ 333
779	787	957	918	544

3.
423	256	333	481	325
+ 60	+ 132	+ 52	+ 113	+ 100
483	388	385	594	425

Problem Solving

4. Mary collects 145 cans for recycling. Sarah collects 234 cans. How many cans are collected in all?

___379___ cans

5. What is the same about the numbers 529 and 259? What is different?

The value of the digit 9 is the same in both numbers; the values of the digits 2 and 5 are different

Spiral Review

Count forward. Write the missing numbers.

6. 4, ___5___ , 6, ___7___ , 8

Grade 2, Chapter 13, Lesson 2 **119**

© McGraw-Hill School Division

Chapter 13 ~ Lesson 3

Practice

3-Digit Addition
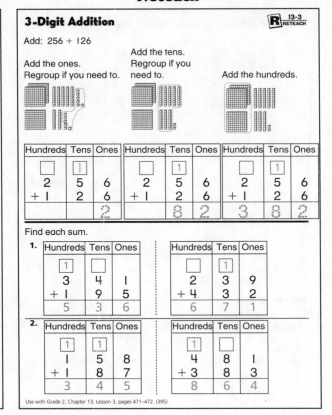

Add. Use hundreds, tens, and ones models.

1.

Hundreds	Tens	Ones
[1]	[ ]	
4	5	2
+2	6	5
7	1	7

Hundreds	Tens	Ones
1		
3	7	5
+1	6	1
5	3	6

2.

Hundreds	Tens	Ones
[1]	[ ]	
3	4	7
+3	8	1
7	2	8

Hundreds	Tens	Ones
[1]		
2	4	7
+4	4	4
6	9	1

3.

Hundreds	Tens	Ones
[ ]	1	
2	1	8
+1	2	5
3	4	3

Hundreds	Tens	Ones
[ ]	1	
1	7	6
+1	0	9
2	8	5

Problem Solving

4. There are 325 second graders. There are 289 third graders. How many children are there in all?

   614 children

5. There are 415 fourth graders. There are 365 fifth graders. How many children are there in all?

   780 children

Use with Grade 2, Chapter 13, Lesson 3, pages 471–472. (394)

Reteach

3-Digit Addition

Add: 256 + 126

Add the ones. Regroup if you need to.

Add the tens. Regroup if you need to.

Add the hundreds.

Hundreds	Tens	Ones
[ ]	[1]	
2	5	6
+1	2	6
		2

Hundreds	Tens	Ones
[ ]	1	
2	5	6
+1	2	6
	8	2

Hundreds	Tens	Ones
[ ]	1	
2	5	6
+1	2	6
3	8	2

Find each sum.

1.

Hundreds	Tens	Ones
1	[ ]	
3	4	1
+1	9	5
5	3	6

Hundreds	Tens	Ones
[ ]	1	
2	3	9
+4	3	2
6	7	1

2.

Hundreds	Tens	Ones
1	1	
1	5	8
+1	8	7
3	4	5

Hundreds	Tens	Ones
1	[ ]	
4	8	1
+3	8	3
8	6	4

Use with Grade 2, Chapter 13, Lesson 3, pages 471–472. (395)

Enrich

3-Digit Addition
What's Missing?

Find the missing digits. Complete the additions.

1.

Hundreds	Tens	Ones
	1	
4	6	2
+ 3	[2]	8
7	9	[0]

Hundreds	Tens	Ones
	1	1
5	8	4
+ 3	5	[8]
9	4	2

2.

Hundreds	Tens	Ones
	1	
[1]	5	6
+ 3	3	[6]
4	9	2

Hundreds	Tens	Ones
	1	1
[2]	3	[8]
+ 2	7	7
5	1	5

Circle the 3-digit number that completes the addition.
Write the digits in the boxes.

3.

Hundreds	Tens	Ones
6	7	1
+ [1]	[8]	[8]
8	5	9

(188)   178   288

Hundreds	Tens	Ones
2	5	6
+ [3]	[4]	[8]
6	0	4

448   399   (348)

Use with Grade 2, Chapter 13, Lesson 3, pages 471–472. (396)

Daily Homework

13-3 3-Digit Addition

Add. Use hundreds, tens, and ones models.

1.

hundreds	tens	ones
1	[ ]	
2	6	4
+4	5	4
7	1	8

hundreds	tens	ones
[ ]	1	
3	7	5
+_	1	6
3	9	1

hundreds	tens	ones
1	[ ]	
2	8	3
+3	4	6
6	2	9

2.

hundreds	tens	ones
[ ]	1	
2	6	7
+3	2	4
5	9	1

hundreds	tens	ones
1	[ ]	
5	4	6
+1	2	6
6	7	2

hundreds	tens	ones
1	[ ]	
4	4	3
+1	4	9
5	9	2

Problem Solving

3. Draw a picture.
   Show the sum of 154 and 221.   375

Spiral Review

Add.

4.

200	300	300	100	700	600
+ 200	+ 400	+ 300	+ 500	+ 200	+ 300
400	700	600	600	900	900

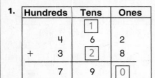

© McGraw-Hill School Division

Chapter 13 ~ Lesson 4

Practice

MORE 3-Digit Addition

Find each sum.

1.

Hundreds	Tens	Ones
	1	
3	6	6
+ 1	2	5
4	9	1

Hundreds	Tens	Ones
1		
4	8	5
+ 4	8	1
9	6	6

2.

345	178	236	494	117
+ 219	+ 411	+ 289	+ 119	+ 336
564	589	525	613	453

3.

823	355	517	438	551
+ 127	+ 315	+ 119	+ 224	+ 295
950	670	636	662	846

4.

114	744	482	312	541
+ 267	+ 155	+ 432	+ 226	+ 388
381	899	914	538	929

Problem Solving

5. On Saturday, 437 pounds of paper were collected. On Sunday, 378 pounds of paper were collected. How many pounds of paper were collected in all?

___815___ pounds

6. Last week, the first grade collected 236 pounds of cans for recycling. The second grade collected 316 pounds of cans. How many pounds of cans did they collect in all?

___552___ pounds

Use with Grade 2, Chapter 13, Lesson 4, pages 473–474. (397)

Reteach

MORE 3-Digit Addition

Add: 163 + 248

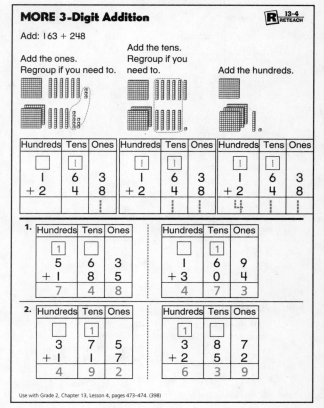

Add the ones. Regroup if you need to.

Add the tens. Regroup if you need to.

Add the hundreds.

Hundreds	Tens	Ones
	1	
1	6	3
+ 2	4	8

Hundreds	Tens	Ones
1	1	
1	6	3
+ 2	4	8

Hundreds	Tens	Ones
1	1	
1	6	3
+ 2	4	8

1.

Hundreds	Tens	Ones
1		
5	6	3
+ 1	8	5
7	4	8

Hundreds	Tens	Ones
	1	
1	6	9
+ 3	0	4
4	7	3

2.

Hundreds	Tens	Ones
	1	
3	7	5
+ 1	1	7
4	9	2

Hundreds	Tens	Ones
1		
3	8	7
+ 2	5	2
6	3	9

Use with Grade 2, Chapter 13, Lesson 4, pages 473–474. (398)

Enrich

MORE 3-Digit Addition
Our Little Town

Ms. Murphy delivers mail from the Post Office. Find how far she walks between each place.

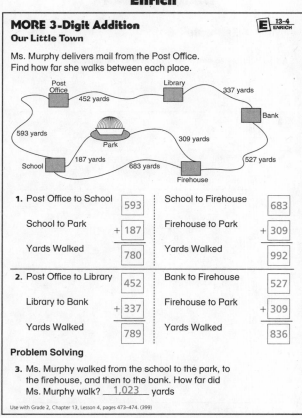

1. Post Office to School ___593___

School to Park + ___187___

Yards Walked ___780___

School to Firehouse ___683___

Firehouse to Park + ___309___

Yards Walked ___992___

2. Post Office to Library ___452___

Library to Bank + ___337___

Yards Walked ___789___

Bank to Firehouse ___527___

Firehouse to Park + ___309___

Yards Walked ___836___

Problem Solving

3. Ms. Murphy walked from the school to the park, to the firehouse, and then to the bank. How far did Ms. Murphy walk? ___1,023___ yards

Use with Grade 2, Chapter 13, Lesson 4, pages 473–474. (399)

Daily Homework

13-4 More 3-Digit Addition

Add. Regroup if you need to.

1.

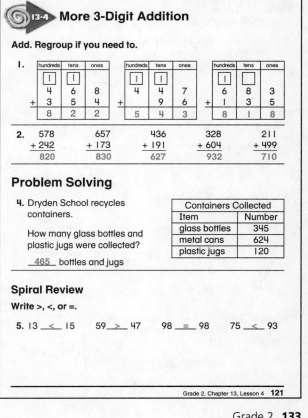

hundreds	tens	ones
1	1	
4	6	8
+ 3	5	4
8	2	2

hundreds	tens	ones
1	1	
4	4	7
+ 9	7	6
5	4	3

hundreds	tens	ones
1		
6	8	3
+ 1	3	5
8	1	8

2.

578	657	436	328	211
+ 242	+ 173	+ 191	+ 604	+ 499
820	830	627	932	710

Problem Solving

4. Dryden School recycles containers.

How many glass bottles and plastic jugs were collected?

___465___ bottles and jugs

Containers Collected	
Item	Number
glass bottles	345
metal cans	624
plastic jugs	120

Spiral Review

Write >, <, or =.

5. 13 _<_ 15   59 _>_ 47   98 _=_ 98   75 _<_ 93

Chapter 13 ~ Lesson 5

Practice

Estimate Sums

P 13-5 PRACTICE

Add. Estimate to see if your answer is reasonable.

1.
```
  537    500       187    200
+ 219  + 200     + 442  + 400
  756    700       629    600
```

2.
```
  376    400       522    500
+ 125  + 100     + 367  + 400
  501    500       889    900
```

3.
```
  138    100       672    700
+ 289  + 300     + 176  + 200
  427    400       848    900
```

4.
```
  242    200       139    100
+ 289  + 300     + 445  + 400
  531    500       584    500
```

5.
```
  217    200       621    600
+ 332  + 300     + 173  + 200
  549    500       794    800
```

Problem Solving

6. There are 452 bottles and 397 cans. How many bottles and cans are there?

   __849__ bottles and cans

7. There are 128 newspapers and 228 magazines. How many newspapers and magazines are there?

   __356__ newspapers and magazines

Reteach

Estimate Sums

R 13-5 RETEACH

Estimate: 427 + 289

```
  427   Round 427 down to __400__ →      400
+ 289   Round 289 up to __300__ →      + 300
  716                                    700
```

716 is close to 700, so your answer is reasonable.

Add. Estimate to see if your answer is reasonable.

1.
```
  369   Round 369 to __400__ →      400
+ 495   Round 495 to __500__ →    + 500
  864                               900
```

2.
```
  213   Round 213 to __200__ →      200
+ 441   Round 441 to __400__ →    + 400
  654                               600
```

3.
```
  519    500       271    300
+ 267  + 300     + 132  + 100
  786    800       403    400
```

Enrich

Estimate Sums
Miss Winchell's Flower Shop

E 13-5 ENRICH

The table shows how many flowers Miss Winchell sold each month.

	Roses	Daisies	Tulips	Daffodils
June	287	376	539	645
July	419	294	288	337
August	532	421	99	582

Use the table to estimate the sums.

1. About how many roses were sold in June and July?

   June __287__   July __419__

   __300__ + __400__ = __700__

   About how many tulips were sold in July and August?

   July __288__   August __99__

   __300__ + __100__ = __400__

2. About how many daisies were sold in June and August?

   June __376__   August __421__

   __400__ + __400__ = __800__

   About how many daffodils were sold in July and August?

   July __337__   August __582__

   __300__ + __600__ = __900__

3. Write your own estimation problem. Use the numbers in the table. Solve it. Then give it to a friend to solve.

   __Answers may vary.__

Daily Homework

13-5 Estimate Sums

Add. Estimate to see if your answer is reasonable.

1.
```
  508    500       187    200
+ 291  + 300     + 491  + 500
  799    800       678    700
```

2.
```
  215    200       639    600
+ 279  + 300     + 228  + 200
  494    500       867    800
```

3.
```
  423    400        87    100
+ 190  + 200     + 540  + 500
  613    600       627    600
```

4.
```
  787    800       536    500
+ 102  + 100     + 290  + 300
  889    900       826    800
```

5.
```
  595    600       444    400
+ 341  + 300     + 391  + 400
  936    900       835    800
```

Spiral Review

Subtract.

6.
```
  12     15     13     18     14     16
 - 9    - 8    - 6   - 10    - 6    - 7
   3      7      7      8      8      9
```

Chapter 13 ~ Lesson 6

Practice

Problem Solving: Reading for Math
Main Idea and Details

P 13-6 PRACTICE · Reading Skill

The second grade is collecting food for the food bank. Emmy's class collects 186 cans of food. Rodrigo's class collects 225 cans of food. How many cans of food do they collect in all?

Solve.

1. What is the main idea?
   The second grade collects canned food.

2. What do you want to find out?
   The number of cans of food they collect in all.

3. What details will help you find out?
   Emmy's class collects 186 cans; Rodrigo's class collects 225 cans.

4. How many cans of food do they collect in all? __411__ cans

5. Write a number sentence to show your thinking.
   186 + 225 = 411 or 225 + 186 = 411

Use with Grade 2, Chapter 13, Lesson 6, pages 477–478. (403)

Practice

Problem Solving: Reading for Math
Main Idea and Details

P 13-6 PRACTICE · Math Skills Test Prep

Karl and his neighbors are planting a community garden. Karl and the people on his block bring 178 tulip bulbs. Mrs. Richards and the people on her block bring 194 daffodil bulbs. How many bulbs do they have in all?

Choose the best answer. Fill in the ◯.

1. What do you want to find out?
   Ⓐ how many bulbs the neighbors have
   Ⓑ how many gardens they will plant
   Ⓒ how many people live in the neighborhood

2. What details will help you find out?
   Ⓕ how many people are planting the garden
   Ⓖ how many people live on the two blocks
   Ⓗ how many bulbs the people bring

3. What are the neighbors doing?
   Ⓐ counting bulbs
   Ⓑ picking flowers
   Ⓒ planting a garden
   Ⓓ talking to each other

4. How many bulbs do they have in all?
   Ⓕ 178
   Ⓖ 272
   Ⓗ 362
   Ⓙ 372

Use with Grade 2, Chapter 13, Lesson 6, pages 477–478. (404)

Practice

Problem Solving: Reading for Math
Main Idea and Details

P 13-6 PRACTICE · Math Skills Test Prep

Bonnie's school is having a play. 245 people come to the play the first night. 267 people come to the play the second night. How many people come to the play in all?

Choose the best answer. Fill in the ◯.

1. What are the people doing?
   Ⓐ acting in a play
   Ⓑ coming to a play
   Ⓒ playing in an orchestra
   Ⓓ playing at school

2. What do you need to find out?
   Ⓕ how many people come to the play the first night
   Ⓖ how many more people come to the play the second night
   Ⓗ how many people come to the play in all

Solve.

3. What details will help you find out?
   245 people come the first night; 267 people come the second night

4. How many people come to the play in all? __512__ people

5. Write a number sentence to show your thinking.
   245 + 267 = 512 or 267 + 245 = 512

Use with Grade 2, Chapter 13, Lesson 6, pages 477–478. (405)

Daily Homework

13-6 Problem Solving: Reading for Math
Main Idea and Details

Henry and Jill paint tiles for a new school mural. Henry paints 231 tiles. Jill paints 178 tiles. How many tiles do they paint in all?

1. What is the main idea? Two children paint tiles for a mural.

2. What do you want to find out?
   how many tiles they paint in all

3. What details will help you find out?
   how many tiles they each paint

4. How many tiles do they paint in all? ____409____

5. Write a number sentence to show your thinking.
   231 + 178 = 409 or 178 + 231 = 409

Spiral Review

Choose + or −.

6. 8 ⊕ 6 = 14   16 = 8 ⊕ 8   9 ⊖ 5 = 4   9 ⊕ 6 = 15

Chapter 13 ~ Lesson 7

Practice

Problem Solving: Strategy
Make a Graph

 13-7 PRACTICE

Complete the graph to solve.

1. Sally sold 18 cookies at the bake sale. Maggie sold 32 cookies. Jana sold 39 cookies. About how many cookies did they sell in all?

   about __90__ cookies

   Number of Cookies
Sally					
Maggie					
Jana					

   0 10 20 30 40 50 60

2. Ian sold 23 cherry ice pops, 17 grape ice pops, and 12 orange ice pops. About how many ice pops did he sell in all?

   about __50__ ice pops

   Number of Ice Pops
Cherry					
Grape					
Orange					

   0 10 20 30 40 50 60

3. Ryan collected 32 shells at the beach. Kyra collected 29 shells. Eve collected 11 shells. About how many shells did they collect in all?

   about __70__ shells

   Number of Shells
Ryan					
Kyra					
Eve					

   0 10 20 30 40 50 60

Mixed Strategy Review

Solve.

4. Hana has 98 gray rocks and 124 white rocks in her rock collection. How many rocks does she have in all?

   __222__ rocks

5. **Create a problem** for which you would make a graph to solve. Share it with others.

Reteach

Problem Solving: Strategy
Make a Graph

 13-7 RETEACH

Page 482, Problem 1

In the Book Walk, Jon walked the first lap in 5 minutes and the next lap in 10 minutes. Betty waked the first lap in 10 minutes and the next lap in 5 minutes. Kathy walked the first lap in 5 minutes and the next lap in 10 minutes.
Which lap took longer to walk?

Step 1 **Read**	**Be sure you understand the problem.**
	What do you know?
	• Jon, Betty, and Kathy walked for __2__ laps.
	What do you need to find?
	• You need to find __which lap took longer to walk__

Step 2 **Plan**	**Make a plan.**
• Draw a Picture	Choose a strategy.
• Write a Number Sentence	Make a bar graph.
• Use Logical Reasoning	Show how many minutes each child took
• Act it Out	to walk each lap.
• Choose the Operation	
• Make a Table	Use the graph to find about how many
• Guess and Check	minutes each lap took.
• Find a Pattern	
• Make a Graph	

Reteach

Problem Solving: Strategy
Make a Graph

 13-7 RETEACH

Step 3 **Solve**	**Carry out your plan.**

• Make a bar graph. Show how many minutes each child took to walk each lap.

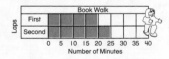
Book Walk
| First | | | | | |
| Second | | | | | |

0 5 10 15 20 25 30 35 40
Number of Minutes
Laps

• Use the graph to find about how many minutes each lap took.

• Jon, Betty, and Kathy walked the first lap in __20__ minutes.

• Jon, Betty, and Kathy walked the second lap in __25__ minutes.

• Which lap took longer to walk?

   __second__ lap

Step 4 **Look Back**	**Is the solution reasonable?**
	Does your answer make sense (Yes) No

Daily Homework

13-7 Problem Solving: Strategy
Make a Graph

Complete the bar graph to solve.

1. In the Jump-Rope-a-Thon, Jim jumped for 10 minutes, hopped for 5 minutes, and skipped for 5 minutes. Mark jumped for 15 minutes and hopped for 10 minutes. Julie skipped for 25 minutes. How many minutes were spent on each of the three activities?

   __jump: 25; hop: 15; skip: 30__

   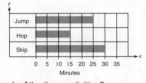
Jump					
Hop					
Skip					

   0 5 10 15 20 25 30 35
   Minutes

2. At the flower sale, Tanya sold 8 red flowers and 2 yellow ones. Dan sold 7 pink flowers and 5 white ones. Marcus sold 3 yellow flowers and 6 blue ones. How many flowers did each of them sell?

   __Tanya: 10; Dan: 12; Marcus: 9__

   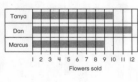
Tanya					
Dan					
Marcus					

   1 2 3 4 5 6 7 8 9 10 11 12
   Flowers sold

Spiral Review

Write the number that comes between.

3. 34 __35__ 36   59 __60__ 61   100 __101__ 102

Chapter 13 ~ Lesson 8

Practice

Subtract Hundreds

P 13-8 PRACTICE

Subtract.

1.
$$300 - 100 = 200$$
$$800 - 300 = 500$$
$$700 - 100 = 600$$
$$600 - 300 = 300$$
$$600 - 200 = 400$$

2.
$$400 - 100 = 300$$
$$500 - 100 = 400$$
$$600 - 200 = 400$$
$$800 - 100 = 700$$
$$500 - 300 = 200$$

3.
$$500 - 200 = 300$$
$$400 - 200 = 200$$
$$600 - 100 = 500$$
$$700 - 200 = 500$$
$$800 - 200 = 600$$

4.
$$400 - 300 = 100$$
$$500 - 100 = 400$$
$$700 - 300 = 400$$
$$900 - 300 = 600$$
$$900 - 100 = 800$$

Problem Solving

5. There are 400 children in the park. There are 200 adults in the park. How many more children are there than adults?

   __200__ more children

6. There are 600 cars in the parking lot. 300 of the cars are driven away. How many cars are left in the parking lot?

   __300__ cars

Use with Grade 2, Chapter 13, Lesson 8, pages 483–484. (409)

Reteach

Subtract Hundreds

R 13-8 RETEACH

Count back by hundreds.

Subtract: 600 − 300

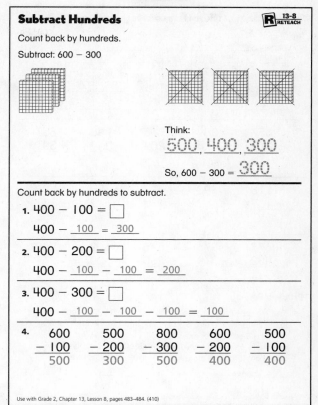

Think:

__500__, __400__, __300__

So, 600 − 300 = __300__

Count back by hundreds to subtract.

1. $400 - 100 = \square$

   $400 - \underline{100} = \underline{300}$

2. $400 - 200 = \square$

   $400 - \underline{100} - \underline{100} = \underline{200}$

3. $400 - 300 = \square$

   $400 - \underline{100} - \underline{100} - \underline{100} = \underline{100}$

4.
$$600 - 100 = 500$$
$$500 - 200 = 300$$
$$800 - 300 = 500$$
$$600 - 200 = 400$$
$$500 - 100 = 400$$

Use with Grade 2, Chapter 13, Lesson 8, pages 483–484. (410)

Enrich

Subtract Hundreds
Subtraction Puzzle

E 13-8 ENRICH

Subtract. Then find that number at the bottom.
Write the letter in the box. Find the secret message.

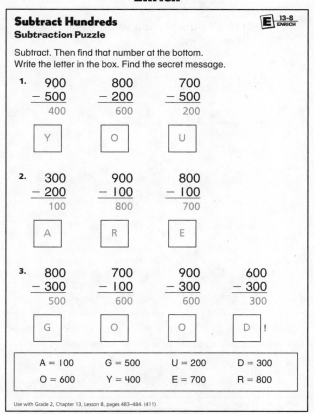

1.
$$900 - 500 = 400 \quad \boxed{Y}$$
$$800 - 200 = 600 \quad \boxed{O}$$
$$700 - 500 = 200 \quad \boxed{U}$$

2.
$$300 - 200 = 100 \quad \boxed{A}$$
$$900 - 100 = 800 \quad \boxed{R}$$
$$800 - 100 = 700 \quad \boxed{E}$$

3.
$$800 - 300 = 500 \quad \boxed{G}$$
$$700 - 100 = 600 \quad \boxed{O}$$
$$900 - 300 = 600 \quad \boxed{O}$$
$$600 - 300 = 300 \quad \boxed{D} !$$

A = 100	G = 500	U = 200	D = 300
O = 600	Y = 400	E = 700	R = 800

Use with Grade 2, Chapter 13, Lesson 8, pages 483–484. (411)

Daily Homework

13-8 Subtract Hundreds

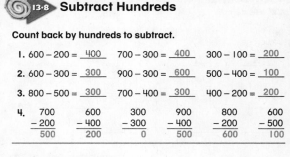

Count back by hundreds to subtract.

1. $600 - 200 = \underline{400}$ $700 - 300 = \underline{400}$ $300 - 100 = \underline{200}$

2. $600 - 300 = \underline{300}$ $900 - 300 = \underline{600}$ $500 - 400 = \underline{100}$

3. $800 - 500 = \underline{300}$ $700 - 400 = \underline{300}$ $400 - 200 = \underline{200}$

4.
$$700 - 200 = 500$$
$$600 - 400 = 200$$
$$300 - 300 = 0$$
$$900 - 400 = 500$$
$$800 - 200 = 600$$
$$600 - 500 = 100$$

Problem Solving

5. Find the next number in each pattern.

   600 500 400 300 __200__   345 445 545 645 __745__

   200 300 400 500 __600__   762 662 562 462 __362__

6. The third grade washes 200 windows. The second grade washes 400 windows. How many more windows does the second grade wash? __200__ windows

Spiral Review

Write each number. Write each word.

8.

453	hundreds	tens	ones
	4	5	3

four hundred fifty-three

162	hundreds	tens	ones
	1	6	2

one hundred sixty-two

Grade 2, Chapter 13, Lesson 8   125

Chapter 13 ~ Lesson 9

Practice

3-Digit Subtraction Without Regrouping

Subtract.

1.

Hundreds	Tens	Ones
6	3	7
− 4	1	1
2	2	6

Hundreds	Tens	Ones
5	7	7
− 2	5	6
3	2	1

2.

657	389	915	443	857
− 327	− 126	− 204	− 332	− 341
330	263	711	111	516

3.

778	593	477	736	499
− 167	− 142	− 153	− 612	− 137
611	451	324	124	362

4.

677	976	575	672	488
− 432	− 314	− 250	− 130	− 261
245	662	325	542	227

Problem Solving

5. There are 457 coloring books in the store. By the end of the week, 143 coloring books were sold. How many coloring books are left in the store?

_314_ books

6. There are 567 pencils in the store. At the end of the week, 134 pencils were left in the store. How many pencils were sold that week?

_433_ pencils

Use with Grade 2, Chapter 13, Lesson 9, pages 487–488. (412)

Reteach

3-Digit Subtraction Without Regrouping

Subtract: 547 − 234

Subtract the ones.	Subtract the tens.	Subtract the hundreds.

Hundreds	Tens	Ones
5	4	7
− 2	3	4
		3

Hundreds	Tens	Ones
5	4	7
− 2	3	4
	1	3

Hundreds	Tens	Ones
5	4	7
− 2	3	4
3	1	3

Subtract to find the difference.

1.

Hundreds	Tens	Ones
3	4	9
− 1	2	5
2	2	4

Hundreds	Tens	Ones
4	3	7
− 2	0	6
2	3	1

2.

Hundreds	Tens	Ones
8	7	9
− 1	1	4
7	6	5

Hundreds	Tens	Ones
7	5	3
− 2	5	1
5	0	2

Use with Grade 2, Chapter 13, Lesson 9, pages 487–488. (413)

Enrich

3-Digit Subtraction Without Regrouping

What's Missing?

Circle and write the 3-digit numbers that complete the subtractions.

1.

H	T	O
6	5	7
− 1	4	3
5	1	4

243
(143)
132

H	T	O
7	9	5
− 3	2	1
4	7	4

221
341
(321)

2.

H	T	O
9	4	5
− 3	0	4
6	4	1

(304)
404
315

H	T	O
8	2	5
− 1	2	2
7	0	3

(122)
143
132

Order of answers for exercises 3–4 may vary. Possible order is shown.

3.

H	T	O
8	4	8
− 4	1	5
4	3	3

(433)
533
(415)

H	T	O
4	9	7
− 1	5	2
3	4	5

(152)
(345)
138

4.

H	T	O
5	7	4
− 2	1	2
3	6	2

255
(212)
(362)

H	T	O
4	6	8
− 1	3	7
3	3	1

(331)
237
(137)

Use with Grade 2, Chapter 13, Lesson 9, pages 487–488. (414)

Daily Homework

13-9 **3-Digit Subtraction Without Regrouping**

Subtract.

1.

hundreds	tens	ones
5	5	5
− 4	5	4
1	0	1

hundreds	tens	ones
2	7	6
−	2	5
2	5	1

hundreds	tens	ones
2	8	7
− 1	0	6
1	8	1

2.

538	614	936	318	555
− 201	− 113	− 21	− 200	− 333
337	501	915	118	222

3.

423	256	767	486	325
− 10	− 132	− 52	− 113	− 100
413	124	715	373	225

Solve.

4. What is the same about the numbers 625 and 265? What is different?

The value of the digit 5 is the same in both; the values of the digits 2 and 6 are different.

5. Cathy decorates the lunchroom with 124 red balloons. Bill puts up 257 blue balloons. How many more blue balloons are there than red balloons?

_133_ balloons

Spiral Review

Write the amount. Use a dollar sign and decimal point.

6.  $ _0.83_

© McGraw-Hill School Division

Practice

3-Digit Subtraction

Subtract. Use hundreds, tens, and ones models.

1.

Hundreds	Tens	Ones
[5]	[12]	[ ]
6	2	7
− 2	6	2
3	6	5

Hundreds	Tens	Ones
[5]	[13]	[ ]
6	3	5
− 1	5	2
4	8	3

2.

Hundreds	Tens	Ones
[8]	[13]	[15]
9	4	5
− 3	8	6
5	5	9

Hundreds	Tens	Ones
[ ]	[8]	[13]
5	9	3
− 2	4	7
3	4	6

3.

Hundreds	Tens	Ones
[2]	[15]	[15]
3	6	5
− 1	9	7
1	6	8

Hundreds	Tens	Ones
[ ]	[2]	[10]
7	3	0
− 1	2	9
6	0	1

Problem Solving

4. There are 468 children. 278 children are in the second grade. How many children are not in the second grade?

___190___ children

5. There are 538 people at the concert. 294 people are adults. How many people at the concert are not adults?

___244___ people

Reteach

3-Digit Subtraction

Subtract: 427 − 154

Subtract the ones. Regroup if you need to.	Subtract the tens. Regroup if you need to.	Subtract the hundreds.

Hundreds	Tens	Ones
[ ]	[ ]	[ ]
4	2	7
− 1	5	4

Hundreds	Tens	Ones
[3]	[12]	[ ]
4	2	7
− 1	5	4
		3

Hundreds	Tens	Ones
[3]	[12]	[ ]
4	2	7
− 1	5	4
2	7	3

1.

Hundreds	Tens	Ones
[4]	[11]	[ ]
5	1	7
− 2	9	4
2	2	3

Hundreds	Tens	Ones
[ ]	[4]	[12]
6	5	2
− 2	1	7
4	3	5

2.

Hundreds	Tens	Ones
[ ]	[6]	[14]
8	7	4
− 3	2	7
5	4	7

Hundreds	Tens	Ones
[8]	[14]	[ ]
9	4	5
− 5	8	3
3	6	2

Enrich

3-Digit Subtraction

Subtraction Tic-Tac-Toe

Subtract. Color the boxes in which you regroup tens red. Color the boxes in which you regroup hundreds blue. Color the boxes in which there is no regrouping yellow.

1.

5	2	6	7	7	6	6	9	4
− 2	8	4	− 5	3	9	− 1	8	1
2	4	2	2	3	7	5	1	3
blue			red			yellow		

2.

8	4	6	9	3	5	6	5	3
− 2	1	7	− 5	8	0	−	2	4
6	2	9	3	5	5	6	2	9
red			blue			red		

3.

7	9	3	9	8	7	7	8	8
− 2	6	2	− 2	8	4	− 2	9	7
5	3	1	7	0	3	4	9	1
yellow			yellow			blue		

Which color makes a line with three subtractions in a row? ___blue___

You get Tic-Tac-Toe!

Daily Homework

 13-10 3-Digit Subtraction

Subtract. Use hundreds, tens, and ones models.

1.

hundreds	tens	ones
[5]	[12]	[ ]
6	2	4
− 3	5	4
2	7	0

hundreds	tens	ones
[3]	[11]	[ ]
4	1	6
− 1	2	5
2	9	1

hundreds	tens	ones
[ ]	[8]	[15]
3	9	5
− 1	0	6
2	8	9

2.

hundreds	tens	ones
[ ]	[6]	[11]
2	7	1
− 1	6	4
1	0	7

hundreds	tens	ones
[ ]	[7]	[12]
8	8	2
− 5	3	6
3	4	6

hundreds	tens	ones
[3]	[10]	[ ]
4	0	7
− 1	3	6
2	7	1

Problem Solving

3. How is 627 − 511 different from 627 − 531?

I need to regroup to solve 627 − 531.

4. Natalie tutors students for 120 minutes on Tuesdays. She tutors for 480 minutes on Thursdays. How many more minutes does she tutor on Thursdays than on Tuesdays? ___360___ minutes

Spiral Review

Circle each figure that shows equal parts.

Write how many equal parts.

5. [triangle] ___4___   [trapezoid] ___   [rectangle] ___

Chapter 13 ~ Lesson 11

Practice

MORE 3-Digit Subtraction

Subtract.

1.

Hundreds	Tens	Ones
4	13	
5	3	6
− 1	8	5
3	5	1

Hundreds	Tens	Ones
5	10	18
6	1	8
− 4	3	9
1	7	9

2.
```
  457      836      519      640      749
− 189    − 362    − 193    − 138    − 552
  268      474      326      502      197
```

3.
```
  773      351      815      553      925
− 567    − 315    − 299    − 262    − 618
  206       36      516      291      307
```

4.
```
  793      847      534      660      428
− 289    − 177    − 476    − 413    − 287
  504      670       58      247      141
```

Problem Solving

5. The second grade class collects 527 bottles and cans. They have 328 bottles. How many are cans?

_199_ cans

6. The third grade has 479 children. There are 265 girls. How many children are boys?

_214_ boys

Reteach

MORE 3-Digit Subtraction

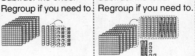

Subtract: 635 − 378

Subtract the ones. Regroup if you need to.	Subtract the tens. Regroup if you need to.	Subtract the hundreds.

Hundreds	Tens	Ones	Hundreds	Tens	Ones	Hundreds	Tens	Ones
	2	15	5	12	15	5	12	15
6	3	5	6	3	5	6	3	5
− 3	7	8	− 3	7	8	− 3	7	8
		7		5	7	2	5	7

Subtract.

1.

Hundreds	Tens	Ones
4	13	12
5	4	2
− 1	8	7
3	5	5

Hundreds	Tens	Ones
7	13	16
8	4	6
− 3	5	9
4	8	7

2.

Hundreds	Tens	Ones
8	11	15
9	2	5
− 1	8	8
7	3	7

Hundreds	Tens	Ones
5	11	14
6	2	4
− 4	9	8
1	2	6

Enrich

MORE 3-Digit Subtraction
Mr. Ito's Apple Farm

One weekend, Mr. Ito's workers picked 947 apples. Here are the numbers of apples Mr. Ito sold each day. Keep subtracting. Find out how many apples were left on Friday.

Day of Week	Apples Sold	Apples Left
Monday	179	768
Tuesday	295	473
Wednesday	87	386
Thursday	119	267
Friday	93	174

Use the chart to answer the questions.

1. How many more apples did Mr. Ito sell on Tuesday than on Monday?

_116_ apples

2. How many more apples did Mr. Ito sell on Thursday than on Friday?

_26_ apples

3. How many apples did Mr. Ito sell in all?

_773_ apples

4. On which day did Mr. Ito sell the most apples?

Tuesday

Daily Homework

13-11 More 3-Digit Subtraction

Subtract to find the difference.

1.

hundreds	tens	ones
6	11	15
7	2	5
−	3	2	9
3	9	6

hundreds	tens	ones
4	11	
5	2	1
− 1	4	6
3	7	5

hundreds	tens	ones
5	13	
6	3	2
− 1	5	1
4	8	1

2.
```
  538      610      926      328      552
− 241    − 103    − 328    − 239    − 383
  297      507      598       89      169
```

3.
```
  387      251      737      486      320
− 226    − 182    − 259    − 193    − 145
  161       69      478      293      175
```

Problem Solving

4. Find each missing number.
```
  572      364      971
− 454    − 225    − 360
  118      139      611
```

5. There were 345 glass bottles collected in all. 126 of the bottles were green. How many bottles were not green?

_219_ bottles

Spiral Review

Write the sum.

6.
```
  21      43      28      47      62      32
+ 37    + 49    + 38    + 22    +  8    + 45
  58      92      66      69      70      77
```

Chapter 13 ~ Lesson 12

Practice

Estimate Differences

Subtract. Estimate each difference to check.

1.	542 − 197 345	500 − 200 300	723 − 431 292	700 − 400 300
2.	645 − 125 520	600 − 100 500	378 − 138 240	400 − 100 300
3.	519 − 277 242	500 − 300 200	695 − 314 381	700 − 300 400
4.	861 − 276 585	900 − 300 600	921 − 429 492	900 − 400 500
5.	816 − 157 659	800 − 200 600	944 − 173 771	900 − 200 700

Problem Solving

6. A town collects 647 bags of garbage. Another town collects 438 bags of garbage. How many more bags of garbage did the first town collect?

___209___ bags

7. On Saturday, 578 people go to the park. On Sunday, 398 people go to the park. How many more people go to the park on Saturday?

___180___ people

Reteach

Estimate Differences

Estimate: 543 − 187

523 − 187 336	Round 523 down to 500 → Round 187 up to 200 →	500 − 200 300

336 is close to 300, so your answer is reasonable.

Subtract. Estimate to see if your answer is reasonable.

1.	735 − 212 523	Round 735 to _700_ → Round 212 to _200_ →	700 − 200 500
2.	479 − 332 147	Round 479 to _500_ → Round 332 to _300_ →	500 − 300 200

3.	815 − 327 488	800 − 300 500	592 − 133 459	600 − 100 500
4.	903 − 188 715	900 − 200 700	458 − 195 263	500 − 200 300

Enrich

Estimate Differences
Brown's Sewing Shop

Mr. and Mrs. Brown count the buttons in their shop.
They both make an estimate.
Show the estimate for each question.
Circle the better estimate.

Buttons

Red	Blue	Green	Yellow	Purple	Orange
735	873	182	549	317	284

1. About how many more red buttons than purple buttons?

___700___ − ___300___ = ___400___

Mr. Brown (400) Mrs. Brown 300

2. About how many more blue buttons than green buttons?

___900___ − ___200___ = ___700___

Mr. Brown 600 Mrs. Brown (700)

3. About how many more yellow buttons than orange buttons?

___500___ − ___300___ = ___200___

Mr. Brown 300 Mrs. Brown (200)

4. About how many more red buttons than yellow buttons?

___700___ − ___500___ = ___200___

Mr. Brown (200) Mrs. Brown 100

5. About how many more blue buttons than orange buttons?

___900___ − ___300___ = ___600___

Mr. Brown 500 Mrs. Brown (600)

Daily Homework

13-12 ### Estimate Differences

Subtract. Then find the nearest hundred. Estimate each difference to check.

1.	598 − 293 305	600 − 300 300	687 − 491 196	700 − 500 200
2.	295 − 279 16	300 − 300 0	639 − 228 411	600 − 200 400
3.	423 − 190 233	400 − 200 200	887 − 540 347	900 − 500 400
4.	787 − 102 685	800 − 100 700	536 − 291 245	500 − 300 200

Problem Solving

5. Tim collects 778 plastic bags. Jack collects 529 paper bags. How many more bags does Tim collect than Jack?

___249___ bags

6. There are 898 flowers. 679 were used to make flower arrangements. How many flowers were not used?

___219___ flowers

Spiral Review

Compare. Use >, <, or =.

7. 27¢ _<_ 29¢   _=_ 10¢   35¢ _>_

Chapter 13 ~ Lesson 13

Practice

Add and Subtract Money Amounts

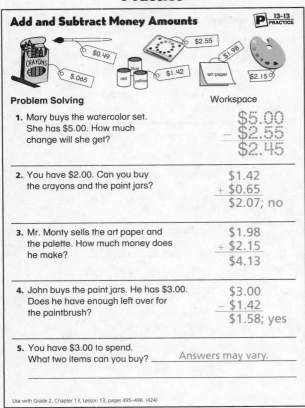

P 13-13 PRACTICE

Problem Solving | Workspace

1. Mary buys the watercolor set. She has $5.00. How much change will she get?

$$\begin{array}{r} \$5.00 \\ -\ \$2.55 \\ \hline \$2.45 \end{array}$$

2. You have $2.00. Can you buy the crayons and the paint jars?

$$\begin{array}{r} \$1.42 \\ +\ \$0.65 \\ \hline \$2.07; \text{ no} \end{array}$$

3. Mr. Monty sells the art paper and the palette. How much money does he make?

$$\begin{array}{r} \$1.98 \\ +\ \$2.15 \\ \hline \$4.13 \end{array}$$

4. John buys the paint jars. He has $3.00. Does he have enough left over for the paintbrush?

$$\begin{array}{r} \$3.00 \\ -\ \$1.42 \\ \hline \$1.58; \text{ yes} \end{array}$$

5. You have $3.00 to spend. What two items can you buy? ___Answers may vary.___

Use with Grade 2, Chapter 13, Lesson 13, pages 495–496. (424)

Reteach

Add and Subtract Money Amounts

R 13-13 RETEACH

Jim buys the cat and the dog. How much does he spend?

$$\begin{array}{r} \$1.59 \\ +\ \$2.35 \\ \hline \$3.94 \end{array}$$

Add the cents, dimes, and dollars.

Write the dollar sign and the decimal point in the answer.

Problem Solving | Workspace

1. Betty has $5.00. She buys the pig. How much money does she have left?

$$\begin{array}{r} \$5.00 \\ -\ \$3.31 \\ \hline \$1.69 \end{array}$$

2. Sammy buys the duck and the rabbit. How much does he spend?

$$\begin{array}{r} \$1.72 \\ +\ \$0.89 \\ \hline \$2.61 \end{array}$$

3. Pam has $4.00. She buys the dog. How much money does she have left?

$$\begin{array}{r} \$4.00 \\ -\ \$2.35 \\ \hline \$1.65 \end{array}$$

Use with Grade 2, Chapter 13, Lesson 13, pages 495–496. (425)

Enrich

Add and Subtract Money Amounts
Heather's Health Food Shop

E 13-13 ENRICH

yogurt $1.49

granola bar $1.36

health shake $2.80

pita pocket $4.16

salad $3.59

carob bar $2.09

Use the prices in the chart to add or subtract.

1. Millie buys a carob bar and a salad. How much does she spend? $5.68

Jessie buys a granola bar. She pays with a $5.00 bill. How much is her change? $3.64

2. Marky buys a health shake and a yogurt. How much does he spend? $4.29

Justin buys a salad. He pays with four $1.00 bills. What is his change? $0.41

3. Robin buys a pita pocket, a yogurt, and a carob bar. How much does she spend? $7.74

Phyllis buys 2 yogurts and a granola bar. She pays with a $10.00 bill. What is her change? $5.66

Use the chart to buy two items.

4. I buy a _____ and a _____. I spend _____.

I pay with a $_____ bill. My change is _____.

Use with Grade 2, Chapter 13, Lesson 13, pages 495–496. (426)

Daily Homework

13-13 Add and Subtract Money Amounts

Solve. Show your work.

1. Nancy buys pizza and milk. How much does she spend?

$ __2.25__

$$\begin{array}{r} \$1.75 \\ +\ 0.50 \\ \hline \$2.25 \end{array}$$

2. Rosa buys a salad. She has $3.00. How much change will she get?

$ __0.65__

$$\begin{array}{r} \$3.00 \\ -\ 2.35 \\ \hline \$0.65 \end{array}$$

3. Marcus has $4.00. Does he have enough to buy tacos and a juice?

__Yes.__

$$\begin{array}{r} \$2.25 \\ +\ 0.85 \\ \hline \$3.10 \end{array} < \$4.00$$

4. Paige buys a sandwich and milk. How much does her lunch cost?

$ __4.05__

$$\begin{array}{r} \$3.55 \\ +\ 0.50 \\ \hline \$4.05 \end{array}$$

MENU

★ Pizza	$1.75
★ Sandwich	$3.55
★ Tacos	$2.25
★ Salad	$2.35
★ Milk	$0.50
★ Juice	$0.85
★ Ice Cream	$1.10

Spiral Review

Count on or back by hundreds. Write each number.

5. One hundred more than 541 is __641__.

One hundred less than 732 is __632__.

One hundred more than 263 is __363__.

130 Grade 2, Chapter 13, Lesson 13

Chapter 13 ~ Lesson 14

Part A Worksheet

Problem Solving: Application
Plan a Food Drive

Choose the food for your class to donate to the Main Street food bank.

Cut out the food collected.

Choose three types of food that weigh 650 pounds.

Rice
212 Pounds

Cereal
275 Pounds

Vegetables
163 Pounds

Bread
147 Pounds

Use with Grade 2, Chapter 13, Lesson 14, pages 497–498. (427)

Part A Worksheet

Problem Solving: Application
Plan a Food Drive

1. Which foods did you choose?

   Correct choices: rice, cereal, vegetables

2. Does the food weigh 650 pounds? _____

   Show how you know.

Work Space

3. What if you wanted to donate 850 pounds of food?

   Would you have collected enough food? ____no____

   If not, how much more would you need? ___53___ pounds

   Show how you know.

Work Space

Use with Grade 2, Chapter 13, Lesson 14, pages 497–498. (428)

Part B Worksheet

Problem Solving: Application
How Much Water Does Your Class Use?

1. Record your class's use of water.

Day	Water Used (Tally)	How Water Was Used
Monday		
Tuesday		
Wednesday		
Thursday		
Friday		

2. On which day did your class use the most water?

   Answers may vary.

3. On which day did your class use the least water?

   Answers may vary.

4. For what did your class use water the most often?

   Answers may vary.

5. Do you think you use more water at home or at school? Explain your thinking.

   Answers may vary.

   _____

Use with Grade 2, Chapter 13, Lesson 14, pages 499–500. (429)

Chapter 14 ~ Lesson 1

Practice

Skip Counting

Skip count. Write how many.

1.
○○ ○○ ○○ ○○ ○○
○○ ○○ ○○ ○○ ○○
○○ ○○ ○○ ○○ ○○
○○ ○○ ○○ ○○ ○○
○○ ○○ ○○ ○○ ○○

__10__   __20__   __30__   __40__   __50__

There are __50__ counters in all.

Skip count by 2s or 5s.
Write the numbers.

2.
```
0  1  3  5  7  9  11  13  15  17
```
__2__ __4__ __6__ __8__ __10__ __12__ __14__ __16__ __18__

3.
```
0
```
__5__ __10__ __15__ __20__ __25__ __30__ __35__ __40__ __45__

Use with Grade 2, Chapter 14, Lesson 1, pages 513–514. (430)

Reteach

Skip Counting

You can skip count when the number in each group is the same.

Think: Each group has 2 in it.

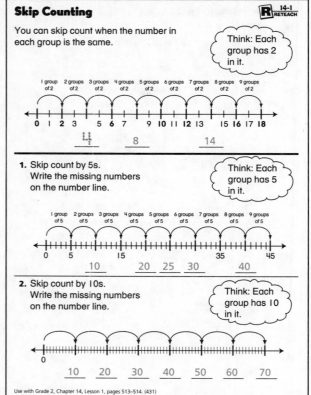

1 group of 2, 2 groups of 2, 3 groups of 2, 4 groups of 2, 5 groups of 2, 6 groups of 2, 7 groups of 2, 8 groups of 2, 9 groups of 2
```
0  1  2  3  4  5  6  7  9  10 11 12 13  15 16 17 18
```
__8__   __14__

1. Skip count by 5s.
Write the missing numbers on the number line.

Think: Each group has 5 in it.

1 group of 5, 2 groups of 5, 3 groups of 5, 4 groups of 5, 5 groups of 5, 6 groups of 5, 7 groups of 5, 8 groups of 5, 9 groups of 5
```
0     5        15              35        45
```
__10__   __20__ __25__ __30__   __40__

2. Skip count by 10s.
Write the missing numbers on the number line.

Think: Each group has 10 in it.

```
0
```
__10__ __20__ __30__ __40__ __50__ __60__ __70__

Use with Grade 2, Chapter 14, Lesson 1, pages 513–514. (431)

Enrich

Skip Counting
How Many Groups?

Write how many groups.
Write how many in each group.
Write how many in all.

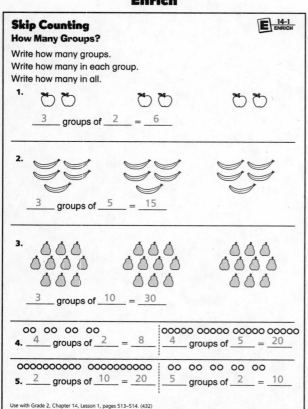

1. __3__ groups of __2__ = __6__

2. __3__ groups of __5__ = __15__

3. __3__ groups of __10__ = __30__

4. __4__ groups of __2__ = __8__ | __4__ groups of __5__ = __20__

5. __2__ groups of __10__ = __20__ | __5__ groups of __2__ = __10__

Use with Grade 2, Chapter 14, Lesson 1, pages 513–514. (432)

Daily Homework

14-1 Skip Counting

Skip count by 2s, 5s, or 10s.
Write the numbers.

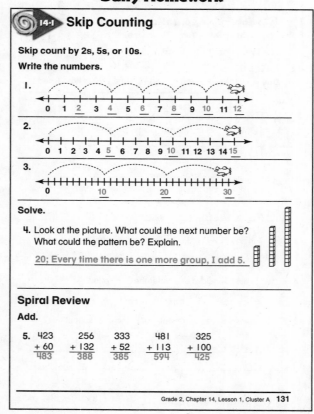

1.
```
0  1  2  3  4  5  6  7  9  10 11 12
```

2.
```
0  1  2  3  4  5  6  7  8  9  10 11 12 13 14 15
```

3.
```
0      10        20        30
```

Solve.

4. Look at the picture. What could the next number be?
What could the pattern be? Explain.

__20; Every time there is one more group, I add 5.__

Spiral Review
Add.

5.	423	256	333	481	325
	+ 60	+ 132	+ 52	+ 113	+ 100
	483	388	385	594	425

Grade 2, Chapter 14, Lesson 1, Cluster A **131**

Chapter 14 ~ Lesson 2

Practice

Add. Then multiply.

1.

$$\underline{2} + \underline{2} + \underline{2} + \underline{2} + \underline{2} = \underline{10}$$
$$\underline{5} \times \underline{2} = \underline{10}$$

2.

$$\underline{4} + \underline{4} + \underline{4} = \underline{12}$$
$$\underline{3} \times \underline{4} = \underline{12}$$

Write the multiplication sentence.

3.

$$\underline{4} \times \underline{3} = \underline{12}$$

4.

$$\underline{2} \times \underline{4} = \underline{8}$$

Use with Grade 2, Chapter 14, Lesson 2, pages 515–516. (433)

Reteach

Remember × means multiply.

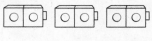

$$\underline{2} + \underline{2} + \underline{2} = \underline{6}$$
$$\underline{3} \times \underline{2} = \underline{6}$$

Use cubes to make groups. Add. Then multiply.

1.

$$\underline{2} + \underline{2} + \underline{2} + \underline{2} = \underline{8}$$
$$\underline{4} \times \underline{2} = \underline{8}$$

2.

$$\underline{3} + \underline{3} + \underline{3} + \underline{3} = \underline{12}$$
$$\underline{4} \times \underline{3} = \underline{12}$$

3.

$$\underline{2} + \underline{2} + \underline{2} + \underline{2} + \underline{2} = \underline{10}$$
$$\underline{5} \times \underline{2} = \underline{10}$$

Use with Grade 2, Chapter 14, Lesson 2, pages 515–516. (434)

Enrich

Repeated Addition and Multiplication
Draw a Picture

Draw the groups.
Write an addition and a multiplication sentence.

1. Draw 3 groups of 2.

$$\underline{2} + \underline{2} + \underline{2} = \underline{6}$$
$$\underline{3} \times \underline{2} = \underline{6}$$

Draw 2 groups of 4.

$$\underline{4} + \underline{4} = \underline{8}$$
$$\underline{2} \times \underline{4} = \underline{8}$$

2. Draw 3 groups of 3.

$$\underline{3} + \underline{3} + \underline{3} = \underline{9}$$
$$\underline{3} \times \underline{3} = \underline{9}$$

Draw 3 groups of 1.

$$\underline{1} + \underline{1} + \underline{1} = \underline{3}$$
$$\underline{3} \times \underline{1} = \underline{3}$$

3. Draw 5 groups of 3.

$$\underline{3} + \underline{3} + \underline{3} + \underline{3} + \underline{3} = \underline{15}$$
$$\underline{5} \times \underline{3} = \underline{15}$$

Use with Grade 2, Chapter 14, Lesson 2, pages 515–516. (435)

Daily Homework

 **14-2** **Repeated Addition and Multiplication**

Add. Then multiply.

1.

$$\underline{4} + \underline{4} = \underline{8}$$
$$\underline{2} \times \underline{4} = \underline{8}$$

2.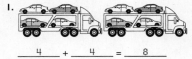

$$\underline{5} + \underline{5} + \underline{5} + \underline{5} = \underline{20}$$
$$\underline{4} \times \underline{5} = \underline{20}$$

Problem Solving

3. Use the addition sentence to complete the multiplication sentence.

$$4 + 4 + 4 + 4 + 4 = 20$$

$\boxed{5} \cdot 4 = 20$ What is the missing number? _____ 5

Spiral Review

Add. Estimate to see if your answer is reasonable.

4.	476	500	587	600	384	400
	+ 283	+ 300	+ 291	+ 300	+ 211	+ 200
	759	800	878	900	595	600

Chapter 14 ~ Lesson 3

Practice

Use Arrays — P 14-3 PRACTICE

Write a multiplication sentence to show each array.

1. $5 \times 3 = 15$

2. $4 \times 5 = 20$

3. $3 \times 6 = 18$

4. $2 \times 7 = 14$

Find each product.

5. $6 \times 4 = \underline{24}$ $3 \times 7 = \underline{21}$ $4 \times 3 = \underline{12}$

6. $3 \times 5 = \underline{15}$ $2 \times 8 = \underline{16}$ $5 \times 5 = \underline{25}$

7. $4 \times 4 = \underline{16}$ $10 \times 3 = \underline{30}$ $9 \times 2 = \underline{18}$

Use with Grade 2, Chapter 14, Lesson 3, pages 517–518. (436)

Reteach

Use Arrays — R 14-3 RETEACH

Count how many rows.
Count how many in each row.

$3 \times \underline{4} = \underline{12}$

Use counters to make arrays.
Write a multiplication sentence.

1. $\underline{2} \times \underline{4} = \underline{8}$

2. $\underline{3} \times \underline{3} = \underline{9}$

3. $\underline{4} \times \underline{3} = \underline{12}$

4. $\underline{2} \times \underline{5} = \underline{10}$

Use with Grade 2, Chapter 14, Lesson 3, pages 517–518. (437)

Enrich

Use Arrays — E 14-3 ENRICH
Array Patterns

Look at each pattern. Draw the next array.
Write the multiplication sentence.

1.

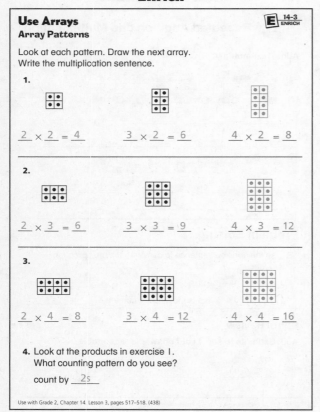

$\underline{2} \times \underline{2} = \underline{4}$ $\underline{3} \times \underline{2} = \underline{6}$ $\underline{4} \times \underline{2} = \underline{8}$

2.

$\underline{2} \times \underline{3} = \underline{6}$ $\underline{3} \times \underline{3} = \underline{9}$ $\underline{4} \times \underline{3} = \underline{12}$

3.

$\underline{2} \times \underline{4} = \underline{8}$ $\underline{3} \times \underline{4} = \underline{12}$ $\underline{4} \times \underline{4} = \underline{16}$

4. Look at the products in exercise 1.
   What counting pattern do you see?

   count by $\underline{2s}$

Use with Grade 2, Chapter 14 Lesson 3, pages 517–518. (438)

Daily Homework

14-3 **Use Arrays**

Write a multiplication sentence to show each array.

1. 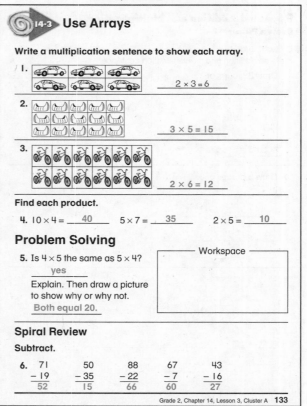 $2 \times 3 = 6$

2. $3 \times 5 = 15$

3. $2 \times 6 = 12$

Find each product.

4. $10 \times 4 = \underline{40}$ $5 \times 7 = \underline{35}$ $2 \times 5 = \underline{10}$

Problem Solving

5. Is 4×5 the same as 5×4?
   $\underline{yes}$
   Explain. Then draw a picture to show why or why not.
   $\underline{Both\ equal\ 20.}$

   Workspace

Spiral Review

Subtract.

6.
71	50	88	67	43
− 19	− 35	− 22	− 7	− 16
52	15	66	60	27

Chapter 14 ~ Lesson 4

Practice

Multiplication

P 14-4 PRACTICE

Find each product.

1.
$$\underline{3} \times \underline{4} = \underline{12}$$
rows   in each row   in all

$$\underline{5} \times \underline{2} = \underline{10}$$
rows   in each row   in all

2.
$$\underline{3} \times \underline{6} = \underline{18}$$
rows   in each row   in all

$$\underline{4} \times \underline{2} = \underline{8}$$
rows   in each row   in all

3. $5 \times 4 = \underline{20}$ $3 \times 8 = \underline{24}$ $9 \times 3 = \underline{27}$

4. $6 \times 2 = \underline{12}$ $5 \times 5 = \underline{25}$ $4 \times 6 = \underline{24}$

5.
$\begin{array}{c}4\\\times 3\\\hline 12\end{array}$
$\begin{array}{c}6\\\times 5\\\hline 30\end{array}$
$\begin{array}{c}3\\\times 7\\\hline 21\end{array}$
$\begin{array}{c}8\\\times 2\\\hline 16\end{array}$
$\begin{array}{c}6\\\times 3\\\hline 18\end{array}$
$\begin{array}{c}2\\\times 5\\\hline 10\end{array}$

Use with Grade 2, Chapter 14, Lesson 4, pages 519–520. (439)

Reteach

Multiplication

R 14-4 RETEACH

Count the number of rows.
Count how many in each row.

$$\underline{3} \times \underline{4} = \underline{12}$$
rows   in each row   in all

Use cubes. Multiply.

1.
$$\underline{3} \times \underline{4} = \underline{12}$$
rows   in each row   in all

2.
$$\underline{5} \times \underline{2} = \underline{10}$$
rows   in each row   in all

3.
$$\underline{2} \times \underline{6} = \underline{12}$$
rows   in each row   in all

4.
$$\underline{3} \times \underline{3} = \underline{9}$$
rows   in each row   in all

Use with Grade 2, Chapter 14, Lesson 4, pages 519–520. (440)

Enrich

Multiplication
Building Arrays

E 14-4 ENRICH

Play this game with 2 or 3 people.
Take turns.

You will need:

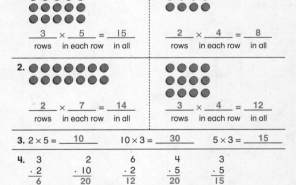

• Use the spinners. Spin two numbers.

• Build an array to find the product.

• Write a multiplication sentence.

• The player with the greatest product
  scores a point.

The player to reach 5 points first is the winner.

Multiplication Sentences

Player 1	Player 2	Player 3
___ × ___ = ___	___ × ___ = ___	___ × ___ = ___
___ × ___ = ___	___ × ___ = ___	___ × ___ = ___
___ × ___ = ___	___ × ___ = ___	___ × ___ = ___
___ × ___ = ___	___ × ___ = ___	___ × ___ = ___
___ × ___ = ___	___ × ___ = ___	___ × ___ = ___
___ × ___ = ___	___ × ___ = ___	___ × ___ = ___

Score Card

Player 1	Player 2	Player 3

Use with Grade 2, Chapter 14, Lesson 4, pages 519–520. (441)

Daily Homework

14-4 Multiplication

Find each product.

1.
$$\underline{3} \times \underline{5} = \underline{15}$$
rows   in each row   in all

$$\underline{2} \times \underline{4} = \underline{8}$$
rows   in each row   in all

2.
$$\underline{2} \times \underline{7} = \underline{14}$$
rows   in each row   in all

$$\underline{3} \times \underline{4} = \underline{12}$$
rows   in each row   in all

3. $2 \times 5 = \underline{10}$ $10 \times 3 = \underline{30}$ $5 \times 3 = \underline{15}$

4.
$\begin{array}{c}3\\\cdot 2\\\hline 6\end{array}$
$\begin{array}{c}2\\\cdot 10\\\hline 20\end{array}$
$\begin{array}{c}6\\\cdot 2\\\hline 12\end{array}$
$\begin{array}{c}4\\\cdot 5\\\hline 20\end{array}$
$\begin{array}{c}3\\\cdot 5\\\hline 15\end{array}$

Problem Solving

5. The marching band has 5 rows.
   In each row there are 10 musicians.
   How many musicians are there in all?   _____50_____ musicians

Spiral Review

Write the time 2 ways.

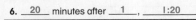

6. __20__ minutes after __1__ , __1:20__

Chapter 14 ~ Lesson 5

Practice

MORE Multiplication:
Multiply in Any Order

Find each product.

1. 3 groups of 5   5 groups of 3

$3 \times 5 = \underline{15}$ $5 \times 3 = \underline{15}$

2. 2 groups of 7   7 groups of 2

$2 \times 7 = \underline{14}$ $7 \times 2 = \underline{14}$

3.
4	3	9	3	4	4
$\times 6$	$\times 3$	$\times 3$	$\times 2$	$\times 4$	$\times 5$
24	9	27	6	16	20

4.
7	2	4	3	5	5
$\times 3$	$\times 8$	$\times 7$	$\times 4$	$\times 6$	$\times 7$
21	16	28	12	30	35

Use with Grade 2, Chapter 14, Lesson 5, pages 521–522. (442)

Reteach

MORE Multiplication:
Multiply in Any Order

Remember, you can multiply factors in any order.

3 groups of 2   2 groups of 3

$3 \times 2 = 6$ $2 \times 3 = 6$

Use counters. Draw groups.
Find each product.

1. 4 groups of 2   2 groups of 4

$4 \times 2 = 8$ $2 \times 4 = 8$

2. 3 groups of 2   2 groups of 3

$3 \times 2 = 6$ $2 \times 3 = 6$

3.
2	6	8	3	4	5
$\times 6$	$\times 2$	$\times 3$	$\times 8$	$\times 5$	$\times 4$
12	12	24	24	20	20

Use with Grade 2, Chapter 14, Lesson 5, pages 521–522. (443)

Enrich

MORE Multiplication:
Multiply in Any Order
Fill the Chart

Use counters to find the product or to find a pattern.

Fill in the multiplication chart.

×	1	2	3	4	5	6	7	8	9	10
1	1	2	3	4	5	6	7	8	9	10
2	2	4	6	8	10	12	14	16	18	20
3	3	6	9	12	15	18	21	24	27	30
4	4	8	12	16	20	24	28	32	36	40
5	5	10	15	20	25	30	35	40	45	50
6	6	12	18	24	30	36	42	48	54	60
7	7	14	21	28	35	42	49	56	63	70
8	8	16	24	32	40	48	56	64	72	80
9	9	18	27	36	45	54	63	72	81	90
10	10	20	30	40	50	60	70	80	90	100

Use with Grade 2, Chapter 14, Lesson 5, pages 521–522. (444)

Daily Homework

14-5 More Multiplication

Find each product.

1. 5 groups of 3   3 groups of 5

$5 \times 3 = \underline{15}$ $3 \times 5 = \underline{15}$

2. 2 groups of 3   3 groups of 2

$2 \times 3 = \underline{6}$ $3 \times 2 = \underline{6}$

3.
2	5	6	2	8	2
$\cdot 5$	$\cdot 2$	$\cdot 2$	$\cdot 6$	$\cdot 2$	$\cdot 8$
10	10	12	12	16	16

Solve.

There are 9 bicycles at the bike rack.
Each bicycle has 2 wheels. How many wheels in all? __18__

Spiral Review

Subtract.

5.
465	788	349	576	639	974
-341	-564	-214	-143	-528	-241
124	224	135	433	111	733

Grade 2, Chapter 14, Lesson 5, Cluster A **135**

Chapter 14 ~ Lesson 6

Practice

Problem Solving: Reading for Math
Make a Prediction

Ten cars are parked in the pizzeria parking lot. The first car has 4 wheels. Each car has the same number of wheels. Predict how many wheels there are in all.

Solve.

1. What do you want to find out?
   how many wheels in all

2. What do you know?
   the number of cars and the number of wheels on the first car

3. How many cars are in the parking lot? __10__ cars

4. Predict the number of wheels each car has. __4__ wheels
   Explain your prediction.
   The first car has 4 wheels, so I predict the other cars will also have 4 wheels.

5. How can you predict how many wheels in all? by multiplying
   __10__ cars × each with __4__ wheels = __40__ wheels

Use with Grade 2, Chapter 14, Lesson 6, pages 525–526. (445)

Practice

Problem Solving: Reading for Math
Make a Prediction

The second grade is going on a field trip. The children will ride in 5 vans. There will be 9 children in the first van. The same number of children will ride in every van. Predict how many children will go on the field trip.

Choose the best answer. Fill in the ◯.

1. What do you want to find out?
   Ⓐ how many vans there are
   Ⓑ how many children will go on the field trip
   Ⓒ how many children will ride in each van

2. How many vans are there?
   Ⓕ 1   Ⓗ 5
   Ⓖ 2   Ⓙ 9

3. How many children will ride in each van?
   Ⓐ 9   Ⓒ 5
   Ⓑ 8   Ⓓ 6

4. Predict how many children will go on the field trip.
   Ⓕ 25   Ⓗ 45
   Ⓖ 14   Ⓙ 9

Use with Grade 2, Chapter 14, Lesson 6, pages 525–526. (446)

Practice

Problem Solving: Reading for Math
Make a Prediction

People are sitting on the bleachers watching a basketball game. There are 10 rows of bleachers. 8 people are sitting in the first row. The same number of people are sitting in every row. Predict how many people there are in all.

Choose the best answer. Fill in the ◯.

1. What do you want to find out?
   Ⓐ how many people are sitting in one row
   Ⓑ how many rows of bleachers there are
   Ⓒ how many people there are in all

2. How many rows of bleachers are there?
   Ⓕ 8
   Ⓖ 10
   Ⓗ 18
   Ⓙ 80

Solve.

3. How many people are sitting in each row? __8__
   Explain your prediction. The first row has 8 people in it, so I predict the other rows also have 8 people in them.

4. How can you predict how many people there are in all? by multiplying
   __10__ rows × each with __8__ people = __80__ people

Use with Grade 2, Chapter 14, Lesson 6, pages 525–526. (447)

Daily Homework

14-6 Problem Solving: Reading for Math
Make a Prediction

Vanessa sees a parade. There are 5 bands in the parade. The first band has 6 drummers. Each band has the same number of drummers. Predict how many drummers are in the parade.

1. What do you want to find out?
   how many drummers are in the parade

2. What do you know?
   the number of bands and the number of drummers in the first band

3. How many bands are in the parade? __5__

4. Predict the number of drummers in each band. __6__

5. How can you predict how many drummers in all? by multiplying
   __5__ bands × __6__ drummers in each band = __30__ drummers.

Spiral Review
Choose + or –.

6. 24 ⊖ 6 = 18   16 = 9 ⊕ 7   9 ⊕ 5 = 14   9 ⊕ 6 = 15

136 Grade 2, Chapter 14, Lesson 6, Cluster A

Chapter 14 ~ Lesson 7

Practice

Problem Solving: Strategy
Draw a Picture

Draw a picture to solve each problem.

1. 4 bookshelves hold 6 books each. How many books are there in all?

   __24__ books

2. 6 rows of people are watching a soccer game. There are 5 people in each row. How many people are there in all?

   __30__ people

3. There are 3 groups of dancers in the ballet recital. There are 4 dancers in each group. How many dancers are there in all?

   __12__ dancers

Mixed Strategy Review

Solve.

4. Yoshi has 85¢. He spends 67¢ on a drink. How much money does he have left?

   __18__ ¢

   What coins could he have left?
   3 nickels, 3 pennies; 1 dime, 8 pennies; 1 dime, 1 nickel, 3 pennies; 2 nickels, 8 pennies or 18 pennies

5. **Create a problem** for which you would draw a picture to solve. Share it with others.

   _____

   _____

Reteach

Problem Solving: Strategy
Draw a Picture

Page 530, Problem 3

10 trucks each delivered 5 crates of carrots to the supermarket. How many crates are there in all?

Step 1 Read	**Be sure you understand the problem.**

What do you know?
- There are __10__ trucks.
- Each truck delivered __5__ crates of carrots to the supermarket.

What do you need to find?
- You need to find __how many crates there are in all__

Step 2 Plan	**Make a plan.** Choose a strategy.

- Draw a Picture
- Write a Number Sentence
- Use Logical Reasoning
- Act it Out
- Choose the Operation
- Make a Table
- Guess and Check
- Find a Pattern
- Make a Graph

Draw a picture.

Describe what the picture shows.

Reteach

Problem Solving: Strategy
Draw a Picture

Step 3 Solve	**Carry out your plan.**

- Draw a picture.

- Describe what the picture shows.
- To tell how many crates in all, you can multiply.

  __10__ trucks × __5__ crates = __50__ crates

  There are __50__ crates in all.

Step 4 Look Back	**Is the solution reasonable?**

Does your answer make sense? (Yes) No

Did you answer the question? (Yes) No

Daily Homework

14-7 Problem Solving: Strategy
Draw a Picture

1. 6 buckets of apples are loaded onto each truck. There are 3 trucks. How many buckets are there in all?

   __18__ buckets

2. 4 mail trucks collect the mail. Each truck collects 5 bags of mail. How many bags of mail are there in all?

   __20__ bags

3. There are 7 milk trucks. Each truck delivers 10 crates of milk every morning. How many crates of milk are delivered every morning?

   __70__ crates

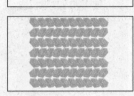

Spiral Review

Count back by 4s.

5. 33, 29, __25__, __21__, __17__, __13__, __9__

Chapter 14 ~ Lesson 8

Practice

Repeated Subtraction

P 14-8 PRACTICE

Use ⬚.
How many equal groups can you make?

1. Use 16 ⬚.

Subtract groups of 2.

You get __8__ groups of 2.

Use 20 ⬚.

Subtract groups of 4.

You get __5__ groups of 4.

2. Use 18 ⬚.

Subtract groups of 3.

You get __6__ groups of 3.

Use 12 ⬚.

Subtract groups of 4.

You get __3__ groups of 4.

3. Use 24 ⬚.

Subtract groups of 6.

You get __4__ groups of 6.

Use 25 ⬚.

Subtract groups of 5.

You get __5__ groups of 5.

Problem Solving

4. A farmer has 12 bales of hay. He puts 4 bales in each wagon. How many wagons does he have?

__3__ wagons

A farmer has 16 bags of feed. She puts 4 bags in each wagon. How many wagons does she have?

__4__ wagons

Reteach

Repeated Subtraction

R 14-8 RETEACH

Subtract groups of 3 to make equal groups.

$9 - 3 = $ __6__ $6 - 3 = $ __3__ $3 - 3 = $ __0__

__3__ groups of __3__

How many equal groups can you make?

1.

$8 - 2 = $ __6__ $6 - 2 = $ __4__ $4 - 2 = $ __2__

$2 - 2 = $ __0__   __4__ groups of __2__

2.

$18 - 6 = $ __12__ $12 - 6 = $ __6__ $6 - 6 = $ __0__

__3__ groups of __6__

3.

__5__ groups of __3__ | __2__ groups of __6__

Enrich

Repeated Division
Subtraction Patterns

E 14-8 ENRICH

Subtract. Find the rule.
Then name the counting pattern.

1.

Rule: Subtract __2__

In	Out
10	8
8	6
6	4
4	2
2	0

Pattern: count back by __2s__

Rule: Subtract __3__

In	Out
15	12
12	9
9	6
6	3
3	0

Pattern: count back by __3s__

2.

Rule: Subtract __4__

In	Out
20	16
16	12
12	8
8	4
4	0

Pattern: count back by __4s__.

Rule: Subtract __5__

In	Out
25	20
20	15
15	10
10	5
5	0

Pattern: count back by __5s__.

Daily Homework

14-8 Repeated Subtraction

How many equal groups can you make?

1. Use 12 ⬚.
Subtract groups of 4.

You get __3__ groups of 4.

Use 18 ⬚.
Subtract groups of 6.

You get __3__ groups of 6.

2. Use 9 ⬚.
Subtract groups of 3.

You get __3__ groups of 3.

Use 20 ⬚.
Subtract groups of 5.

You get __4__ groups of 5.

3. Use 15 ⬚.
Subtract groups of 3.

You get __5__ groups of 3.

Use 16 ⬚.
Subtract groups of 4.

You get __4__ groups of 4.

Problem Solving

4. Mrs. Arnold's class is taking a canoe trip. They need to carry 18 canoes to the river. Each trailer holds 6 canoes. How many trailers are needed to carry the canoes? __3__ trailers

Spiral Review

Add.

5.

423	256	333	481	325
+ 60	+ 132	+ 52	+ 113	+ 100
483	388	385	594	425

Chapter 14 ~ Lesson 9

Practice

Subtraction and Division

There are 19 bags to load onto a truck.
Each truck can carry 3 bags.

1. How many times can you subtract 3? __6__

2. How many are left? __1__

3. How many trucks do you need? __7__ trucks

Divide. Use repeated subtraction.
Write how many trucks you need.

4. 15 horses
2 in a truck

You need __8__ trucks.

5. 9 cows
4 in a truck

You need __3__ trucks.

6. 12 pigs
5 in a truck

You need __3__ trucks.

Reteach

Subtraction and Division

10 cubes
4 cups

Put groups of 2 in each cup.

How many times can you subtract 2? __4__

How many are left? __2__

How many cups do you need? __5__ cups

Use cubes and cups.

1. 13 cubes
2 cups
Put groups of 6 in each cup.
How many times can you subtract 6? __2__
How many are left? __1__
How many cups do you need? __3__ cups

2. 11 cubes
3 cups
Put groups of 3 in each cup.
How many times can you subtract 3? __3__
How many are left? __2__
How many cups do you need? __4__ cups

3. 15 cubes
5 cups
Put groups of 3 in each cup.
How many times can you subtract 3? __5__
How many are left? __0__
How many cups do you need? __5__ cups

Enrich

Subtraction and Division
How Many in Each Group?

Solve. Draw a picture if you need to.

1. There are 12 beach balls.
There are 6 classes.
How many beach balls
will each class get?

__2__ beach balls

2. Tyler has 20 seashells.
He wants to give them to 5 friends.
How many seashells will
each friend get?

__4__ seashells

3. There are 4 fish tanks in the
school. The school teachers
bought 24 fish for the tanks.
If there are the same number
in each tank, how many fish
are in each tank?

__6__ fish

4. Josie has 3 books for her fish stamps.
There are the same number of
stamps in each book. She has
18 stamps in all. How many stamps
are in each book?

__6__ stamps

Daily Homework

14-9 Subtraction and Division

Subtract. Then divide.

1. There are 24 people who want to go sailing.
Each sailboat can carry 6 people.

How many times can you subtract 6? __4__

$24 \div 6 =$ __4__

How many sailboats are needed? __4__

Draw a picture and solve.
Use repeated subtraction. Divide.

2. 25 people
5 in each car

$25 \div 5 =$ __5__

How many cars are needed?

__5__ cars

Workspace

Drawings may vary.

3. 21 goats
3 in each truck

$21 \div 3 =$ __7__

How many trucks are needed?

__7__ trucks

Workspace

Drawings may vary.

Spiral Review

Write the number that comes just before.

4. __396__ 397   __287__ 288   __342__ 343   __658__ 659

Chapter 14 ~ Lesson 10

Practice

Division

Make equal groups.
Write how many in each group.

1. 8 boats
4 people

_2_ in each group

2. 9 cars
3 people

_3_ in each group

3. 10 trucks
2 people

_5_ in each group

Circle Fair or Not fair.

4. There are 12 pigs to load on 4 trucks.
The farmer puts 3 pigs on one truck.

(Fair)   Not fair

5. There are 8 horses to put inside 2 fences.
The farmer puts 5 horses inside one fence.

Fair   (Not fair)

6. There are 16 chickens to load in 4 wagons.
The farmer puts 4 chickens in one wagon.

(Fair)   Not fair

Use with Grade 2, Chapter 14, Lesson 10, pages 535–536. (457)

Reteach

Division

Divide to make 2 in each group.

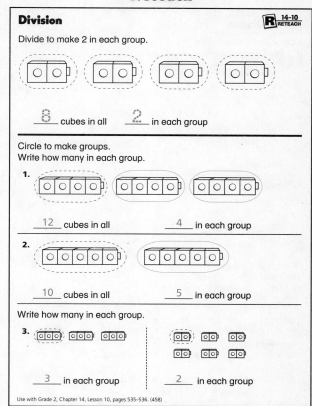

_8_ cubes in all   _2_ in each group

Circle to make groups.
Write how many in each group.

1.

_12_ cubes in all   _4_ in each group

2.

_10_ cubes in all   _5_ in each group

Write how many in each group.

3.

_3_ in each group   _2_ in each group

Use with Grade 2, Chapter 14, Lesson 10, pages 535–536. (458)

Enrich

Division
Find the Name

Find the quotient. Then solve the puzzle.

1. $8 \div 2 = $ _4_ **S**	$12 \div 3 = $ _4_ **S**	$3\overline{)21}$ = 7 **T**
2. $18 \div 3 = $ _6_ **H**	$5 \div 5 = $ _1_ **C**	$2\overline{)4}$ = 2 **A**
3. $10 \div 2 = $ _5_ **U**	$16 \div 2 = $ _8_ **E**	$3\overline{)9}$ = 3 **M**
4. $6 \div 3 = $ _2_ **A**	$16 \div 4 = $ _4_ **S**	$2\overline{)14}$ = 7 **T**
5. $20 \div 5 = $ _4_ **S**		

Write the letter that goes with each quotient. The letters will tell you the name of the state where the Pilgrims landed at Plymouth Rock.

M	A	S	S	A	C	H	U	S	E	T	T	S
3	2	4	4	2	1	6	5	4	8	7	7	4

Use with Grade 2, Chapter 14, Lesson 10, pages 535–536. (459)

© McGraw-Hill School Division

Daily Homework

14-10 Division

Make equal groups. Divide.
Write how many in each group.

1. 9 sailboats
3 groups

$9 \div 3 = $ _3_
_3_ in each group

2. 8 tow trucks
4 groups

$8 \div 4 = $ _2_ in each group
_2_ in each group

Circle *Fair* or *Not Fair*.

3. There are 8 oranges for 4 friends.
Joel takes 3 oranges.

Fair   (Not Fair)

4. There are 5 baskets for 30 apples.
One basket has 6 apples.

(Fair)   Not Fair

Problem Solving

5. A farmer has 10 pigs. There are 3 trucks to carry them. Can each truck carry the same number of pigs? _No._

Explain: _1 pig left over when I try to make 3 equal groups._

Spiral Review

Add. Regroup if you need to.

6.
608	783	568	618	289	189
+ 139	+ 143	+ 376	+ 109	+ 418	+ 463
747	926	944	727	707	652

Chapter 14 ~ Lesson 11

Practice

MORE Division

Make equal groups.
Write how many are in each group and
how many are left over.

1. 13 🚚

6 🪴

__2__ in each group

__1__ left over

17 🥣 flour

4 🛒

__4__ in each group

__1__ left over

2. 23 people 🚐

3 🚐

__7__ in each group

__2__ left over

20 📟

6 🚗

__3__ in each group

__2__ left over

Divide into equal groups.
Write how many are in each group.
Write how many are left over.

3. 16 into 3 equal groups: __5__ in each group, __1__ left over

4. 16 into 4 equal groups: __4__ in each group, __0__ left over

5. 16 into 5 equal groups: __3__ in each group, __1__ left over

6. 16 into 6 equal groups: __2__ in each group, __4__ left over

Use with Grade 2, Chapter 14, Lesson 11, pages 537–538. (460)

Reteach

MORE Division

Make equal groups.

7 counters
3 groups

__2__ in each group

__1__ left over

Make equal groups.

1. 11 counters
5 groups

__2__ in each group

__1__ left over

2. 14 counters
4 groups

__3__ in each group

__2__ left over

3. 9 counters
2 groups

__4__ in each group

__1__ left over

4. 17 counters
3 groups

__5__ in each group

__2__ left over

Use with Grade 2, Chapter 14, Lesson 11, pages 537–538. (461)

Enrich

MORE Division
Division Puzzle

Write the quotient and the remainder.

7 R2 $2\overline{)16}$	3 $4\overline{)12}$	4 $5\overline{)20}$	3 $9\overline{)27}$	9 R1 $3\overline{)28}$
7 R2 $4\overline{)30}$	9 R1 $2\overline{)19}$	7 $1\overline{)7}$	8 $3\overline{)24}$	4 R1 $2\overline{)9}$
4 R3 $5\overline{)23}$	7 $3\overline{)21}$	8 R1 $2\overline{)17}$	5 $5\overline{)25}$	3 R2 $5\overline{)17}$
1 R3 $6\overline{)9}$	4 $4\overline{)16}$	2 $6\overline{)12}$	5 R1 $3\overline{)16}$	6 R1 $2\overline{)13}$
4 R2 $3\overline{)14}$	2 $7\overline{)14}$	5 $2\overline{)10}$	3 $7\overline{)21}$	3 R3 $4\overline{)15}$

Color all the boxes where
the remainders equal 1, 2, or 3.
What letter do you see?

__N__

Use with Grade 2, Chapter 14, Lesson 11, pages 537–538. (462)

Daily Homework

More Division

Make equal groups. Write how many are in each group and
how many are left over.

1. 26 baseballs
3 buckets

__8__ baseballs in
each bucket

__2__ baseballs left over

Drawings may vary.
Workspace

2. 26 fish
4 tanks

__6__ fish in each tank

__2__ fish left over

Workspace

Divide into equal groups. Write how many in each group.
Write how many are left over.

3. 14 into 7 equal groups __2__ in each group __0__ left over

4. 9 into 2 equal groups __4__ in each group __1__ left over

Solve.

5. A farmer has 32 oranges and 4 crates to pack them in. How
many can go into each crate if she makes equal groups? __8__

Spiral Review

Write The number that comes in between.

6. 659 __660__ 661   599 __600__ 601   428 __429__ 430

Grade 2, Chapter 14, Lesson 11, Cluster B **141**

© McGraw-Hill School Division

Chapter 14 ~ Lesson 12

Part A Worksheet

Problem Solving: Application
At the Farmer's Market

Decide how to put crates of vegetables into the truck.

There are 12 crates.

You will put the same number in each of 4 rows.

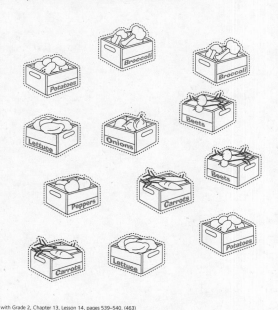

Use with Grade 2, Chapter 13, Lesson 14, pages 539–540. (463)

Part A Worksheet

Problem Solving: Application
At the Farmer's Market

1. How many crates did you put in each row?

3 crates

2. Write the multiplication fact that shows how many crates you put in 4 rows.

_4 × 3 = 12 or 3 × 4 = 12_

3. In what other ways could you have put 12 crates in rows that have the same number of crates in each?

1 row of 12 crates; 2 rows of 6 crates; 3 rows of 4
crates; 6 rows of 2 crates; 12 rows of 1 crate

Use with Grade 2, Chapter 14, Lesson 12, pages 539–540. (464)

Part B Worksheet

Problem Solving: Application
What is the Shortest Distance Between Two Places?

1. Tally the winners on each team.

Team 1	Team 2	Team 3	Team 4

2. Which team had the most winners?

3. How did the path of the team with the most winners compare to the paths of the other teams?

It was straight.

4. What if you drew on a map the shortest path from your school to your home? What would it look like? Explain your thinking.

It would look like a straight line because a straight
line is a shorter path than one that has curves.

Use with Grade 2, Chapter 14, Lesson 12, pages 541–542. (465)